CULTURE, PLACE, AND NATURE

Studies in Anthropology and Environment

K. Sivaramakrishnan, Series Editor

Centered in anthropology, the Culture, Place, and Nature series encompasses new interdisciplinary social science research on environmental issues, focusing on the intersection of culture, ecology, and politics in global, national, and local contexts. Contributors to the series view environmental knowledge and issues from the multiple and often conflicting perspectives of various cultural systems.

FUKUSHIMA FUTURES
SURVIVAL STORIES IN A REPEATEDLY RUINED SEASCAPE

Satsuki Takahashi FOREWORD BY K. SIVARAMAKRISHNAN

University of Washington Press | Seattle

Fukushima Futures was made possible in part by a grant from the Association for Asian Studies First Book Subvention Program. Additional support was provided by the Donald R. Ellegood International Publications Endowment.

Copyright © 2023 by the University of Washington Press
Design by Mindy Basinger Hill | Composed in Minion Pro

All rights reserved. No part of this publication may be reproduced or transmitted in any form or by any means, electronic or mechanical, including photocopy, recording, or any information storage or retrieval system, without permission in writing from the publisher.

UNIVERSITY OF WASHINGTON PRESS | uwapress.uw.edu

LIBRARY OF CONGRESS CATALOGING-IN-PUBLICATION DATA

Names: Takahashi, Satsuki, author.

Title: Fukushima futures : survival stories in a repeatedly ruined seascape / Satsuki Takahashi ; foreword by K. Sivaramakrishnan.

Description: Seattle : University of Washington Press, [2023] | Series: Culture, place, and nature | Includes bibliographical references and index.

Identifiers: LCCN 2022056003 (print) | LCCN 2022056004 (ebook) | ISBN 9780295751337 (hardcover ; alk. paper) | ISBN 9780295751344 (paperback ; alk. paper) | ISBN 9780295751351 (ebook).

Subjects: LCSH: Jōban Region (Japan)—Social conditions—21st century. | Jōban Region (Japan)—Economic conditions—21st century. | Fishers—Japan—Jōban Region—Social conditions. | Fisheries—Japan—Jōban Region. | Communities—Japan—Jōban Region. | Fukushima Nuclear Disaster, Japan, 2011. | Environmental disasters—Social aspects—Japan—Jōban Region.

Classification: LCC HN730.J63 J365 2023 (print) | LCC HN730.J63 (ebook) | DDC 338.3/7270952117—dc23/eng/20230407

LC record available at https://lccn.loc.gov/2022056003

LC ebook record available at https://lccn.loc.gov/2022056004

♾ This paper meets the requirements of ANSI/NISO Z39.48-1992 (Permanence of Paper).

CONTENTS

vii	FOREWORD	by K. Sivaramakrishnan
xi	ACKNOWLEDGMENTS	
xv	PROLOGUE	A Month after 3/11
1	INTRODUCTION	The Removal of Fukushima Future
17	CHAPTER 1	Tankers, Clams, and Octopuses
38	CHAPTER 2	Survival Conditions
54	CHAPTER 3	Mamas' Elegy
73	CHAPTER 4	The (Un)expected
87	CHAPTER 5	Fourfold Pain
105	CHAPTER 6	Fukushima FORWARD
121	CHAPTER 7	In Limbo
138	EPILOGUE	The Return of the Octopuses
143	NOTES	
153	WORKS CITED	
163	INDEX	

FOREWORD

Spectacular disasters, especially those associated with nuclear energy or weapons, train attention on the fragility of human life and the devastation of nonhuman life in the most unrelenting fashion. After all, these disasters leave their deadly traces for generations, if not centuries. Precarity and uncertainty come to haunt landscapes altered by such nuclear fallout. Such is the fate of the Joban Sea in Japan, blighted by its proximity to Fukushima and the nuclear power plant located there.

This sensitive and thoughtful study began as research conducted in the years preceding the terrible tsunami, earthquake, and nuclear disaster in Fukushima. It resumed after that catastrophic event for several years and thereby provided Satsuki Takahashi a window into the world created by the Joban Sea and the fisherfolk of Ibaraki in northeastern Japan living with the excruciating uncertainties of a coastal zone deeply contaminated by the nuclear accident occasioned by the violence that possessed the sea in those fateful days in March 2011. As Takahashi shows in her fine ethnography, a decade later this uncertainty continues to pervade the way people there imagine a future, having participated in efforts to measure the damage, assess the safety, and study the viability of fashioning lives in the region.

The entanglement of environmental and human futures and the exacerbated risk and unpredictability in which these futures are caught are now the subjects of a growing literature in the anthropology of climate change, as well as the anthropology of disasters (see, for instance, Barnes 2016). When this discussion of risky futures enters a region like the Joban Sea coast, it recognizes the sculpting of the coastal landscape that was performed in the last century, during which a wealth of marine resources met intense industrial development. Disasters became a recurring feature of the seascape, as Takahashi shows, and fisherfolk developed a whole vocabulary and disposition for dealing with these events that repeatedly disrupted their lives along the coast.

Coastal dwellers learn, she writes, to survive with the seascape as they and the sea collaborate in navigating a growing precarity shaped by poisonous industrial legacies.[1] Through this attention to the regional history of economic development and the vagaries of being fishers in the midst of major social and environmental changes, Takahashi elicits her concept of futurism, a definitely modern view of change as improvement that is vigorously implemented by the government and fitfully embraced by the coastal residents.

If nuclear energy was presented as a clean and safe alternative to the sullied land and seascape of the Joban coast in the mid-twentieth century, offshore wind farms became the symbols of a new vision for an ecologically prudent and sustainable future. This is the face of green modernity in the aftermath of the nuclear meltdown of 2011 and recovery from a disaster that destroyed both energy and fishing infrastructure. Takahashi is in conversation with the rapidly growing scholarly literature on the Anthropocene, as well as examinations of life amid the ruins of capitalism and large-scale development projects. She provides a study, not of apocalyptic visions or unspeakable distress but of the cautious rearticulation of hope during continuing precarity and uncertainty in an area repeatedly subject to both intensive development activity and periodic catastrophic events.[2]

Having carried out research in the area before the 2011 nuclear disaster, during the immediate recovery in 2011–12, and later when the region was being reimagined again for new kinds of clean energy production, Takahashi achieves a rare perspective informed by knowledge of what happened before, during, and after the cataclysmic events of 2011 to the troubled energy industries and modernizing fisheries of the Joban seascape. The book gives an account of the cumulation of industrial hazards and incidents and the recovery of fishing economy and culture against all odds, albeit with muted expectations. As a result, Takahashi shows, with particular attention to gender dynamics, how uncertainty is internalized in new perspectives that invest in hope and rebuild the fishing communities that remain committed to realizing a viable future in the area.[3]

In that sense she reveals the ethical, technical, and cultural striving to comprehend toxicity as historically contingent relations between living organisms, ecosystems, and institutional change. The fisherfolk of Fukushima become informed evaluators of risk as they learn all about radiation and contamination assessment.[4] But she also goes beyond a defensive response through what has been discussed as citizen science to engage, in the last three chapters of the book, with the new green energy projects along the coast as the fisherfolk are once again drawn into new visions of the future in a fresh wave of modernizing endeavors.

Big questions relating to energy, economic development, uncertain futures in the wake of industrial pollution and repeated disasters, coastal ecosystems, and how ordinary people think about what is now being theorized as the Anthropocene are all tackled in this book. It takes up these urgent and important themes through empathetic ethnography and clear writing. Knowledge of fisheries and sociocultural processes in the Joban Sea prefectures of Ibaraki and Fukushima gives Takahashi wonderful insight into society and ecology, as well as the political economy of futurism in this corner of Japan.

As a result, big questions are tackled and discussed with unassuming directness and engaging insight to provide a study that will enrich many debates in the anthropology of environment, disasters, coastal ecology, and energy studies. The discussion of the way precarity and hope are coproduced in the interaction between aspiration and adaptation in conditions of human and ecological uncertainty will remain a lasting contribution of this book. Repeated and growing environmental crises have generated, in the last fifty years, some of the most sustained questioning of modernity and capitalism.

Utopic and somewhat sweeping visions have also been generated for a future freed of the destructive consequences of capitalist modernity. Takahashi engages these critiques and alternatives from her vantage in northeastern Japan. She shows both local fisherfolk and nonlocal government or industry struggling to comprehend the lessons taught by the sea and its suffering at the hand of modernizing endeavors. In her account the sea remains a source of sustenance that cannot be abandoned. It also compels the adaptation of human enterprise to seek pathways to a livable future.

K. Sivaramakrishnan   YALE UNIVERSITY

ACKNOWLEDGMENTS

This book is based on survival stories that I gathered through ethnographic field research among coastal fishing families of the Joban Sea in Japan between 2004 and 2018. By showing me the ways that they muddled through in a seascape that has been repeatedly ruined by industrial and natural disasters, they taught me that survival is a work of collaboration. Their collaboration with me was invaluable to this book project and to me personally. I am deeply grateful to them for their generosity and cooperation. I especially thank those who kindly welcomed me into their homes or other personal spaces and shared their stories, often accompanied by tea, snacks, and tasty meals. There are so many of these stories that I could not possibly include all in this book, but they greatly motivated and influenced me as I wrote the following pages.

This book also depended on cooperation from other individuals and institutions, and particularly the fellowships and grants that provided essential financial support for its research, writing, and publication. I am grateful to the National Science Foundation for DDIG and RAPID grants. I owe special thanks to Laura Ahearn and Bonnie J. McCay, who encouraged me to apply for RAPID Grant to conduct postdisaster research during the immediate aftermath of the 2011 catastrophe. I am also thankful to the Wenner-Gren Foundation for a Hunt Fellowship, the Research Institute for Humanity and Nature in Kyoto for the research grants to conduct summer fieldwork each year from 2014 to 2017, the Japan Society for the Promotion of Science for KAKENHI Research Grants, and Rutgers University for the Special Opportunity Award for fieldwork and a Bigel Fellowship. I would also like to express my gratitude to the Association for Asian Studies for their generous support through their First Book Subvention Program.

This book would not have been possible without my incredible mentors and their unending support. I am grateful to Osamu Baba, especially for continuously reminding me of the importance of grounded and interdisciplinary insights in thinking about intricate human-ocean relations ever since I was a college student at the Tokyo University of Fisheries Science (currently, the Tokyo University of Marine Science and Technology). At Rutgers, I cannot thank Bonnie McCay enough for her warm encouragement and for being such a wonderful role model as an environmental anthropologist and, more generally, as a person. I am thankful to David Hughes for pushing me to think critically with his deep questions about development, risk, conservation, and energy. Laura Ahearn and Dorothy Hodgson both inspired me as committed ethnographers who helped me to widen my analytical perspectives by introducing me to feminist anthropology and linguistic anthropology. Kevin St. Martin also helped me to critically engage with fishing communities and their relationship to the ocean, technologies, and politics. My respect and admiration for them continue to grow as I try to become a better scholar.

My friends and colleagues whom I met at different times of my career provided me warm encouragement and critical feedback, which were invaluable for me in writing this book. The Institute of Social Science at the University of Tokyo, where I was a research fellow, gave me not only the workspace to think and write but also important opportunities to connect with scholars and researchers who were based in and outside of Japan. I am deeply thankful to Hiroshi Ishida, Yuji Genda, Naofumi Nakamura, Gregory Noble, Tamie Matsuura, Mihoko Miura, Yuki Sato, and Shigeki Uno. The Department of East Asian Studies at Princeton University kindly welcomed me as a research fellow. I am especially grateful to Amy Borovoy, David Howell, and Shinji Sato.

Colleagues and friends whom I met during the three years I spent as an assistant professor at George Mason University also supported my progress in research and writing. I am especially grateful to Andrew Bickford, Amy Best, John Dale, Hugh Gusterson, Jaeeun Kim, Jeffrey Mantz, Rashmi Sadana, and Linda Seligmann for countless fun and stimulating conversations, which greatly helped me to muddle through as I juggled between teaching, researching, and child-rearing. I also made substantial progress on writing this book while I was a Toyota Visiting Professor at the Center for Japanese Studies at the University of Michigan, and I am grateful for their generosity in providing me with a superb academic environment and the university's extensive research resources. I am especially thankful to Allison Alexy, Stuart Kirsch, Rebecca Hardin, Erik Mueggler, Elizabeth Roberts, Jennifer Robertson, Perrin Selcer, and Kiyoteru Tsutsui for inviting me to their colloquia, workshops, classrooms, radio shows, and homes and for offering thoughtful comments and questions on my research. I completed this book while teaching in the Faculty of Sustainability Studies at Hosei University in Tokyo. I would like to thank my colleagues, especially

Miya Itabashi, Makoto Nishikido, Eiko Saeki, and Naruhiko Takesada, for their friendship and support.

Many more friends and colleagues sustained me and my research with their encouragement and thoughtful comments and questions on earlier drafts of the chapters at conferences, workshops, classrooms, seminars, and more casual occasions. I am grateful to everyone who attended these meetings and provided feedback on material I develop in this book. Among them, I would like to specially thank Jun Akamine, Majed Akhter, Samer Alatout, Anne Allison, Emily Anderson, Andrea Arai, Yuki Ashina, Sharon Baskind, Shawn Bender, Theodore Bester, David Biggs, Chelsea Booth, Stella Capoccia, Sakura Christmas, C. Anne Claus, Eric Cunningham, Greg de St. Maurice, Michael Degani, Neriko Musha Doerr, Alexis Dudden, Edwin Everhart, Takashi Fujitani, Naomi Fukunaga, Timothy George, Christopher Gerteis, Arjun Guneratne, Junko Habu, Shingo Hamada, Takeshi Hamada, Stefan Huebner, Tan Ying Jia, Teresa Johnson, William Kelly, Shuhei Kimura, Andrew Littlejohn, Shi-Lin Loh, Dillon Mahoney, Sarasij Majumder, Ian Miller, Laura Miller, Hirokazu Miyazaki, Ryo Morimoto, Atsuro Morita, Karen Nakamura, Moe Nakazora, Miki Namba, Susan Napier, Victoria Nguyen, David Odo, Keiichi Omura, Kimiko Osawa, Philip Paje, Katherine Tegtmeyer Pak, Alyssa Paredes, Prasannan Parthasarathi, Robert Pekkanen, Jon Pitt, Ken Pomeranz, Hugh Raffles, Annelise Riles, Shoko Sakurai, Ryan Sayre, Ellen Schattschneider, Vyjayanthi Ratnam Selinger, Debarati Sen, David Slater, Nathaniel Smith, Nicolas Sternsdorff-Cisterna, Philip Streich, Takao Suami, Daichi Sugai, Wakana Suzuki, Heather Swanson, Kimberley Thomas, Julia Thomas, Karen Thornber, William Tsutsui, Chika Watanabe, Takehiro Watanabe, Paige West, Kath Weston, Merry White, Gavin Whitelaw, Sarah Wise, Mami Yabuki, Aiko Yamauchi, and Chigusa Yamaura. Organizers of talks at Dickinson College, Cornell, Harvard, Yale, UCLA, the University of Tsukuba, the University of Washington also made it possible for me to learn from the great questions of audience members at each event, and I am grateful for their invitations and work.

At the University of Washington Press, Lorri Hagman as the executive editor, Kalyanakrishnan (Shivi) Sivaramakrishnan as the series editor, and their team (Jennifer Comeau, Susan Murray, Beth Fuget, Scott Smiley, and many others) also provided helpful suggestions along with encouragement and patience throughout the long process. Their kind support made it possible for me to continue with this work, especially at difficult times when I was struggling with the demands of child-rearing and full-time teaching during the pandemic. I thank as well two anonymous reviewers for the Press. Their perceptive, thoughtful, and detailed comments and suggestions laid the basis for significant and substantial improvements through the revision process.

Finally, I thank my dearest family, who have supported me for all these years with much love and encouragement. My parents, Hidemoto and Yurie Takahashi, have always been there for me wherever I was. I cannot thank them enough for the physical and emotional assistance they gave me and their grandchildren while I was doing my fieldwork, conference travels, and other work needed to complete this book. I also thank my brothers, Kohei and Junpei, for their unconditional confidence in me for whatever I try to do. My family of in-laws provided me much inspiration and courage to go through difficult times. I am grateful to Joe, Sandra, Vivienne, and Cara for welcoming me and always being supportive of my work. Last but not least, I thank my dearest partner and children. Dave listened to my ideas and read countless pages of my drafts while sharing various family duties. I would not have been able to complete this book without his assistance and love. Nari and Sayu were wonderful companions and provided me energy with their smiles and goofy humor. My family expanded as I carried on with this work. I depended on each family member for their support in different ways at different times, which was all necessary for me to complete this book. I therefore dedicate this book to all of them.

PROLOGUE A Month after 3/11

"Can you ever finish your book?" laughed Hiroshi,[1] a coastal fisherman whom I have known since I was a college student in 1999. On April 11, 2011, I was visiting him and his family at their home in Minato, a coastal town in Ibaraki.[2] This was exactly one month after the March 11 disaster, when a massive earthquake generated a historic tsunami that struck the northeastern coast of Japan, subsequently causing one of the world's most severe nuclear catastrophes at the Fukushima Daiichi Nuclear Power Plant. Back in 2006–7, when I conducted my yearlong fieldwork in the region, Hiroshi was one of the fishermen with whom I had worked most closely. Throughout that year, he, his family, and his fellows of other fishing families taught me a great deal about the sea, the history of coastal modernization, the politics and culture of coastal fisheries, and also the lives of fishing families depending on the industrialized seascape. After I returned to the United States in the summer of 2007, we stayed in touch through occasional email correspondence and seasonal greeting cards, but we had not seen each other in person for four years, until the disaster forced me to go back to the coast.

When I had called him a couple of weeks earlier, he suggested that we meet at his home rather than the usual fishing port. He explained that since the disaster, he rarely visited the harbor because of a fishing moratorium. At first, the moratorium was due to the acute physical damage the tsunami had caused to the harbor. The waves wrecked dozens of fishing boats and split the wharf's concrete floor, making long and deep cracks. Nevertheless, in Minato, like in other fishing communities in Ibaraki, the extensive and visible wreckage was less severe than farther north in the disaster zone, where the tsunami had virtually washed away entire coastal towns. Thus, at first, the fishing families in Ibaraki had viewed themselves as comparatively lucky and hoped for a relatively speedy recovery. The subsequent development of the Fukushima nuclear crisis, however, prolonged the moratorium, especially after an unexpectedly high level of radiation was detected in Japanese sand lance (*kōnago*, *Ammodytes personatus*) caught off the Ibaraki shore in early April.

Hiroshi and his fellow fishers informed me that it was they, Ibaraki fishers, who initially demanded that the government test radiation levels in fish within local waters. Because of their location south of the Fukushima Daiichi Nuclear Power Plant, they immediately suspected that their waters would be more vulnerable than the ocean to the north. They knew from experience that the coastal current runs southward during the early spring and would therefore flush radioactive material from Fukushima into Ibaraki's waters. Eventually, the radiation monitoring results sadly vindicated these concerns. And so the very current that had enabled the success of Ibaraki fishers by bringing abundant marine resources and nutrient-rich waters to the Ibaraki coast now brought radioactive particles spewed into the ocean from the crippled reactors. During the extended fishing moratorium, radiation levels in fish and seawater were carefully monitored, and local fishers took turns helping to collect fish and seawater samples. Hiroshi told me that he had taken part in such sampling duties but otherwise mostly stayed away from the harbor.

When I visited Hiroshi and his family a month after the tsunami, I arrived at their house in the early afternoon and stayed with them until after dinner. We spent a good chunk of the time talking about the disaster, but we also had a lot to catch up on after four years. "How have you been?" Hiroshi asked as he was showing me into the living room. I told him that I had finally finished my dissertation and received my doctoral degree just six months earlier. I also thanked him for his generous support during my fieldwork. He smiled but did not reply directly. "So," he asked, "what're you up to now?"

I was not sure how best to answer the question, partly because I felt like I was in suspension. But I explained, to the best of my ability, that I had intended to turn my dissertation thesis into a book manuscript. But when I was about to start working on it, the March 11 tsunami and the Fukushima meltdown occurred. Immediately, I understood that it would be hard to publish a book on Japanese fishing families without talking about the unprecedented disaster that had just befallen them. I had therefore decided to conduct research on the disaster's aftermath in order to think about how I might be able to talk about predisaster stories with postdisaster ones, reconceptualizing and greatly expanding the book's subject. But as I had just begun my postdisaster fieldwork, I was not sure what the new book would even look like.

It was then that Hiroshi laughed at me, saying that I would never be able to finish my book. He was joking but also serious. He said that the conditions in the wake of the Fukushima nuclear crisis were so uncertain and unpredictable that I would not be able to come up with a coherent conclusion anytime soon. I agreed with him. I then told him that although a book has to conclude somehow, my book's conclusion would not be the end of story. Fishing would continue, and so would my research. This was not a lie, but I knew that I probably sounded a little pretentious. Right then, Hiroshi's wife, Kimie, punctured the awkward moment with her familiar humor. "Oh my goodness, what a great business plan!" Hiroshi subsequently asked with a sarcastic smile on his face, "How many books in total are you thinking of publishing, then?" "Two volumes, perhaps," I said jokingly. "Nah," Kimie added, "you could do five, at least!" We all laughed.

When I asked how they had been for the past four years, they updated me about their three children and their school lives. They also filled me in on the major events in the lives of the other fishing families in their fishing cooperative. Some had "got off the boat"—that is, retired—but most of them had been doing well enough until the disaster occurred. As the afternoon went on, Hiroshi also told me various stories about the disaster, ranging from the day of the tsunami, cleanup efforts during the immediate post-tsunami days, radioactive contamination, consumers' fears about the nuclear disaster's effects on fish from their area, wholesalers' refusal to buy their catches, disaster compensation and lawsuits, and also some friction that had emerged in the town. At 5:17 p.m., while he was explaining the complicated compensation procedures required by TEPCO (Tokyo Electric Power Company, which owns the crippled Fukushima Daiichi Nuclear Power Plant), the whole house violently shook.

Kimie immediately turned on the TV in the living room. A loud beeping sound came from the stereo. A male anchor repeated a set of short sentences: "A large earthquake has just occurred. The magnitude is 7.1. The epicenter is Hamadori, Fukushima. There is a possibility of tsunami. Do not go near the ocean or the river." The TV screen was showing a map of Japan with the northeastern coast highlighted in red. Next to it, a "tsunami warning" sign was flashing. As soon as the tremor stopped, Hiroshi quickly grabbed his waterproof jacket and ran to the door. It was raining outside. Hiroshi did not say a word, but we understood that he was going to the harbor to take his fishing boat offshore in order to save it from an incoming tsunami. "Here," Kimie said, handing him a pack of snacks in case he had to stay offshore for a while. Exactly a month earlier, on March 11, those who took their boats offshore could not return to the harbor for twenty-four hours or more because of the tsunami debris; they later said that their hunger was particularly challenging. "Be careful," Kimie added. Hiroshi returned a quiet "yeah" and took off in his truck. The rest of us—Kimie, their three children,

Hiroshi's parents, and I—resumed quietly staring at the TV screen.

The anchor reported that the evening's quake was the biggest aftershock since March 11. A few minutes later, the tsunami warning was turned off. The anchor announced that there was no risk of tsunami. After another few minutes had passed, Hiroshi called Kimie's cell phone. He told her that he did not actually take his boat offshore and that he had just left the harbor to return home after making sure that his boat was tightly roped to the quay. I left their place soon after Hiroshi returned home. The rain was still coming down, not too heavy but hard enough to make me nervous while driving on dark streets without streetlights because they had been either destroyed or left without power since the March 11 disaster.

That night, I had trouble falling asleep in my hotel bed. The feeling of uncertainty was overwhelming. Thinking of the future, it felt as if I were still driving in darkness. A series of questions arose in my mind. What is going to happen to Hiroshi and his family? What is going to happen to the fishing industry? How long does it take for the damaged ocean to recover? How are fishing families going to survive? I knew that I would not know the answers anytime soon, but I could not help but wonder about the future. Ten years later, I still ponder the same questions. Although there are some changes in the conditions, the future remains opaque. But during the past years, I learned a lot about the future through my post-2011 fieldwork with Hiroshi and other fishers in Ibaraki and Fukushima and also through revisiting my old fieldwork that I carried out before the disaster. Based on my unexpectedly protracted fieldwork, this ethnography is about the uncertain future and people who are living with it. My goal in writing this ethnography is not to anticipate the future but, rather, to explore how people imagine, discuss, and act toward the future as they live with the ever-precarious ocean.

FUKUSHIMA FUTURES

INTRODUCTION The Removal
of Fukushima Future

This book is about survival in precarious times. In particular, it focuses on the sea of Fukushima and Ibaraki in Japan, which is also known as Jōban Oki, or the Joban Sea.[1] Located adjacent to the Fukushima Daiichi Nuclear Power Plant, the Joban Sea suddenly became widely known to the world as one of the most fraught seascapes in the wake of the 2011 meltdown. But stories that I gathered before and after the nuclear accident illuminate that precarity had always been the condition of the seascape. This book tells two entangled yet distinct stories of survival in this milieu, based on long-term ethnographic fieldwork conducted between 2004 and 2018. One story is of coastal fishing families who lived with the precarious seascape while encountering multiple industrial disasters and other punishing challenges, ranging from declining marine resources to economic recessions. The other story is one of modernization, which the government has repeatedly introduced as necessary to ensure the future survival of coastal fishing families in precarious times, even when the source of that precarity might visibly be modernization itself. Following the two survival stories, this book asks: How did coastal fishing families experience, respond to, and live with precarity of the seascape? How did modernization play a role in shaping the precarious seascape, and vice versa? How and to what extent did modernization contribute to the survival of coastal fishing families? What do the survival stories of coastal fishing families and modernization from one of the world's most notorious seascapes tell us about possibilities of imagining more livable futures?

The Joban Sea is simultaneously abundant and ruined. The marine ecology is rich and full, thanks to the warm and cold ocean currents meeting off the coast. For generations, commercial fishing families along the shore have lived on the abundant coastal resources, and their catches were historically regarded as "the Joban material" (Jōban mono) for their premium quality at the world's largest fish market in Tokyo.[2] Besides its rich marine resources, the Joban Sea is also known for hosting one of Japan's largest industrialized coastlines. Ringed and

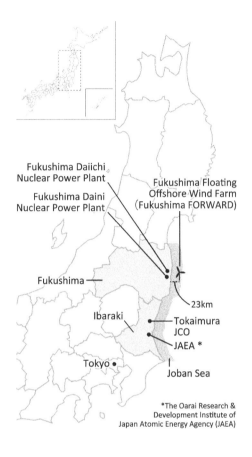

FIG. 1. The Joban Sea, showing four nuclear power plants and a floating offshore wind farm within the area. Created by OFFICE SA based on maps of the Geospatial Information Authority of Japan.

marked by concrete seawalls, multiple industrial port complexes, twenty-two modern concrete fishing harbors, and also four nuclear power plants in addition to seven thermal power plants, the coastline represents a microcosm of postwar Japan's modernization genealogy. As a result, though industrialization brought capitalist development to the formerly poor coastal region, the heavy engineering of the coastal landscape has also caused substantial change in the natural habitat through tidal alteration, shoreline erosion, sand loss, and water pollution. Moreover, coastal industrialization made the Joban Sea prone to manmade disasters in addition to natural ones.

Disasters, as anthropologists have argued, are processual phenomena rather than events that are isolated and temporally demarcated in exact time frames (Oliver-Smith 1999). As Anthony Oliver-Smith and Susanna Hoffman have put it, "disasters do not just happen" (2002, 3). In the case of industrial disasters, pollutants are produced through previous efforts of modernization (Beck 1992; Hecht 1998; Fortun 2001). In the Joban Sea, too, through historical industrial modernization, man-made disasters have been among the processes making the precarious seascape.[3] Looking at the present seascape in the aftermath of the Fukushima nuclear meltdown, the inseparability of precarity and disasters seems obvious, but their interconnections have been accruing for far longer than the decade since the 2011 disaster. In a highly industrialized seascape like the Joban Sea, disasters—natural and man-made alike—are in fact ordinary because they occur with frequency.[4]

Thus, my interactions with the seascape have been repeatedly marked by disasters since the beginning. My first visit to the Joban Sea was in 1999, when the now almost overlooked Tokaimura nuclear accident occurred. Located in central Ibaraki, the Tokaimura Nuclear Power Plant was Japan's oldest commercial nuclear generator, having opened in 1965. On September 30, 1999, the plant suffered a critical accident that killed two plant workers who were exposed to high-level radiation. The Tokaimura nuclear accident was shocking since it was the first nuclear accident that caused casualties in Japanese history. A significant amount of media attention was paid to the accident being categorized as a Level 4 disaster, one notch below that of the 1979 Three Mile Island accident on the International Nuclear Event Scale (INES) by the International Atomic Energy Agency (IAEA). In the wake of this disaster, all fishing activities in Ibaraki were immediately shut down, and the moratorium lasted for a week. Subsequently, fishing families also struggled with declines in fish prices due to consumers' fear of the risk of radiation in fish from Ibaraki, eventually resulting in a prolonged compensation lawsuit that lasted nearly five years after fishers filed the claim against the plant owner.

At the time, I was a college student at a fisheries university in Tokyo, and the accident happened right before I was going to visit the coast for a field trip as part of a course on the social dimensions of coastal fishing communities. As a result of the accident, the field trip was postponed, but we eventually visited the coastal communities a couple of months later, when the immediate effects of the accident had receded. During the field trip, through listening to local fishers tell us about the fishing moratorium and consumers' hesitancy to buy fish due to their fear of its contamination by radiation, we learned how consequential the nuclear accident had been to those people who rely on the sea. At the same time, I was also intrigued by an optimistic belief in the possibility of recovery that the fishers presented. They emphasized that the disaster was already over and that fishing had returned to normal. Indeed, normality did seem to have returned to the seascape at the time we visited the shore.

In 2006, another major industrial disaster occurred in the Joban Sea when I was about to begin my yearlong fieldwork, during which I was planning to study community-based marine conservation. This was a rolling disaster, with three successive tanker accidents occurring in a short time near the industrial port in Minato, a coastal town in Ibaraki Prefecture, which happened to be one of my two main field sites and where I was scheduled to begin. At first, a large tanker ran aground in a typhoon and killed ten crew members, ultimately leaking substantial amounts of oil and ore into the sea. A couple of weeks later, two more tankers ran aground in another typhoon. In the wake of the three accidents, commercial fishing activities in the adjacent coastal water were entirely banned for as long as a month. Subsequently, I ended up observing the anxieties and hope that emerged among coastal fishing families in the aftermath of the tanker disaster, while exploring how those fishing families muddled through the difficult time in Minato as well as the neighboring town, which I call Hama. For fishing families, the processes of recovery from the tanker accidents involved even more time and work than had those in the wake of the Tokaimura nuclear accident in 1999. But eventually, by the time I finished my yearlong fieldwork, a sense of normality seemed to have returned.

It was almost five years after the tanker accidents that the next major disaster struck the Joban Sea in March 2011. When the triple disaster—a combination of earthquake, tsunami, and nuclear accident—happened, I was a postdoctoral fellow at a university in Tokyo, which made it possible for me to revisit the coast in early April 2011 to observe the immediate postdisaster situation.[5] Retrospectively speaking, given the multiple major disasters that I repeatedly encountered in my interactions with the Joban Sea, I sometimes wondered whether I simply had (and carried with me) some kind of bad luck as an ethnographer. But I eventually came to understand that, along this coast that has been heavily industrialized in the name of modernization, man-made disasters have historically been part of the seascape. For coastal fishing families living on the Joban Sea, dwelling in the industrialized sea means living with not only natural but also man-made disasters.

For commercial fishers from coast to coast around the world, dealing with natural disasters is a part of a learning process that shapes who they are (Pálsson 1991). For those living on the Joban Sea, dealing with industrial disasters is also part of the process. They expect both natural and industrial disasters, but they cannot predict when and how the disasters will occur. Encountering one disaster after another, they have become experienced in dealing with not only natural but also man-made ones. This does not mean that they are fully prepared for the next disaster, but their past experiences teach them how to cope with new challenges. For instance, in 2006, while muddling through in the wake of the tanker accidents, more than a few men and women of fishing families mentioned to me their experiences with the 1999 Tokaimura nuclear accident. They explained that the knowledge that they had gained following the previous disaster had helped them to deal with the latest tanker accidents. It is true that the magnitude of the 2011 catastrophe is such that it deserves the frequent references to it as "unprecedented." But as they have always done before, coastal fishing families used experiences with previous disasters to guide them in coping with the present one. Although coastal fishers themselves often emphasized notable differences between the current disaster and earlier ones, they also expressed that the ongoing nuclear catastrophe would not be the region's last calamity. For coastal fishing families, living with disasters is part of life with the Joban seascape.

Living with the precarious sea is by no means easy. In fact, it is frequently unsettling. When I lived on the Joban coast, I learned about the hardships fishing families faced in living with the seascape, especially through everyday conversations with them, which were often devoted to various anxieties—not only about disasters but also about declining resources, stagnant fish prices, increasing costs, coastal erosion, and industrial contamination. Such conversations were especially frequent during the process of recovering from a disaster. But they also taught me that precarity does not mean hopelessness. I was intrigued by the fact that, no matter how anxiety-producing the conditions became, coastal fishing families eventually survived. That does not mean that the anxiety-producing conditions receded; indeed, anxiety over these conditions never disappears. But coastal fishing families were and still are continuously staying alive with the ever-precarious Joban Sea.

So how did these fishing families end up surviving despite long-term threats punctuated by immediate and seemingly existential crises? In order to explore this question, I revisited the field notes that I collected during 2006–7 in Minato and Hama in the aftermath of the tanker accidents as well as the ones from 2011. I also carried out ethnographic fieldwork during the summers between 2014 and 2018 in coastal towns of Fukushima. Through this long exploration, I eventually learned that coastal fishing families were not surviving in spite of precarity. Rather, my argument is that they were surviving together with the precarious sea. Survival is, indeed, an act of collaboration (Tsing 2015, 20). In this context, the Joban seascape is precarious, not only because it has been repeatedly ruined by coastal industrialization and man-made disasters, but also because it provides unpredictable opportunities for survival. The Joban Sea is precarious because it is filled with "life without the promise of stability" (Tsing 2015, 2).

The Joban Sea is by no means healthy. But it is animated with eventful surprises.[6] In many ways, the survival stories of the region's fishing families that this book narrates resonate with Anna Tsing's insight that "one value of keeping precarity in mind is that it makes us remember that changing with circumstances is the stuff of survival" (Tsing 2015, 27). The sea is, by nature, uncertain. Fish behave differently depending on the weather, tidal flows, water temperature, and other surrounding conditions. It is fishing families' everyday routine to coordinate their plans according to the capricious circumstances. In addition to daily changes, there is also seasonal and other cyclical precarity, which makes the seascape an especially lively space for survival. For example, some fish species—such as clams and octopuses, in the case of the Joban Sea—unexpectedly emerge in large quantity once every few years or decades and support the survival of fishing families. But because such a phenomenon results from various chains of events that occur within the ever-changing marine environment, it is almost impossible for marine biologists or anybody else to predict accurately when these large populations will emerge or how big the size of the school might be.[7]

Modernization has also survived together with the precarious sea, although its symbiotic relationship is more often parasitic than commensal or mutual.[8] It has persisted in the precarious seascape when coastal fishing families and nonhuman species of the seascape were often harmed. Although modernization projects have repeatedly ruined the seascape, modernization has continued as the state's main policy agenda for the region, its existence repeatedly justified as the necessary means for human and nonhuman species in the blasted seascape to survive disasters and other disaster-like situations, including economic recessions and resource depletion. This use of disasters by advocates of modernization shares common principles with what Naomi Klein has called the "shock doctrine" (Klein 2007), which points to the ways that politicians and government officials use crises in order to push through unpopular political reforms such as free-market privatization. Likewise, the phenomenon that has taken shape in the repeatedly ruined seascape in Japan—what I call "surviving modernization"—highlights how crisis also provides opportunities for the idea of modernization to stay alive.[9]

Furthermore, the stories from the Joban Sea underscore that the survival of modernization does not occur simply or naturally but relies on on-site collaboration between the government's field agents and those who follow their suggestions. Similar to extension agents (Escobar 1995) or NGO workers (West 2006; Li 2007), fisheries agents in Japan have historically devoted their time and effort into gaining the support of local fishing families in order to put the government's modernization agenda into practice. In fact, developing alliances with local fishing families is not an easy task, but the ordinary disasters of the Joban seascape have helped fisheries agents to eventually gain collaboration from those fishing families who struggle to stay alive, as I discuss through the contrasting stories from the two neighboring fishing towns, Minato and Hama (in chapters 1, 2, and 3). The survival of modernization is dependent, too, on the precarious seascape. In the end, while continuous modernization is often assumed and naturalized in a modern world,[10] the fact that modernization has survived is actually unnatural.

THE SEA OF FUTURISM

Modernization has successfully stayed alive in Japan due largely to the extensive time and effort politicians, government officials, and extension agents devote to advocating and promoting the concept.[11] But why are they attracted to the concept? It seemed especially contradictory when they reintroduced modernization as a means to recover from the Fukushima nuclear crisis, even though it was unquestionable that what now imperiled the region was the result of a crucial earlier modernization project. Nonetheless, the Japanese government claimed that further modernization would support the ruined seascape and struggling fishing families in their efforts to survive in the future. This contradiction and the embedded idea of the future are together the key to understanding how to survive modernization. In the context of modernization, the image of the future is built on "futurism." As famously argued by the German historian Reinhart Koselleck, futurism is different from the concept of the future itself, which has been around since before premodern times; futurism is the future-oriented positivism that modernity produces (Koselleck 2004). Futurism, therefore, is closely associated with the developmental timeline of progress. In the name of futurism, the future is interpreted as "the newness," and the past and the present are reduced to "the oldness," which become subjects of modernization whose transformation is required to achieve the imagined future progress.

Modernization and futurism are together seductive (Tsing 2000). They provide government officials and policy makers alike a narrative of justification for their work as a mission to accomplish the goal of making something new and better for the future. Thus, modernization advocates rely on and reproduce images of a bright future and also justify the existence of modernization by actively employing them. They are also attracted or even addicted to the nostalgia of earlier futurisms, especially those that emerged during postwar Japan's era of rapid industrialization.[12] That is why the building of infrastructure continues to dominate the central designs of modernization projects even as they have allegedly taken an "ecological turn," claiming to build a more sustainable future. Likewise, the environmental crisis has been translated as an opportunity for further modernization, through developing new eco-technology, rather than as a crucial moment for reflection on what a sustainable future actually means.

The Joban seascape is filled with the remains and detritus of modernization's historical efforts to design new futures. Along the coastline, in addition to the coastal industrial complexes and modern concrete fishing ports, the nuclear and thermal power plants exist as remainders from Japan's earlier modernization projects, which were carried out between the 1960s and the early 1980s. By including the construction of this power infrastructure, these projects allegedly aimed to open a new future not only for the energy industry, and therefore Japan as a modern nation more broadly, but also for the "underdeveloped" coastal region. Moreover, by referring to the heightened industrial pollution cases around the country in the 1950s and 1960s, the development of nuclear energy was also narrated as a new ecological technology that would usher Japan into a cleaner and more sustainable future (Takahashi 2014b). To take the example of Futaba, the township that invited the construction of two of the six reactors of the Fukushima Daiichi Nuclear Power Plant, the spirit of futurism was represented on a large billboard reading, "Nuclear: The Bright Future's Energy."[13]

In the Joban Sea area, as well as other coastal regions in Japan, industrial futurism has historically been entangled with fisheries futurism. When coastal industrial complexes were introduced in the 1960s as part of the compensation to fishers for giving up some of their fishing grounds, local fishing families received modern concrete fishing ports and subsidies allowing them to upgrade from small rowboats to bigger motorboats. The modern ports are typically surrounded by seawalls and include a wharf as well as a local fish market, which allows fishing families to land and sell their fish within their own port. Therefore, though losing fishing grounds was a painful blow, those fishing families largely accepted the compensation, anticipating greater gains from modernizing their fishing infrastructure. Similarly, when the government promoted the development of nuclear power reactors in the 1970s, local fishing families accepted modern marine fish hatcheries as part of the compensation for their willingness to accept the proximity of, for example, the newly constructed Fukushima Daiichi Nuclear Power Plant. In fact, the Fukushima Fish Nursery Laboratory—which was built in the town of Okuma, where the initial four units of nuclear reactors are located—was one of the nation's largest and most cutting-edge marine fish hatcheries. Just like the nuclear reactors that were presented as emblems of the region's bright future, the marine fish hatchery was also introduced as a means to open a better and sustainable future for the seascape, as I learned when I visited the facility in 2004.

On a sunny summer day in July 2004, I was in Okuma in order to visit the Fukushima Fish Nursery Laboratory both as a fieldworker to conduct preliminary research for my dissertation and also as a translator for ninety fisheries experts from around the world who were on a field trip as part of an international conference on fisheries management held in Tokyo. Given that year's conference theme—"What Are Responsible Fisheries?"—the fish laboratory seemed to be an ideal location for the excursion. Our itinerary for the afternoon was to visit and learn about the fish laboratory, where marine biologists bred fish juveniles of more than eighty species in their hatcheries.

"It feels nice," said a professor from Indonesia in front of me as we were getting off our large charter bus. The early-afternoon air in coastal Fukushima was summery but fresh, especially compared with unbearably hot and muggy Tokyo, from where we had left in the morning. In the middle of the laboratory's spacious parking lot, a Japanese fisheries professor—also the conference organizer and the excursion's tour leader—spoke to the crowd of international fisheries experts through a handy megaphone. We were in Fukushima Prefecture's fish hatchery, as he explained, and we were going to break up into groups and take a tour of the facilities. Among many marine fish hatcheries in Japan, the one in Fukushima was easily the largest facility that I had ever seen.

A young ichthyologist who worked for the hatchery escorted our group. He first took us to the twelve-acre front yard next to the parking lot. In that space, there were a few dozen lines of long, rectangular concrete tanks that looked like tall stone coffins. The ichthyologist explained to us that they raised abalone and sea urchin juveniles in as many as 160 concrete tanks. Next, the young ichthyologist took us into a 7.5-acre building that looked like a large indoor sports stadium. After disinfecting the soles of our shoes in chlorinated water, we entered the facility. Inside were two dozen large, round concrete pools in which were kept thousands of flounder juveniles, organized by size. In one corner were also two dozen plastic containers for growing plankton for feed. Gathering us in front of one flounder tank, the ichthyologist gave us a mini-lecture about the facility, opening with the proud announcement that his laboratory was one of Japan's most advanced hatcheries and that it played an important role in achieving Fukushima's sustainable fisheries. He also told us that his laboratory could produce fish juveniles three to four months faster than the natural speed because it used thermal discharge from the neighboring Fukushima Daiichi Nuclear Power Plant. According to him, the warmed seawater speeds up not only the spawning cycles but also the growth of fish juveniles. In addition, he also emphasized that the method of recycling thermal discharge was an advanced, environmentally conscious technology. Thermal discharge is normally considered to be an environmental hazard because it increases the temperature of coastal waters adjacent to a power plant.[14] But by recycling it, the fish hatchery transforms hazardous wastewater into a useful resource. As I was translating his explanation into English, a few fisheries experts expressed their admiration.

At that time in 2004, none of us expected that the fish hatchery would end up with a famously tragic future, and no one even mentioned any risk of a future accident. To the contrary, since the facility had opened in 1982, the laboratory had been considered a symbol of the area's bright future, with a positive reputation nationwide. For example, in 1999, when an annual national fisheries conference, the National Convention on Nurturing the Abundant Ocean, was held at the fishing harbor of Matsukawaura in northern Fukushima, the nuclear fish hatchery as well as local fishers received the highest honor for their efforts to promote Japan's modern marine conservation. As the highlight of the event, Japan's emperor and empress made a speech, praising local fishers for their contributions to promoting sustainable fisheries. After the speech, the royal couple took a few steps onto a custom-made wooden platform on the quay, which was built specially for this occasion, and gently released a bucket of hatchery-born fish juveniles raised at Fukushima Fish Nursery Laboratory into the ocean. The slogan of the year's fisheries convention read, "Nurturing the Ocean, We Build a Dream Bridge to the Future." The embodied futurity of the nuclear fish hatchery was unmistakable.

But the future is, indeed, unpredictable. On March 11, 2011, the tsunami utterly destroyed not only the nuclear power plant but also the adjacent fish hatchery, washing away the buildings, the tubs, fish, and six staff members. In the aftermath, the hatchery exists only as a ruin. The only thing that remained on the site was the frame and the rooftop of the stadium-like building, where thousands of flounder juveniles were once nurtured. At sea, the nuclear substances released from the crippled nuclear reactors further damaged the precarious seascape while threatening the future survival of fishing families. A couple of months after the catastrophe, a fisheries official from Fukushima Prefecture told a reporter from the *Yomiuri*, Japan's most popular daily newspaper, "Until the accident, we and the nuclear power plant co-existed in peace and prosperity" (Miura 2011).

But it did not take a long after the 2011 accident for the government to introduce a new direction for modernization. Nine months after the nuclear meltdown the government announced a project of a public-private consortium for building the world's first floating wind farm off the Fukushima coast. The consortium leaders proudly claimed that their project would open yet another new future for not only Fukushima and Japan but also for the nation's fishing industry. On June 20, 2012, while the consortium began its mission to build the new future, the University of Tokyo—one of the consortium members—celebrated the innovativeness of the new ecological technology in an online article on their school's website. The headline of this article reads: "Tomorrow's Wind Blows at Sea" (Ashita no kaze ga umi ni fuku) (University of Tokyo 2012). A year later, in June 2013, this notion of building the future would be reiterated when the consortium introduced the public to their first floating windmill, named Fukushima Future (Fukushima Mirai).

The history of the Joban seascape reminds us that futurism is, indeed, "a modern cultural tradition" (Pels 2015, 782; see also Koselleck 2004; and Harding and Rosenberg 2005) and that it continues in the present. In many cases, we see this tradition in infrastructure: transportation systems (Latour 1996), nuclear power plants (Hecht 1998), dams (Tilt 2014), and agricultural and fisheries extension facilities (Escobar 1995; Takahashi 2014a, 2018; Fukunaga 2019; Swanson 2022). Therefore, by looking at infrastructures, we can learn a great deal about aspirations, anticipations, and imaginations of the future that are shared among the people involved (Appadurai 2013; see also Gupta 2015, 2018). In recent years, more projects of futurism have made "an ecological turn," emphasizing that their

FIG. 2 Fukushima Future, the first floating turbine in the Fukushima offshore wind farm. Photo by author.

innovations—for example, electric cars and renewable energy—are designed to build the new sustainable future. But by and large, such eco-futurism projects have continued to be preoccupied with the familiar idea of progress and thus have employed typical developmental procedures by exploiting the local landscapes and seascapes in order to produce electricity. As a result, "green" energy projects are often short-lived, as seen with a large wind park in Oaxaca, Mexico, which could cause further delay in dealing with climate change into the future (Howe 2019; see also Boyer 2019). The ill-fated Fukushima offshore floating wind farm would also become one such ephemeral eco-futurism project.

Futurism implies newness, but the imagined future in eco-futurism projects is built on nostalgia for the usual. Eco-futurism projects aim at sustaining the accustomed capitalist lifestyles through technologically fixing the current ecological problems without changing conventional energy-dependent practices (Hughes 2014). But there is no way to "fix" the Anthropocene (Thomas, Williams, and Zalasiewicz 2020). Nevertheless, the stories from the Joban Sea suggest that there is still hope in the damaged seascape. Therefore, instead of dreaming about the fictional future, this book argues that it is important to reorient ourselves to be truly present, gazing at the current problems and considering ways to collaboratively survive with the damaged landscape and seascape.

HOPE IN THE PRECARIOUS SEA

This book's title, *Fukushima Futures*, is inpired by the name of the first windmill of the Fukushima's floating wind farm for two reasons. One is that it represents the survival of modernization in Japan and also the limits of futurism. The other is because I wish this book to help open our imaginations for "more livable futures" (Haraway 2016). I hope to do so by both making visible the limits of futurism and nurturing our hope for "collaborative survival" (Tsing 2015, 20) in the repeatedly damaged seascape between human and more-than-human others, including not only fish and other marine species, tides, waves, wind, rain, seabed, beaches, but also man-made objects such as ports, hatcheries, energy plants, wind farms, and other marine infrastructure.

The Fukushima Daiichi Nuclear Power Plant accident, as one of the world's worst man-made disasters, left in its wake substantial debates on the Anthropocene, the new geological epoch in which the earth's natural systems have been changed by harmful human activities (Ghosh 2016; Morton 2013; Scranton 2015; Tsing, Swanson, Gan, and Bubandt 2017). In many ways, people across the world projected images of postdisaster Fukushima onto those of the doomed future of the Anthropocene. Media reports from Fukushima along with iconic images—such as the demolished nuclear power reactors, people in hazmat suits and masks, Geiger counters over fresh vegetables and seafood, mounds of black bags filled with radioactive soil, and abandoned houses in evacuation zones—were undeniably unnerving and terrifying, even apocalyptic. The Japanese disaster also affected the energy policies of several countries, including Italy and Germany, which quickly made decisions to reduce their reliance on nuclear power, gradually shifting to renewable energy sources, in order to reduce the future risk of causing another Fukushima-like catastrophe. In Japan, though the antinuclear movement was not as active as it was in many European nations, public and policy support for adapting more renewable energy sources grew in the immediate aftermath of the Fukushima accident. Largely for this reason, the Japanese government introduced the floating wind farm off the damaged coast as a utopian antidote to the seemingly doomed future of Fukushima and, more broadly, of the troubled earth.

The national project of Fukushima Future eventually stalled, largely due to the reduction of government support, with repercussions that ripple through the accounts that unfold in this book. This failure suggests perhaps that the future of the Anthropocene remains opaque, as does the future of Fukushima itself. But living in limbo with the ever-precarious seascape is not necessarily hopeless. Rather, the condition of suspension allows us to become attuned to unforeseen possibilities, which we often overlook when we are preoccupied by our concerns with the expansion of anthropogenic powers (Choy and Zee 2015; see also Kirksey 2015). Although many postdisaster utopias are, in fact, short-lived, some of them may survive in different forms and suggest future hope even though their scales might be small and localized (Morris-Suzuki 2017). Moreover, stories of coastal fishing families in the Joban seascape before and after the 2011 disaster tell us that surviving in the ever-precarious sea depends on collaboration not only among humans but also with more-than-human others—including oceanic fauna and flora, water currents, winds, and forth—which are all part of the dynamic oceanographic milieu. Such oceanographic collaborations are hard to plan in advance, and they often emerge accidentally. But in such precarity, I place hope. Through meditating on the collaborative survival stories of coastal fishing families in the Joban seascape, this book suggests possibilities of more survivable futures, which are different from familiar narratives of apocalyptic or "salvific futures" (Haraway 2016).

The Joban seascape remains precarious, simultaneously hopeful and anxious. In 2022, as I am writing this introduction, the Fukushima nuclear crisis is still lingering, though radioactive effects on the coastal waters seem to have been reduced. According to the most recent official reports, the amount of radioactive materials in all the tested fish samples has been consistently lower than the government's safety standard since April 2015, with the majority of them registering as "N.D." (Not Detected) (Fisheries Agency n.d.). In December 2020, given the satisfactory results of radiation monitoring, local fishers in Fukushima made a collective decision to end the fishing moratorium with limited pilot operations and to move toward the reopening of "normal" operations. A few months later, on March 31, 2021, the limited pilot operations were officially discontinued, and coastal fishing families began working toward gradual recovery of normalcy, while muddling through the additional challenges caused by the COVID-19 pandemic, which had substantially reduced fish sales.

While the reopening of fishing in Fukushima encourages local fishers, the future of coastal fishing remains uncertain, especially considering the issue of nuclear wastewater from the crippled nuclear reactors. During the ten years following the immediate aftermath of the Fukushima nuclear accident, the Japanese government repeatedly proposed a plan to release low-level nuclear wastewater into the sea, claiming that the potential risk to marine species is minimal or zero, and also that the ocean-dumping is necessary due to the scarcity of storage space for continuously accumulating wastewater (Ministry of Economy, Trade, and Industry 2020). But local fishers sustained their strong opposition to the proposal. Local fishers' concerns are twofold. First, it is hard for them to trust the actual safety of the dumping. Their skepticism toward the government and TEPCO regarding safety measures is understandable, especially considering that they have been betrayed once before when they were informed belatedly about the leakage of high-level nuclear wastewater into the sea. Additionally, even if low-level nuclear wastewater is actually safe, local fishers worry justifiably that ocean-dumping of nuclear wastewater would further damage consumers' trust in the safety of fish landed in the area, continuing to drive down the future value of their fish. But eventually, in April 2021, despite local fishers' remaining strong opposition, Prime Minister Yoshihide Suga announced an executive decision to put the water release plan into practice, starting in 2023.

In December 2020, in the midst of heated discussions on the release of wastewater and the reopening of regular fishing operations, another headline regarding the future of Fukushima leapt into the news. The Ministry of Economy, Trade, and Industry made an announcement that it had decided to discontinue the Fukushima offshore floating wind farm project and to remove all the remaining windmills, including Fukushima Future, from Fukushima's offshore waters by the end of March 2022. The spokesperson explained that the government had to remove the entire offshore wind farm because maintaining the project was too costly and unprofitable. Those coastal fishers who imagined the possibility of a survivable future together with the offshore wind farm were disappointed. But, as they told me, they still retain hope in staying alive together with the precarious Joban seascape.

Gazing at the Joban seascape in limbo, this book reflects on our attitude toward the future. The story of "surviving modernization" demonstrates that modernization itself has survived by generating hope through promising sustainable progress, in which the seascape itself is tamed and stabilized, reducing the precarity of life within and around it. But in contrast, the stories of surviving fishing families remind us that hope of more survivable futures exists within precarity (see also Allison 2013). They also show us that hope can emerge in the blasted seascape (see also Kirksey, Chapiro, and Brodine 2014). If we define precarity as "life without the promise of stability" (Tsing 2015, 2), coastal fishing families living on the Joban Sea have long, historical experience with it. As they often said to me, the ocean is by nature precarious. The wind, currents, and fish are all capricious, changing their movements in every moment. They have also survived multiple disasters, not only natural but also man-made ones. Their survival stories suggest that possibilities of more livable futures exist in the Joban seascape, no matter how doomed the future seems to be.

OUTLINE OF THE BOOK

This book traces the survival of modernization and fishing families and their entanglements through stories that I gathered based on three stretches of ethnographic fieldwork along the Joban seascape. The first segment reflects material collected during 2006–7, when I spent a year in two coastal town, Minato and Hama, in Ibaraki Prefecture (chapters 1–3). The second draws from material from 2011, in the immediate aftermath of the triple disaster of earthquake, tsunami, and the Fukushima Daiichi Nuclear Power Plant accident, when I carried out fieldwork in Ibaraki, Fukushima, and Tokyo (chapters 4 and 5). Finally, I use material collected from 2013–17, when I focused primarily on the Fukushima offshore floating wind farm and those fishers who were associated with the newly introduced postdisaster futurism project (chapters 6 and 7).

CHAPTER 1 Tankers, Clams, and Octopuses

In October 2006, my fieldwork began with seasonal typhoons and three tanker accidents. The first accident happened a day after I arrived in Japan. In the evening, a TV anchor announced a newsflash: "A large tanker has just run aground off the port of Minato." She reported that, hit by a large-scale low-pressure front, the tanker, holding close to ten metric tons of ore, had struck the sea bottom and was leaking its fuel into the waters near shore. By the next morning, the news had been updated—ten crew members of the tanker had been either killed or were still missing. The footage captured the gigantic tanker split in half, with its bright orange-red bottom exposed above the blackish, oil-slicked water.

My original plan had been to stay a couple of nights with my parents in a suburb of Tokyo and then move into an apartment in Minato to kick off my yearlong ethnographic research. But the disaster news reports left me unsure whether I would be able to carry it out. I hesitated for a day and half but eventually called Mr. Oda, who was the president of the Minato fishing cooperative (hereafter, fishing co-op) at the time. Although I expected that he would still be busy dealing with the tanker accident, I wanted to check with him about my fieldwork because he had previously given me permission to start it the following day. To be sure, he was busy. On the phone, he responded with a disengaged, "yeah, yeah," to my greetings and sympathies. He then said that he was in the middle of an emergency meeting and told me to call him back a week later.

After the week had passed, I called Mr. Oda again. He informed me that Minato and three neighboring fishing co-ops had decided to carry out a voluntary fishing moratorium for a few weeks until the spilled fuel and ore from the damaged tanker as well as public concern over the safety of fish was contained. He explained that it was a tough decision to make because a new season of young anchovy fishing had just opened a few days earlier, and fishing families were especially enjoying the beginning of what promised to be a highly successful season. Their expectations for a good young anchovy season were particularly high because they had experienced shrinking catch sizes of the two major species on which their income depended—namely, young anchovies and clams—for the past several years. Nevertheless, even as large schools of young anchovies were swimming through their coastal waters, none of their fishing boats were allowed to leave the harbor.

As for my fieldwork, Mr. Oda told me that it would be difficult for me to meet fishers because they would rarely be at the fishing port during the moratorium. He also mentioned that he himself would be too busy managing the disaster's aftermaths to introduce me to individual fishers. He suggested that I call him again in two weeks to find out when the fishing moratorium would end and also when I might be able to begin my fieldwork at his co-op. As I was trying to wrap up the call, he asked me whether I would be free on the Sunday after next. He said that his fishing co-op's members and their families would go to the beach in Hama, the neighboring town, to collect baby hard clams, which recently appeared in a large quantity, suggesting a possible emergence of an ecological phenomenon that marine biologists call a "dominant year class" (Hjort 1914). The news of the baby clams was like a silver lining in the midst of a crisis.

Clam stocks had recently been in decline despite the continuous conservation efforts that fishing families have maintained since they began in the late 1970s. Thus, as Mr. Oda explained, it was important to save the baby clams to support the recovery of the declining clam populations in a safe environment away from poachers and recreational clam collectors. The fishing families would dig up as many as possible from the beach and reset them in the co-op's protected waters adjacent to Minato's fishing harbor. At the end of our phone conversation, Mr. Oda told me to be ready at the beach in Hama at 7:00 a.m. sharp and not to forget rubber boots, rubber gloves, a hand rake, a hat, and towels.

―

On that Sunday morning under the autumn sun, the sandy beach in Hama— thirty miles away from the oil-covered shore of Minato—was filled with approximately two hundred people from fishing families. The wind was calm, and the water was warm. It was a perfect day for clam-digging. The fishing families were from Minato, Hama, and another neighboring town, who all share the exclusive access rights to hard clams inhabiting this long stretch of the coastal water. There were also a few marine biologists from the prefectural fisheries experimental station on hand to supervise the activity and to take some samples for their scientific research on the clams' population dynamics. By the time I arrived, men, women, and children alike were already at work on the sandy beach. They picked clam after clam while occasionally chatting with their families and friends and splashing water at each other. At the time, the fishing moratorium was still continuing without a known end date, and anxiety lingered palpably among these fishing families. But collecting baby clams to transfer them to protected waters felt like an intermission in the midst of the ongoing disaster. In the morning on the beach, fishing families were cheerful, chatty, and even playful.

As soon as I showed up at the beach, a fisherman from Minato teased me about my chest-high waders, which I had bought the day before at a recreational fishing shop. Looking around, I noticed that everybody else was either in "real" commercial fishers' boots—white, up to just below the knee—or in bare feet. Indeed, I looked very much like an outsider. I felt a little embarrassed, especially because I actually purchased the waders hoping that they would enable me to blend in with those fishing families. But my out-of-place chest-high waders apparently worked as a good icebreaker for a novice ethnographer. "Look," a middle-aged woman said to me. Pointing to her bare feet, she said, "Use your heels." On the wet sand, she stood on her heels with toes up and started swiveling her heels and hips like she was dancing the Twist. "Voila!" She moved her feet, and there were a couple of thumb-sized baby clams exposed in the dented sand. "We used to gather a ton of clams like this when we were kids," she smiled.

By noon, all of the co-ops had finished gathering clams. Collected baby clams were gathered in large plastic baskets, and the prefectural biologists calculated the total weight: "Two (metric) tons in total!" As the chief scientist announced the outcome of that day's effort through a megaphone, people oohed and aahed. Mr. Oda then gave short closing remarks in front of fishing families from Minato, praising their efforts, and the group was dismissed. Before heading to my car, I thanked him for inviting me for the clam gathering and told him that I hoped that the fishing moratorium would end soon. "Me too," he replied.

Fate was unkind. The very next day another massive storm hit the region, and two more tankers ran aground off the Minato industrial port. Both accidents occurred within just a few hours of one another and right near where the first tanker had stranded roughly three weeks earlier. The later accidents involved less oil spillage and no casualties, but the fishing moratorium still had to be extended for another ten days. Fishing families ended up with no yield for the entire month. To make matters worse, hauls after the reopening of fishing turned out to be largely unsuccessful. The fishing harbor in Minato remained mostly stagnant for the next six weeks. At the same time, with inadequate catches and without yet having received compensation money from the tanker owners, fishing families grew anxious and frustrated.

But in the end, to their surprise, nature's capriciousness delivered some good news. Large schools of octopuses unexpectedly emerged for the first time in many years. As soon as the octopus season opened in the late November, the harbor quickly came to life. All the cheerful faces there made it almost hard to believe how gloomy and exasperated the fishing families had been just a few days earlier.

In the Joban seascape, the cumulative effects of risk and possibilities of survival are seemingly in conflict but are coexistent and intertwined, both representing the eventfulness of the precarious seascape. In the heavily engineered seascape, risk has been produced and accumulated through historical modernization efforts designed to manufacture an advanced future. But such risks and future effects usually receive little attention or are even discounted in the process of future-building. "In risk society," as the anthropologist Michael Fischer has stated, "risks accumulate slowly, are not limited in time and space, affect future generations, and are often testable only after the fact" (Fischer 2009, 127; see also Beck 1992). But the stories from the Joban seascape reveal that hope for survival also accumulates in an uncertain environment.

In 2006, fishing families in Minato—as well as Hama—encountered the previously accumulated risks after the fact. In addition to the decline in populations of marine species, which was mainly caused by beach construction for coastal development, the tanker accidents were also a risk produced by earlier modernization projects. But later in the same year, fishing families were unexpectedly given an opportunity to get out of the hole when large schools of octopuses appeared in the troubled sea. This is not a simple story of nature's saving the day; the appearance of octopuses was not isolated from the processes of historical modernization but rather entangled with them, similar to the hope that other scholars have noted as having emerged in blasted landscapes, in the form of mushrooms or other nonhuman species (Tsing 2014; Kirksey, Shapiro, and Brodine 2014; Kirksey 2015).

The stories of Minato before the 2011 disaster show that the combination of risk and possibilities of survival that we see in post-Fukushima Japan is not only connected with earlier modernization but also historically accumulated. Understanding the entanglement of the accumulation is especially important in order to make sense of how and why fishing families are able to maintain hope for their survival with the repeatedly ruined seascape, even as they are simultaneously confronted by acute anxieties associated with life in a hazardous, unpredictable marine environment.

"THANKS TO DEVELOPMENT"

Minato's narratives of development history, like those elsewhere, come with bright and dark stories alike. The coastal town's modern development began largely in 1960, when the then governor of the prefecture welcomed the building of Japan's largest artificial seaport in what was then the poorest area of the prefecture. Instead of building into the sea, this new harbor was constructed by dredging out large dune fields more than three kilometers inland at a depth of almost twenty-five meters. Drastically engineering a large area of the sandy beach, this industrialization resulted not only in social changes but also considerable degradation of the coastal ecology, including beach erosion and industrial pollution in air and water.

According to local history books archived at the municipal library, the negative consequences of this industrialization included industrial smog that caused numerous cases of asthma and other health issues among coastal residents (many of whom are fishing families), and wastewater from the industrial complex that killed a substantial amount of fish. For fishing families, water pollution was a life-and-death matter, but the government was reportedly slow in taking any immediate action on the issue. One day in 1971, a few frustrated fishers brought buckets filled with dead, poisoned fish to the prefectural government building and threw them around on the office floor. The pollution itself would eventually decline after stricter environmental regulations were implemented, but the pollution disputes, by all accounts, left many Minato fishing families disgruntled and uneasy for decades. During my interview with Mr. Nakanishi, one of the prefectural marine biologists who served as a fisheries agent during the 1970s, he confirmed that the Minato fishing families' distrust toward the prefectural government was, in fact, extreme. "Everybody in Minato ignored me, at first," he said. Apparently, it took him almost two years to finally be able to start working together with Minato fishing families.

Despite the history books and Mr. Nakanishi's recollection of the dark side of the postwar history of the town's development, when I was living in Minato, I only heard the fishing families describe the seaside industrial development as a positive event, with not a single one reporting on it unhappily. In their storytelling, the era of industrialization was almost always translated as a transformative moment of glorious progress. They also often emphasized that they were grateful to the region's development for giving them a bright future. "Thanks to development" was a phrase they would begin whenever they responded to my questions about their past. "Thanks to development, we got a modern fishing port with concrete wharfs and seawalls." Or "thanks to development, we could finally upgrade my fishing boat with a modern, powerful engine." Or "thanks to development, our standard of living tremendously improved." Or "thanks to development, our fishing business became successful."

The magnitude of the transformation in fishing families' lives through the seaside industrialization was truly dramatic. As Mr. Nakanishi described it, "It was like a Cinderella story." Indeed, the imagery of a poor woman's metamorphosis into a princess fits with how fishing families themselves often explained to me their own "before" and "after" tales. In between the before and the after, the fact that the coastal industrialization has historically caused considerable negative consequences for fishing families is not forgotten but has been translated as unavoidable risk if they are to stay alive in the industrialized seascape.

COLLABORATION IN MODERNIZATION

In the early 1970s, the newly built fishing harbor was filled with ambitious young fishers eager to be part of the new, bright future on the horizon. This was the beginning of the great boom of the fishing economy in Minato. In the middle of their dramatic transformation from "backward" to modern fishers, young sons reportedly were especially keen to learn new and modern fishing methods relying on previously unaffordable electronic equipment like fish-finders, radar, and sonar. According to those fishers who used to be those young sons in the 1970s, fishers of their fathers' generation were too old to accept the new, modern fishing gadgets so the young sons took the lead in promoting the modernization of coastal fishing in Minato. And later on, by the 1980s and 1990s, their modernization initiatives would eventually turn those young fishers of Minato into major collaborators in the prefectural and national governments' promotion of scientific marine conservation programs. At the same time, through participating in the conservation programs, fishing families also developed a collaborative relationship with marine species for their survival. As anthropologists and historians alike have shown, human and nonhuman species may become intimately entangled for their collaborative survival in highly industrialized environments (Tsing 2015; see also White 1995; and Lien 2015). In the case of Minato, collaborative survival between fishing families and hard clams developed as part of surviving modernization.

According to Mr. Shimada, who was one of those young sons in the 1970s, coastal industrialization brought the town not only technological and economic improvements but also an opportunity to form a new social network, especially among young men of fishing families. "At the time, there were plenty of young, energetic guys at the fishing dock," Mr. Shimada said, "so I wanted to do something with those young fishers, something fun." He explained that as the reason he took the initiative in establishing Minato's Young Fishermen's Association (YFA) in 1973. Other fishers, who later took the lead in developing conservation practices, also recalled that they had collaborated with fisheries agents largely because it was enjoyable. According to fisheries officials, promoting YFAs across the nation or advanced marine conservation was an important step for their mission to modernize "backward" coastal fishing families. In other words, for officials, promoting modernization among fishing families was a government mission, whereas for young fishers, organizing their own YFA and working with fisheries agents for modernization activities was interpreted as something exciting and enjoyable. Eventually, this collaboration in modernization would play an important role in cultivating possibilities of survival for fishing families as they muddle through with the repeatedly ruined seascape.

As anthropologists of Japan have discussed, young people in rural Japan played crucial roles in modernizing primary industries like farming and fishing (Kelly 1990, 1994; Martinez 2004). But in order to understand the modernization of Japanese primary industries, it is also important to acknowledge the role of local government officials, especially extension agents, similar to what Arturo Escobar has described in his work on Colombia (Escobar 1995). In 2006, Mr. Tabata was one of the most experienced fisheries agents stationed at the prefectural fisheries experiment station of Ibaraki. For more than fifteen years, he had worked closely with young fishers of YFAs at different fishing co-ops around the prefecture. He explained to me that the idea of YFAs was originally borrowed from agricultural co-ops' Young Farmers' Associations, which first began in the early 1950s. According to Mr. Tabata, organizing youth groups became popular in the immediate postwar period of Japan among various industries, based on the goal of modernizing Japan's economy and on the presumed capacity of young people for adapting new, modern ideas and technology. More than a half century later, the institutionalized partnership between extension agents and youth groups has remained, as modernization remains a key theme of policy governing the industry.

Moreover, Mr. Tabata underlined, while extension agents are in partnership with youth groups, his and his colleagues' ultimate goal was to achieve modernization. When I asked him how he viewed his job as an extension agent, he described his work of a fisheries agent as being like *kuroko*: the black-clad puppeteer in *bunraku*, Japan's widely known form of traditional puppet theater. He explained that extension agents are like these puppeteers because fishing families have to be presented as the main characters in achieving modernization, even though extension agents are the ones who do everything to set the stage. Mr. Tabata also described his work as a "translator." "Do you mean that you interpret local needs and deliver them to policy makers?" I asked. "No, no, no," he replied. He explained that his work as a translator was to interpret policy language to local fishing people. According to him, policy documents explain guidelines on how to modernize coastal fisheries and why they need to be modernized, but fishers never read such documents, partly due to the texts' combination of dry legalese and technical terminology. Therefore, he believed that it was fisheries agents' job to translate policy guidelines into more local-friendly language so that fishing families would be able to follow appropriate directions to modernize themselves.

That is why, according to Mr. Tabata, extension agents had long focused on working with young fishers of YFAs. He said, "It is easier to 'educate' young fishers than to convince older generations to adjust their behavior in line with new policy directions." He noted that, by educating fishers on modernization early in their careers, fisheries agents also hope to develop a prolonged collaboration with local fishers. Thus, whenever the Fisheries Agency decided to promote a new policy agenda for fisheries modernization—such as "technological modernization," "sustainable fisheries," and "community-based fisheries management"—fisheries agents strategically focused on young fishers at local YFAs. Through organizing meetings and workshops with local YFAs, fisheries agents devoted their time and energy to "enlightening" young fishers and convincing them that their active voluntary efforts in participating in development projects were crucial for surviving as commercial fishing families. That said, developing partnership with fishers is, in fact, not at all an easy task, requiring substantial and continuous efforts.

MODERN CONSERVATIONISTS

By the early 1990s, through young fishers' continuous collaboration with fisheries agents, the Minato fishing co-op had become well-known nationwide, as it was introduced in various government and academic documents as a successful case of "community-based resource management." I myself first learned about Minato through those documents when I was a college student at a fisheries university in Tokyo in the late 1990s. At the time, "community-based resource management" (or CBRM) was a concept that received growing attention as a more democratic and effective way to manage natural resources, compared to top-down or market-based strategies, among scholars of environmental studies and environmental policy makers around the world.[1] Following this global trend, Japanese fisheries scholars and policy makers often presented local-level marine conservation practices like the ones in Minato as successful examples of CBRM, emphasizing the institutional capacity of fishing co-ops for local initiatives and voluntary efforts. But in reality, the development of CBRM cases in Japanese coastal fishing can be better understood in the context of the making of "environmental subjects," which are formulated in the processes of transformations in politics, institutions, and subjectivities (Agrawal 2005). In the case of Minato, their CBRM system was established in the processes of the change in the state's fisheries modernization policy, the expansion of the local fishing co-op, and also the conversion of their identity from backward "fishfolks" to modern, conservation-minded fishers.

It was the late 1970s when the Fisheries Agency first announced a new modernization policy direction in promoting marine conservation. This was a major shift in fisheries policy, especially considering the previous agenda, which focused on increasing landings through advancement of fishing technology. But, based on the overall policy principle of fisheries modernization, marine conservation was introduced as a necessary measure to modernize coastal fishers and to build a better future for coastal fishing. At the time, environmental conservation was one of the major policy trends in western Europe and North America, helping to mark what would be considered "modern," even in Japan, in terms of fisheries practice. But Japanese policy makers of that time seem to have been less interested in the concept of environmental conservation itself than in its representational quality: it became an image of the advanced level that other countries' fisheries had already attained, and to which Japanese fisheries ought to aspire. In the official 1991 white paper of Japan's Fisheries Agency, the Coastal

Fisheries Promotion Act—the primary law to guide coastal fisheries policies—is described as having the central goal of promoting marine conservation in order to achieve the modernization of fishing and fishing families.

At the local level, given this new modernization project, fisheries agents around Japan sought to convince young fishers that understanding the scientific logic of marine conservation and being able to wisely and properly use precious marine resources were necessary qualities of "modern subjects." They typically explained to young fishers that the current state of fishing culture was backward, marked by short-sighted attitudes toward limited resources, but also that young fishers are the ones who could bring the new, forward-thinking measures and approaches to the industry. At first, fisheries agents struggled to receive positive responses from local fishing families to their rhetoric of marine conservation for modernization. Mr. Nakanishi, who was one of the fisheries agents at the time, remembered that most of fishing families in Ibaraki were busy enjoying successful landings, and therefore they were understandably unable to see any benefit in resource conservation. But he eventually met Mr. Shimada and his friends in Minato, who offered more positive feedback. These young fishers had just established their YFA a few years earlier, and they were looking for some activity to work on for their organization. For them, as Mr. Shimada explained to me, the idea that marine conservation was the new, cutting-edge project was especially appealing. Thus, Mr. Shimada and his friends eventually agreed to try some experiments with Mr. Nakanishi. After a few meetings exchanging ideas, they decided that they would first work on a project of improving their clam-dredging equipment by making it ecologically friendly.

Initially, the project idea came up in a conversation between Mr. Nakanishi and Mr. Shimada about an issue raised by some of the fish buyers and auctioneers: the problem of clams with cut feet (or, as the Japanese expression goes, "bitten tongues"). Clamshells are usually open in water, and siphons and a foot are exposed while feeding, but clams close their shells when they are taken out of water or if they sense a threat. A cut foot occurs when a clam closes its shell too quickly while its foot is still out—like biting a tongue for us—when there is a sudden threat like, for example, the appearance of a trawler's dredge. Once clams are harvested by dredgers, their shells mostly remain closed. It is therefore impossible for fishers to tell which clams have their legs cut off, and they often face grumbling from middlemen who have to purchase clams without being able to identify injured clams in advance. According to these middlemen, clams without their feet pose two problems: they often do not survive the next stages of transportation, and clients like restaurants and sushi bars complain because leg-less clams are unpresentable to diners when they are served on a half shell.

Once fishers of the YFA and the fisheries agent decided to work on the clam issue, they first studied the causes of leg-cutting and then spent days of trial-and-error testing to determine the best angle and length of dredge bars—or a dredge's "teeth"—to lower the number of damaged clams. During these experiments, they also reached the conclusion that slowing the dredging speed would be necessary for further reductions. After two years of these tests, Mr. Shimada gave a presentation on their research outcomes—which was prepared by the fisheries agent, Mr. Nakanishi—at a national convention of YFAs in Tokyo. The presentation was a collaborative performance. Mr. Nakanishi wrote the presentation to emphasize that, by catching fewer but higher-quality clams, Minato fishers had accomplished both income improvement and clam conservation. In the presentation, Mr. Shimada successfully delivered the highlights to the judges. In the end, the Minato YFA won a gold prize at the national convention. "It was unfortunate that we didn't get the Emperor's Prize [the highest award of the convention, above even the gold prize], but it wasn't bad," Mr. Shimada smiled. Likewise, in my interviews, other fishers who were part of the YFA at the time similarly remembered fondly and proudly the whole experience of working together on the conservation project and receiving the national award.

After being greatly encouraged by the gold prize and increased government support, fisheries agents and the Minato YFA members extended their collaboration further to experiment on new conservation projects. Their conservation projects at the time included such efforts as experiments on fishing equipment and methods for releasing undersized fish and for reducing bycatch. Additionally, in the early 1980s, they began their fish-stocking and intermediate breeding programs as soon as the prefecture opened its marine hatchery facility.[2] Furthermore, during the 1980s, Mr. Nakanishi and the Minato YFA also ran meticulous trial-and-error efforts to come up with the original design of so-called "income-pooling system" for clam-dredging. The "income-pooling system" is basically a communal—or "socialistic," as some fishers say—conservation strategy that aims at optimizing landing values by reducing fishing pressure on marine resources. In Minato in the 1980s, although the quality of clams had been increased thanks to the improved dredging gear by the YFA, fishing families were still struggling with low clam prices. The cause was what they call "good catch poor," a condition in which an exceptionally good catch leads to oversupply and thus the collapse of the market price, resulting in low profits. Thus, with

Mr. Nakanishi's initial suggestion, Minato YFA members began working on an "income-pooling system" as a possible solution to the problem.

Basically, under an "income-pooling system," co-op members are divided into groups, and each group takes turns catching fish on a scheduled fishing day. On each fishing day, the landing value of all fish caught by the members of the group in charge is pooled at the co-op. Then, after all the rotations are completed, the entire pooled landing value would be equally allocated among all the members of the co-op (hence the name income-pooling system). In principle, by reducing the landing volume at a given time, this system allows fishing families to control the market price at the most profitable level and gain a stable income. Moreover, by avoiding overfishing, the system is also considered to be a sustainable fisheries method, which helps fishing families to develop their healthy symbiotic relationship with clams. In theory, the basic idea of an income-pooling system sounds straightforward, and its social and ecological benefits are fascinating. But a laborious trial-and-error, experimental approach was necessary to work out the details for a system that would actually be viable and successful in the community.

"That was a heck of brain workout!" said Atsushi, whom I interviewed along with two of his friends; they all had been YFA members at the time. "Yes, it sure was," his friends both smilingly nodded. According to Atsushi, in order to come up with the best simulation for a successful income-pooling system, he and his friends had to collect the landing data of many previous years, working with the numbers for weeks. But their efforts paid off in the end. When they finally reached a conclusion, they presented the master plan of the income-pooling system for clam dredging to the then co-op president and explained why it would be beneficial for all members of their co-op. Although they were confident in their proposal, Atsushi said that he was worried about how older members of the co-op would respond to the unorthodox and seemingly socialistic plan that went against the traditionally competitive instincts of commercial fishers. But they ended up receiving high marks from the co-op president. Soon after that, the co-op president proposed actual implementation of the income-pooling system of clam-dredging as a new rule to the co-op board members and successfully received a majority of their votes.

"Did you guys finally win the Emperor's Prize this time?" I asked Atsushi and his friends. "No, unfortunately," one of them sighed exaggeratedly. Another said that it was a close call. They apparently missed the chance again because another YFA from a different prefecture had gotten the award for presenting on their income-pooling system in the previous year's YFA convention. "If only we had done it a year or two earlier," said Atsushi's friend. For those young fishers in Minato, missing the national prize was like Elisha Gray losing to Alexander Graham Bell as being named the inventor of the telephone. But Atsushi proudly confirmed that their accomplishment was still recognized and that the Minato YFA was able to receive the top prefectural award that year from the governor. Subsequently, the Minato YFA continued working closely with fisheries agents and received more prizes for their contributions to the development of marine conservation. The additional clam management programs include techniques such as clam-stocking—releasing of juvenile clams raised at the prefectural fish hatchery—and relaying small clams collected from beach areas into offshore marine protected areas. By the late 1990s, the front wall of the conference room at the Minato fishing co-op office was covered with the framed prize certificates.

In 2006, fishing families in Minato were continuously practicing the clam management rules, but clam populations were in decline due, ironically, to the coastal modernization that had encouraged fishing families to become involved in clam conservation in the first place. Nevertheless, they were largely in agreement that clam conservation was vital for their survival in the precarious seascape. As one fisher taught me, fishing families in Minato often referred to their marine protected areas for clams as "the bank of the sea," in which they "deposit" clams to grow their "savings" and to withdraw them when necessary. The bank of the sea assisted fishing families in Minato struggling through difficult occasions not just once but repeatedly, including at times of disasters, which also helped nurturing opportunities for future survival. It is true that their descriptions of clam management might make them sound more like economists than conservationists and that they do not depict themselves as environmentalists. Given the continuity of their efforts, this does not lessen them as "environmental subjects," but it might be equally accurate to describe them as "survival subjects," assembled to survive through intimate connections with other species in the repeatedly ruined sea. In the making of survival subjects, as Minato fishing families showed me, interactions with nonhuman species and their transformations play a critical role, in addition to transformations in human society.

IRONIC DECLINES

If life has its ups and downs, the 1990s and the early 2000s arguably trended downward for fishing families in Minato. Japan's famed financial bubble burst in

1991, beginning a long recession that would last for more than two decades. The inflation of fish prices stopped and turned to nearly ruinous deflation. Average fish prices gradually declined throughout the 1990s and continued through the 2000s. By 2003, the average fish price for coastal fisheries was approximately 300 yen per kilogram, roughly equivalent to the value of 1975. Although fish values were declining, virtually all the costs (such as boats, gear and other equipment, fuel, living expenses, etc.) continued growing. To make matters worse, the quantity of fish landings also continued to drop, even though fishing families had been devoting efforts to marine conservation since the late 1970s. Given the decline of both fish prices and landing volumes, annual landing values of the major species have largely spiraled downward since the early 2000s.

In 2006, while I was living in Minato, anxieties about the declining landings were apparent in everyday conversations among Minato's fishing families. When older members of Minato's fishing families told me about the past, they often began with what was almost a fixed phrase: "In the good old days, there used to be plenty of fish out there in the sea." In the 1960s, annual landings in Minato immensely improved with the establishment of the town's first fishing port, which was built as an appendix to the industrial seaport. The elders' stories then typically went on to the usual statement about the present: "but there are far fewer fish out there these days." But the cause of the declining landings was unexpected and ironic, not just a simple story of the "tragedy of the commons" (Hardin 1968), which assumes that greedy fishers end up collectively hurting their own business by overfishing open-access marine resources.

Before the construction of the fishing port, most fishing families in Minato used to fish only six months of the year, spending the other half of the year growing rice and vegetables. Even when they went fishing, without advanced equipment, their fishing activities were limited to catching clams and finfish in the nearshore waters. But since the fishing port was built, they upgraded to bigger, motorized boats and became full-time fishing families throughout the year. This transition widened their fishing grounds as well as their target species. "We catch whatever comes into our water," Minato captains often told me. In fact, fishing families in Minato are individually prepared for using multiple fishing methods, by owning various types of fishing gear, unlike those in other coastal towns who usually specialize in one or at most two fishing methods.

In Minato, a fishing family typically is prepared for all of the following fishing methods: dredging for clams; purse-seining for young anchovies, sea bass, breams, halfbeaks, and crabs; pot fishing for octopus; pipe fishing for eels;

longline fishing for flounder; gill-netting for flounder, sea robin, and flatheads; bottom-trawling for flounder; and creel fishing for conch. Among this variety of fish species, clams, young anchovies, and flounder are the top three resources that mainly provide most annual household income. In a typical year, fishing families collect clams year-round, whereas they target young anchovies in spring and fall, and flounder in summer and winter. But because the marine environment is always unpredictable, they quickly switch gear whenever they judge that other fish species might fetch a better landing price. Maintaining a variety of fishing gear is costly, but Minato fishing families argue that it is a necessary investment if one is to successfully survive in the unpredictable seascape.

Given this history, there is little doubt that modernization of fishing technology enabled Minato fishing families to greatly improve their hauls. Nevertheless, Minato's decline in landings does not easily fit with the usual story of "the tragedy of the commons." In fact, Minato fishers had been nationally renowned as among of the country's best marine conservationists. Their fishing activities are highly restricted by their own conservation rules. With free-rider problems and other issues, there is certainly room to doubt the effectiveness of some of their conservation techniques. But the decline of landings is situated in the intricate nexus of the highly industrialized seascape, which the government and fishing families have historically supported in collaboration.

In 2006, fishing families were increasingly concerned about the fact that the annual landing values of hard clams and young anchovies had been declining year after year for a decade. The declining annual landing values of these species were reportedly caused by a reduction of the average landing size. But especially for fisheries agents and fishing families alike in Minato, who had put great effort into developing conservation strategies for clams since the late 1970s, the declining clam population was puzzling. As it turns out, overfishing was not a cause. Apparently the declines were caused by changes in the marine ecology brought about by the construction projects that have been central to coastal industrialization. According to Mr. Nakanishi, who was the marine biologist and former fisheries agent who had worked with young fishers in Minato to develop clam conservation strategies, he and his fellow prefectural scientists finally reached a conclusion after a long investigation that the real culprit was the seaports — not just the industrial port but also the concrete fishing port.

Despite the widespread enthusiasm and gratitude of Minato fishers for the construction of the modern fishing port facilities, this development reportedly changed tidal directions and caused substantial beach erosion. Ecologically speaking, hard clams need wide, sandy beaches to survive at the juvenile stage of their life cycle until they become big enough to move into deeper water for their adult stage. Thus, on the eroding beaches, fewer and fewer young clams could survive, while many others "drowned." The fisheries scientists explained that the change in tide caused by the construction of the massive modern ports was also connected to the declining catch sizes of young anchovies, a trend that was exacerbated by the migration patterns that were partly shaped by ocean currents. They used to migrate closer to the coastal line, but the migration path has been pushed out into waters farther from shore, too far for coastal fishing boats to make the trip without spending too much time and fuel. "How ironic, isn't it?" said Mr. Nakanishi.

The irony was not lost on Minato's fishing families. One afternoon, I was chatting about continuously declining young anchovies and hard clams with an experienced captain on the quay at the fishing port in Minato. He told me that he had recently learned from the prefectural fisheries scientists that the ports were arguably the main cause of the misery. "You know what," he said as he tapped his foot on the concrete quay, "If we want clams and young anchovies to come back, we need to completely wreck this fishing port." And he gave a sarcastic laugh. "But without this," he continued, "we can't catch the fish in the first place!"

EMPTY NETS

In early November 2016, on the first day that fishing finally reopened after the monthlong moratorium caused by the tanker accidents, I went along with two brother fishers, Mamoru and Satoru, on their boat for purse-seining young anchovies. At 6:00 a.m., the sky was still dark and quiet, but the fishing harbor was filled with the loud sounds of engines and was illuminated by the beaming lights of more than two hundred boats. Soon after six o'clock, these boats quickly left the harbor and scattered out into the still, dark ocean. A fall season of young anchovies is usually between August and October, so people were of course concerned that there might be no anchovies left in the area's coastal waters. But at the same time, it is hard to predict when a season actually starts and ends. Anchovies are a migratory species, and their migration pattern changes every season, depending on the water temperature, current flows, and other environmental conditions. Hence, fishers hoped to catch any remaining schools of young anchovies that might be swimming somewhere in the vast coastal waters.

About thirty minutes after we left the harbor, Mamoru, who handled the wheel, slowed down the engine. Promptly, his younger brother, Satoru, cast one end of their fishnet into the water. Mamoru then quickly circled the boat around a target spot. Then Satoru picked up from the water the end of the net that he had dropped earlier and speedily hauled in the rest of the net. All of their fishing sequences were orderly and rhythmic. As other fishers told me, these brothers' work on the boat was masterly and beautiful. But even with their expert abilities, the morning's outcome was far from successful. For the next five hours, the brothers cast and hauled their nets as many as sixteen times. But every time they hauled their net, it was either empty or contained only a handful of young anchovies. When it passed noon, Mamoru quietly told his brother, "Let's quit," and headed back to the harbor. Still, the brothers' half-filled basket turned out to be one of the best hauls of the day. Most other fishing boats returned to the harbor with even less or nothing at all.

During the return trip, I sat down next to Satoru while his brother was steering the boat back to the harbor. Understandably, he looked tired and did not seem to be in a good mood after spending the last six hours hauling an almost empty fishnet over and over again. But he kindly chatted with me anyway. Satoru gave me a quick self-introduction. He was forty-five years old, married with three children, and he had been a fisherman since he was fifteen. I asked him why he became a fisherman. "When I graduated from junior high school," he said, "I thought that a deckhand seemed like easy work . . . although it turned out to be hard." "Did you consider going to a high school?" I asked. "No, I didn't," he replied. "Why not?" He paused. "I just did not really think about it," he said, "but now I wonder why I am doing this." "This?" He took another pause. "Well," he continued, "if you are a salaryman, you have a stable income and promotions, but we don't get such things." His sensitive tone made me hold my tongue, and we stayed silent during the remaining trip to the wharf.

At a later date, though, he told me that he became a fisherman because he did not want to work for a company and also because he could make more money as a fisherman, compared to other middle-school-educated men who worked for medium-sized companies. This sentiment was not uncommon among fishers. Many fishers whom I interviewed in Minato told me that they became fishers because they did not want to work for a company as a laborer or a so-called "salaryman." They emphasized that they especially liked the fact that fishers are independent. "We are autonomous business owners," one fisherman noted, "not subordinate to anybody." "I don't have a boss who tells me what to do; I make my own decisions," he added.

The dynamic fluctuation of income is often narrated as an exciting part of their business as fishing families. But the continuously declining landings in recent years had made life more anxious than exciting for many fishing families. Satoru told me that he and his wife, Reiko, had suggested to their oldest son, who was about to graduate from high school, that he should take a company job instead of joining the family fishing business, expecting that he would be able to receive a stable salary unlike a fisherman. Mamoru had no child, meaning that Satoru's son would ostensibly be the brothers' successor in running their family's fishing business, but all of the adults in the family agreed that the son should get a "regular," stable job.

Later in the fall, Satoru's son got a job offer from a small local construction company. The starting salary was apparently ¥170,000 (roughly $1,500) per month, which surprised Satoru. "I didn't expect that it would be that low," Satoru murmured. Reiko said that their son would not be able to afford to rent an apartment, but he would still be better off than he would be as a fisherman, as even this meager income would probably be too much to expect as a deckhand on the boat. Satoru's mother was disappointed by this decision, but she, too, said that there was no choice. "I would have suggested that he join the family boat," she added, "only if the future looked better."

OCTOPUS HOPE

In fall 2006, it was one kind of repetition—of storms and tanker accidents—that caused severe challenges for fishing families in Minato. But it was another kind of repetition that eventually came to their rescue: namely "a dominant year class" of octopuses (*Octopus vulgaris*). Many marine fishes and mollusks are high-fecundity species, producing thousands of eggs in a single spawning. Survival rates from spawning are very poor, but the occasional highly successful spawning season allows for average population maintenance over the longer term. Among fish that spawn annually, the progeny of such spawning are called a "dominant year class" (Royce 1972, 131). This repetition is part of a species' natural population cycle, but, just as the formation of a storm is complicated, the causes of a dominant year class are complex and the timing of their appearances is unpredictable. According to a marine biologist at the fisheries extension, an unusually successful survival of a juvenile population depends on a combination of surrounding environmental factors, including the populations of prey and predators, the magnitude of fishing, and the numbers of fish stocked.

But beyond that, the information on the complicated processes of a dominant year class is largely "blackboxed" (Latour 1999) in the technologically engineered seascape. Thus, fishing families often exchange speculative narratives on what might have happened or might be happening under the ocean, which I view as their imaginings in search of "more livable futures" (Haraway 2016). Apparently, in this part of the Joban Sea, octopuses famously prey on clams, especially hard clams. A few fishers told me that they had hauled octopuses holding a hard clam within their arms. Some of them mentioned a hypothesis that there was a causal connection between the appearance of a dominant year class of octopuses and the population of hard clams that they had continuously conserved. They also wondered if the baby hard clams that recently appeared in the beach of Hama had possibly helped the growth of octopus populations. If so, would that mean that hard clams had found a way to survive in the midst of the coastal construction and the receded sandy beaches? A fisheries scientist at the experimental station indicated that it would be difficult to reach a conclusion. But it certainly was a hopeful thought.

The cheerful faces that emerged at the fishing port in Minato, thanks to the unexpectedly successful landings of octopuses in the winter, would have been almost unimaginable a few weeks earlier. The transformation of the climate at the harbor was indeed incredible. Just two months since the tanker accidents, despair was replaced by joy. On November 29, the first auction of the octopus season was held at the harbor's fish market. Earlier that morning, about fifty fishing boats left the harbor to haul the octopus pots they had sunk in the water three days earlier. After five to six hours of working at sea, the boats returned to the harbor with two to seven large tubs of octopuses. At 1:00 p.m., the action floor was covered with countless blue plastic tubs. In those tubs, each octopus was kept in a bright-red mesh bag so that the slimy creature could stay alive in water but would not be able to escape. The colorful scene of blue tubs and bright-red mesh bags was mesmerizing. I saw Satoru at the auction site standing in front of a large pile of octopuses in mesh bags. "How is today's catch?" I asked. He said with a big smile, "Not good at all!" "My loss," he added, pointing his elbow at his friend's even bigger pile sitting next to his. For the next couple of months, the landing value of octopuses remained mostly high, due to a lack of competition with fishing families of the neighboring town, Hama.

One day in the middle of December, as the end of the year loomed just around the corner, Minato fishing families had yet another successful trip of octopus fishing. That afternoon, Hiroshi—the young captain in his early forties whom I

FIG. 3. Bagged, landed octopuses at Minato's local fish market. Photo by author.

mentioned in prologue—and I were chatting on the quay by his boat while he was preparing for the next morning's fishing trip. Like many others whom I met at the harbor, he was unmistakably in a good mood. He told me that I should note that this winter was unusual. In the previous many winters, as he taught me, the majority of Minato fishing families had gone for bottom-trawling by early December. Usually only about a dozen families engaged in octopus-potting, and they would eventually join in bottom-trawling after a few days of catching octopuses. But unlike usual winters, all of the fishing boats in Minato this year were still enjoying successful octopus-potting in mid-December. Because of the previous years' poor results from octopus-potting, in addition to the fall's tanker disasters and the subsequent monthlong fishing moratorium, this year's emergence of a dominant year class of octopuses was an especially happy surprise. He told me that, until he actually saw the piles of octopuses at the fish market, he had been worried that his family might have to spend a frugal New Year's Day, Japan's most important family holiday. "But," he said with an exaggerated sigh of relief, "it looks like we can celebrate a decent New Year's, many thanks to octopuses!"

During the winter, fishing families in Minato held out hope for successful octopus seasons during the next a couple of winters. I often heard from different men and women of fishing families happily chatting about next year's octopus landings. Their common predictions for the forthcoming future were positive. They claimed that they knew from their experience that once a lot of octopuses appear, they usually keep coming back for another three years.

In the fall of 2007, after I finished my yearlong fieldwork and left Ibaraki, Hiroshi sent me an email that playfully paraphrased the well-known 1934 short story "Matasaburo of the Wind," (Kaze no Matasaburō). The opening line in his message read: "Dear Satsuki who came with a storm and left like a storm." The story, read by virtually all elementary-school children in Japan, begins with the sound of the strong wind that brought that year's fall storm to a small mountain village in northern Japan. For locals, the fall storm is a symbol of merciless nature, which causes serious damage to their farms and rice paddies. Like other small villages might, the people in the town had a number of legends related to natural events, and the winds of the storm are described as a goblin-like spirit, called "Matasaburo of the Wind."

The story focuses on the lives of the village boys who have a number of crazy, surreal experiences when an unknown boy from outside, acting very much like a goblin, arrives in the town with the fall storm, leaving eleven days later with another storm. As Hiroshi indicated in his email, the particular year that I lived in Minato was indeed stormy and surreal. But in fact, ever since the first wave of modernization arrived in Minato in the 1960s, the history of fishing families had been a repetition of such stormy dramas. And as I would eventually witness in 2011 and the following years, the history of stormy dramas goes on. But disaster after disaster, fishing families in Minato repeatedly survived the aftermaths, with occasional assistance from marine species that capriciously appear in the ruined seascape.

CHAPTER 2 Survival Conditions

"For our future, I am placing my hope in the power of women and young people," the president of Hama's fishing co-op said to the more than sixty female members of fishing families who gathered in the conference room on a Sunday in April 2007 for that year's general assembly of Hama Women's Association (WA). A couple of weeks later, on another Sunday, forty junior fishermen occupied the same conference room for their general assembly of Hama's Young Fishermen's Association (YFA). In his opening speech then, the president also made the same remark.

In 2007, both women and young fishermen of fishing families in Hama—a coastal town neighbor of Minato—were busy on Sundays, even though it was officially a no-fishing day. Twelve women were busy with their "coastal mamas' shop," packing and selling fresh and processed fish at the corner of the fishing harbor. At the local sandy beach, young fishermen spent their time collecting baby clams in order to relay them into their own co-op's protected waters. On some Sundays, young fishermen also got together in the co-op's conference room and discussed plans for opening a fish wholesale business. Besides these activities at the co-op level, the elected representatives of the YFA and WA were also busy on some Sundays attending the prefecture-sponsored meetings and workshops, listening to lectures on fish marketing, and exchanging opinions with fisheries experts as well as with men and women from other fishing co-ops.

While observing those busy women and young fishermen of Hama, I often remembered what a novice fisheries agent at the time, Mr. Wakata, had once said to me about them: "They are working hard." Knowing that I previously lived in the neighboring town of Minato, he drew a contrast, complaining that fishing families there had been unsophisticated in their activity, focusing only on catching fish and showing little interest in his suggestions to develop new fish businesses. From his perspective as a government official, the women and young fishermen in Hama were making productive efforts to transform themselves into

FIG. 4. Hama's young fishermen in wetsuits, collecting clams to relay to protected waters. Photo by author.

modern, "self-responsible" members of fishing communities who can develop their own business plans for their future survival. This coincided with a new emphasis consistent with the government's most recent neoliberal economic policies: the goal of developing people of fishing communities into self-sufficient entrepreneurs. This new policy agenda was yet another call for modernization of otherwise backward local fishers, but its particular focus was successful survival in an economically and environmentally uncertain future.

In reality, however, as I witnessed in 2006 and 2007, fishing families not only in Hama but also in Minato were *both* working very hard to survive in the highly uncertain situations, which were marked by not only the three tanker accidents but also continuous declines in fish landings. But fishing families in the two towns took different approaches to surviving in the precarious seascape. Simply put, fishing families in Minato did not consider the government's neoliberal development suggestions suitable for their survival, whereas those in Hama did. But their different attitudes toward the government's policy rhetoric had not emerged from, as the young fisheries agent implied, more (Hama) or less (Minato) sophisticated understandings of the importance of modernization.

Instead, they interpreted the rhetoric of modernization differently. In Minato, fishing families perceived catching octopuses as a more rational way, compared to developing new fish businesses, to survive the challenging circumstances. In Hama, where a shift to catching octopuses represented a more challenging option for reasons I discuss later in this chapter, they embodied the rhetoric of neoliberal modernization by pursuing new fish businesses in collaboration with fisheries agents as an alternative survival strategy.

The entanglements between the survival stories of fishing families and those of modernization are evident in the way women and young fishermen in Hama ended up volunteering to collaborate with fisheries agents and to transform themselves into piscatorial entrepreneurs. Drawing on illustrations of these entanglements, this chapter highlights one of this book's main arguments: the successful survival of modernization itself relies both on those who devote their time and effort to promote the rhetoric of modernization as well as on those who struggle to survive in the precarious seascape. Thus, in the context of the Joban seascape in the early 2000s, the rhetoric of modernization managed to endure not only because of the hardworking fisheries agents but also because of the tanker accidents, which made the fishing families of Hama even more anxious about their future survival. If those fishing families were able to catch octopuses or had another clear means to continue in their livelihoods, the project of promoting modern entrepreneurs might have failed. Its own survival rested in part on collaboration with the fishing families of Hama, who saw no obvious alternative.

Everyday conversations among fishing families in Hama reveal that modernization is not only a technocratic project but also a work of translation. In fact, translation has historically played an essential role in modernization in Japan, much as it has done in other non-Western societies (Satsuka 2015). Although Japan was not officially colonized by Western powers, bureaucrats and their intellectual supporters have voluntarily promoted modernization within their country's territory and among its people by translating and transplanting Western ideas, technology, and political-economic systems. For them, modernization has historically been an apparatus to pursue their dream for Japan and its industries to be regarded as "world-class." But pursuing the dream is like chasing a mirage. Even though the country accomplishes one modernization project after another, its modernization advocates always find something that needs to be modernized. Thus, modernization is always in process, and so is the translation of what it means to be modern. In addition, processes of translation do not end when Western languages are translated into Japanese at the national level. Translation continues as regional officials try to promote national modernization policies at the local level and also as local people try to make sense of given policy suggestions and meanings of modernization.

This angle on translation echoes and also extends critical discussions on cultural politics of "development," to which anthropologists and political ecologists alike have long contributed through their rich ethnographic accounts (Escobar 1995; Ferguson 1999; Li 2007; Pigg 1992; Walley 2004; Agrawal 2005). As they have suggested, interpretations of what it means to be developed or backward are highly nuanced and uniquely configured through not only transnational but also interregional, intercommunal, and interpersonal interactions. Similarly in Hama, fishing families eventually came to embody modernization by actively translating what it means to be modern through interacting with fisheries agents and other fishing families within their own community as well as those of neighboring towns like Minato. Such everyday translation is not only political but also personal and affective.[1] During the months that I lived in Hama, I occasionally encountered daily conversations among fishing families that were associated with modernization, and they were often filled with a mixture of anxiety and hope about the present and the future. It was through such everyday translation that women and young fishermen gradually cultivated their own reasons for becoming modern entrepreneurs and attached meaning to that decision.

NO PAIN, NO FUTURE

In 2007, when I visited prefecture-sponsored events at which fisheries officials and agents discussed new directions in fisheries policy with men and women of local fishing families, I heard the same sentence in more than a few of the officials' speeches and presentations: "There's no such thing as painless reform." The officials were borrowing a famous quote from the popular former prime minister Junichiro Koizumi, who held office from 2001 through 2006. Under the Koizumi administration's neoliberal reforms, the government sharply cut the budgets that had long been used to support the fisheries industry and rural economies. In their speeches, those fisheries officials always emphasized all the difficult challenges that the prefecture's coastal fishery was facing. They also insisted that the industry had to deal with an uncertain future and that therefore "we" must take action *now*. It was clear that what they really meant was that "you, fishers," must follow what "we, the government," suggest for survival.

What has often been described as Japan's neoliberal turn began in the late

1990s, as the state continued to face accumulating financial deficits since the burst of the economic bubble in early 1990s. By the beginning of the millennium, despite many disputes even within the Liberal Democratic Party (LDP)— Japan's long-ruling conservative party—neoliberal reforms had been seemingly accepted widely as something unavoidable. In 2001, while the government announced a significant cutback of subsidies, the newly elected prime minister repeatedly chanted his famous phrase to the citizens: "There's no such thing as painless reform." Accordingly, the Fisheries Agency under the new neoliberal administration introduced a new policy direction, emphasizing the concept of "self-responsibility" (*jikosekinin*), which Koizumi also made popular in his speeches. The rhetoric of self-responsibility claims that fishing families should assume the burdens of dealing with the problems of not only the past and the present but also of shaping the future. Under the new neoliberal policy, therefore, fishing families were allegedly responsible for the current problems of the declining fisheries industry and the future problem of survival; they were presently in trouble because they had not been sophisticated enough to prevent them from happening. For that reason, fishing families were also considered to be responsible for ensuring their own future survival. In such discourses of self-responsibility, the state's accountability was largely ignored or unmentioned, despite its significant role in creating these current problems through its historical modernization projects in the past.

In the rhetoric of modernization policy, coastal fishing families are always regarded as subjects who must be modernized. It means that, even if they had once before successfully followed an earlier government's modernization scheme (e.g., by increasing their fish yields by modernizing fishing boats and equipment), a new policy direction leads the same group of fishing families to revert into "backwardness," if now an updated version of it. In the early 2000s, while introducing the neoliberal language of fishing families' self-responsibility for their survival, government officials made the familiar claim that fishing families had to modernize their old-fashioned mentality in order to deal with the current problems. "Fishers have to do more than just catch fish," said one fisheries agent, "to survive in this modern age."

Under a neoliberal logic emphasizing individual entrepreneurship, fishing families would also have to become sophisticated about fish marketing businesses. For example, fisheries officials suggest that, if the fish price is low, fishing families need to come up with new business plans on how to generate additional value instead of ignorantly just catching more fish, which could lead to overfishing and lowering the price of fish even further. They also argued that, as long as fishing families were willing to transform from "backward" to "modern" in order to survive in the future, the government would support their transition. But in the end, it was up to fishing families to make their own commitment, just as it was their own responsibility to become modern subjects capable of survival by following policy suggestions.

SEA GODDESS, AMBA-SAMA

In the spring of 2007, while the government's neoliberal rhetoric of "self-responsibility" continued to grow at the local level, fishing families in Hama struggled to make do with their continuously declining fish landings. Frustration and anxiety about their future survival seemed especially prevalent among younger members of the community. In their daily conversations, younger members often complained about the customary rules that older generations had developed, which they interpreted as straitjackets and also as signs of backwardness. The continual role of the sea goddess Amba-sama represented one such relic.

Once upon a time in the Joban region, Hama was considered one of the most "modern" fishing towns in the region. This was during the immediate postwar decades, from the late 1940s through the 1960s, when Japan's central government aimed to promote the technological advancement of coastal fishing and to improve the standard of living among coastal fishing families. Throughout this period, Hama was renowned as one of the most successful examples of the nation's fisheries modernization policy. At the time, Hama was a bustling port town. The fishing port was crowded with more than two hundred coastal fishing boats with newly equipped engines and mechanized gear, in addition to a dozen large-scale offshore vessels.[2] While fishing families in Hama were enjoying the triumphant decades and the status of being described as "the modernized," those in the neighboring towns like Minato were still shamefully regarded as backward "fishfolks" who were catching small amounts of nearshore fish and shellfish with their old-fashioned wooden rowboats without engines or any modern equipment. But notions like "countryside," "traditional," and "backward" are cultural products that are generated through the translation of temporality, and their meanings are malleable and reflective of changes in developmental practices (Escobar 1995; Pigg 1992; see also Williams 1973). Decades later, by the time I started my fieldwork in 2006, Minato was largely regarded as a modern port city, whereas Hama was widely referred to as a "traditional fishing village," or *dentōteki na gyoson*. Moreover, Hama fishing families were often depicted—by people within and outside of Hama—as emblematically "old-fashioned" or "backward."

It was just before I moved to Hama that Hiroshi, the captain in Minato whom I introduced in the prologue, told me that in Hama I would be able to observe the idiosyncratic culture of a traditional fishing village, which did not exist in Minato. He emphasized that fishing families' life in Hama was very different from that in Minato. "In Hama," he said, "Amba-sama shows up." I had never heard of the term and could not even tell whether it referred to a person, a creature, or something else. "It is an old anecdote," he explained. I asked whether it was some kind of a piscatorial ritual. "Sort of, I guess," he replied. "I only know things that I heard from people," he said, "but, I heard, when a particular fishing boat especially succeeds in catching fish and remains successful for consecutive days, one night Amba-sama shows up to prevent the boat from going fishing the next morning." "What that means is that," he continued, "a bunch of drunk young fishermen get together at night and break into the successful boat and build a statue of Amba-sama with the fish baskets and other stuff they find on the boat." And the next morning, he explained, when the captain finds out what happened to his boat, he is supposed to call off the fishing trip for that morning because it is considered to be bad luck to go a fishing trip after "Amba-sama has shown up." He said that he used to hear of occasional appearances of Amba-sama in the past, but he was not sure whether the tradition was still ongoing these days. "Pray for your best luck," he smiled, "and maybe you will get a chance to meet the real Amba-sama."

According to one maritime folklore study, Amba-sama is a sea goddess who brings safety at sea and good catches to fishermen, an image that is widely recognized in coastal communities throughout the central and northern regions of the main island of Japan (Kawashima 2003).[3] Municipal documents on Hama's fisheries testify to the history of Amba-sama, which reflects the long roots of the town's commercial fishing. At least since the late Edo period in the early 1800s, the goddess has been part of the local rituals among Hama fishing families. As these local documents indicate, in Hama, an Amba-sama ritual used to be a kind of a festival for fishers to celebrate successful catches by taking a day off, marching around the town with carnival floats shaped like boats and fish, drinking sake, and placing a miniature shrine on top of each fishing boat. The ritual, however, was transformed at some point into a deliberate effort for deckhands to obtain a day off from their captain after being exhausted with consecutive fishing trips by breaking into boats and engaging in mischievous sabotage. At the later date, the practice was further revised as a way to punish a successful fishing boat when it becomes the only winner.

When that happens, deckhands usually create a pile of fish-buckets and helms yanked off from moored fishing boats and finish with a sacred rope taken from the local Shinto shrine and wrapped around their makeshift mountain. The next morning, those captains who own the targeted boats learn that "Amba-sama has shown up" and return home. Then they later return to the dock to put the fish-buckets and detachable helms back on their usual spots on the boats, and then bless Amba-sama with sake before returning the sacred rope to the shrine. The practice became more frequent and elaborate as the mechanization of fishing boats and equipment enabled fishing for longer hours and more consecutive days during the 1950s and 1960s. In the course of the fishing economic boom in Hama, however, there were a few occasions when a captain would ignore Amba-sama's warning, calling the crews and going fishing anyway after cleaning up the mess. But then those boats were eventually further punished by Amba-sama with more malicious mischief, such as cutting a mooring rope and destroying fishing gear. In the late 1960s, however, according to the municipal documents, Amba-sama's mischief ended for a time after an incident that involved a police investigation; an angry captain who could not find his boat's helm formally filed a complaint at the local police station. In 2007, however, some fishing families in Hama indicated that Amba-sama still existed, although her arrival had become far less frequent.

One day, at Hama's fishing harbor, a few women were chatting at the dock while waiting for their husbands' boats to return. One of them asked me how my research was going. I told them that I had been reading about the history of Hama's fisheries and learned about Amba-sama. I then asked them whether Amba-sama still existed or not in Hama and, if yes, when she had made her last appearance. As I asked the question, the first boat for the day returned, showing up at the farthest corner of the seawalls. A couple of women walked away. I repeated the question to a woman who was still standing next me. She, too, started to walk away from the spot where we were, putting her rubber gloves on. I also took a few steps and followed her, putting my rubber gloves on. After a pause, she said in a quiet voice, "Maybe." I asked whether she meant Amba-sama, and repeated my question about when she had last appeared. As the woman was walking farther away from me to join another group of women, she whispered. "Um, about a year ago, I guess."

A few seconds later, I heard a voice from behind me. "Unbelievable, isn't it?"

It was Mayumi, who had moved to Hama from a city after marrying the son of a fishing family. She maintained a quasi-outsider status, often sharing her opinions with me regarding the idiosyncratic culture of Hama's fishing families. I asked her if her comment referred to Amba-sama. She nodded. As it turns out, it was her father-in-law who had been Amba-sama's most recent victim. Mayumi told me that her father-in-law said to her one day that he found, on the deck of his fishing boat, a mountain of buckets and an upside-down kettle on top. "He was laughing," she continued, "and even said to me that it was impressive." "Impressive, eh?" she said contemptuously. "I just couldn't believe such a thing still exists today. It is the twenty-first century, you know? It's so barbaric, don't you think?" Mayumi told me that in this case of Amba-sama, whoever did it was not his deckhand—namely, his own son, and Mayumi's husband—but rather other boats' fishermen. The reason they did it, according to Mayumi, was because her father in-law and his son had had most successful hauls for a few consecutive days, leading up to the vandalism. Hence, "Amba-sama appeared" to punish them for their "selfish" victory and to bring fairness to other fishing families.

Mayumi was not alone in her judgments of Hama as "backward." There were plenty of other men and women of fishing families within Hama who complained about their traditions. They claimed that their old customs were backward and irrational, which caused them to be less successful than other neighboring towns. One morning in Hama, while waiting for fishing boats to return at the quay in front of the fish market, I asked a group of women about their views on competition and cooperation and differences between Minato and Hama. An active elderly woman in her early seventies quickly responded, "Fishing is surely about competition, but cooperation is important." "You can't keep up with your business without cooperating with others," she continued, "and you can't be just selfish," implying that cooperation is a traditional value of a good old fishing village like Hama. After she walked away from the spot, a younger woman in her late forties led me a couple of steps away from the others and whispered, "In reality, you know, fish folks here are not easy people to deal with," implying that the relationship between cooperation and competition is much more nuanced than the older woman had suggested. Others murmured in agreement that cooperation among fishing families in Hama was based more on jealousies and grudges against one another than on mutual trust or mercy.

A few weeks after the conversation about Amba-sama with those Hama women, I was in Minato to visit Hiroshi, who had originally taught me about Hama's Amba-sama at his house. I asked him again about differences between the two neighboring fishing towns, Minato and Hama. He responded: "Our ways of fishing [in Minato] are individualistic and capitalistic. We became successful by competing with one another. When somebody is catching successfully, others try to be more successful. But they [in Hama] are different. They hamstring one another." "Hamstring" (*ashi o hippariau*) is a term usually used to describe the act of someone trying to prevent somebody else from becoming successful, or, more specifically, from getting a leg up on others. Hamstringing in this context means that when somebody in particular is catching successfully, others disturb it. Hiroshi added, "It sounds irrational to us, but that's their way."

OCTOPUS VETO

Besides the sea goddess Amba-sama, Hama's younger members told me that their co-op's rule against octopus-potting was also a straitjacket and a sign of their backwardness. According to them, seniority mattered in the co-op's administration and everyday practices, and older members created a variety of co-op rules in the name of fairness and cooperation. Although they acknowledged the importance of fairness and cooperation, they also expressed their frustration over the "old-school" rules. They claimed that the rules were preventing them from taking crucial opportunities to make up for declining fish landings. One afternoon at the fishing harbor, a young fisherman complained while we were chatting, "If we don't make a change, we're all gonna go down together."

In the fall of 2006, the three tanker accidents near Minato's industrial seaport caused significant income losses not only to fishing families in Minato but also to those in Hama because the monthlong moratorium was applied to the waters adjacent to both towns. Subsequently in the winter, a large quantity of octopuses that unexpectedly appeared in the coastal waters offered the opportunity for the fishing families in both towns to make up for their lost income. Throughout the winter, however, while the fishing harbor in Minato remained lively with cheerful fishing families, that in Hama stayed mostly quiet. In theory, under the prefectural fisheries regulation, fishing families in Hama could have made up for their income loss by catching octopuses, but those elder members collectively put a veto on octopus fishing in the name of fairness and cooperation.

Traditionally, for octopus fishing, Minato fishing families had used octopus pots, whereas Hama families had used longlines. The major difference between the two fishing methods is that octopus-potting is a type of trap fishing, while longlining is a type of hook-and-line fishing. Octopus pots are usually set on the

Survival Conditions

seabed attached to longlines with approximately fifty pots on each line, tricking the octopus to use a pot as shelter. Fishers usually set their pots overnight and haul them back up the following morning. In contrast, octopus-longlining uses one long main line with branch lines attached at intervals with lure hooks, appealing to predatory octopuses to jump right on. Unlike octopus-potting, octopus-longlining is an operation that is fully carried out and completed in the morning. According to one captain in Hama, in comparison to longlining, octopus-potting requires more initial investment for purchasing the gear but is less labor-intensive and more efficient for catching large volumes of octopuses. In addition, he also told me that he and a few others used to go octopus-longlining in winter, but all of them had stopped doing so a few years earlier. He personally quit octopus-longlining five years earlier because the landings had been low for the previous few years and the physical labor was too demanding, particularly for his wife, who had started working as his deckhand after his father passed away. I asked him whether he thought there was a possibility of resuming octopus-longlining during the winter to take advantage of the dominant year class. He said that it would be impossible because the lines and hooks were too old to use. He also mentioned that he did not think that it would be worth taking on the debt necessary to renew the gear for such a labor-intensive fishing method. But some younger fishermen expressed a different opinion, arguing that the opportunity was right for starting to invest in octopus-potting.

The octopus veto remained controversial. In the winter, expecting that the octopus boom would last for another year or two, some families in Hama actually requested approval from the co-op to start octopus-potting the next winter. But after a few meetings, the co-op board eventually announced that octopus-potting would remain banned in Hama. The strongest opposition to octopus-potting in Hama came from captains of bottom-trawlers because the lines of octopus pots lying on the bottom of the sea would become obstacles and would reduce their trawling areas, whereas in Minato, most fishing families were flexible in dealing with different fishing methods. In winter, they usually maintain equipment for both bottom-trawling and octopus-potting, and they flexibly switch between the two fishing methods based on their calculation of which one is more profitable, carefully considering not only the cost of gas and labor but also ecological and market conditions. In contrast, in Hama, bottom-trawlers had a powerful voice in the co-op administration, and without their approval, octopus-potting would not be allowed. Because Hama's bottom-trawlers specialized only in bottom-trawling, they were usually intolerant of other fishing activities, especially if their fishing grounds overlapped with bottom-trawling.

When I had a chance to talk to a senior fisherman who was one of the board members of the Hama fishing co-op, I asked him if there was any room for compromise between bottom-trawlers and those who want to start octopus-potting. His answer was no. "There's no other choice," he said, "we all have to cooperate, you know." Those elders often emphasized the importance of following the co-op rules that they had maintained for generations. But among others, especially younger members of the co-op, those rules were often interpreted as a cultural straitjacket, representing backwardness and closed-mindedness.

THAT STUPID YELLOW LIGHT

One morning about a week after I moved to Hama, I arrived at the fish market around the usual time of 9:00 a.m. I was about to get out of my car to change from my sneakers to rubber boots and to put on waterproof pants, getting ready for my participant observation of the day. But there was nobody at the corner where women would usually hang out while waiting for fishing boats to return. I was not sure where they had gone. I looked up in the sky. The sun was out. It felt slightly windy, but the weather seemed fine for fishing. When I lived in Minato, I had never seen fishers cancel their trips in conditions like that.

I started the car again and drove to the other end of the fish market and found a few captains who were standing talking together. I wondered what those captains were doing there instead of going on fishing trips. I got out of the car, said good morning, and asked them if the fishing trips of that morning had been canceled. One captain pointed his finger at a yellow light that was attached to the corner of the market's concrete roof and murmured, "Because of that, no fishing today." "But look at this weather," he added, "it is absolutely fine!" He continued: "It was a bit windier earlier, so this morning's fishing trip was canceled. But soon after, it got calmer. Anyway, once it's canceled, it's canceled, so here we are." I asked him what the yellow light was for. Another captain explained that the Hama co-op has a rule that every morning, elected senior captains of the purse-seining boats decide whether the weather is suitable to take out the fishing boats. That morning, they had decided to cancel. But apparently, on that same morning, the boats of Minato and other towns in the area went out to catch young anchovies.

A different Hama captain grumbled about not being able to go fishing when he knew that Minato boats were out there at sea catching fish. "We used to be able to go fishing whenever we wanted, but *somebody* made the stupid rule for whatever reason," said another captain with a sarcastic laugh. For a moment, the captains shared an awkward silence. He added, "I'm bored! Let's just go home and take a nap." The other captains agreed with his call and started to walk away. I wanted to ask them more about the rule. I wanted to know why the Hama co-op did not let individual captains decide whether the weather was suitable as they do in Minato, unless the weather was noticeably unsafe for fishing. Why do they limit their chances to go fishing even though they often say they are worried about declining young anchovy landings? Why would they implement a rule that prevents those who want to go fishing when they can? But I decided to wait for another chance.

Later, such an opportunity arrived when I met a captain who taught me that one of the captains I saw the other morning was a brother of one of the co-op board members who established the "stupid" rule with the yellow light. The rule was, in fact, relatively new; it had been implemented only five years earlier in 2001. According to him, the main purpose of the rule was not really for keeping fishing boats safe in bad weather but rather for making sure to limit the gap in landings among fishing families in Hama. He explained that the rule was basically to prevent those well-equipped boats with young crews from being significantly more successful than those older boats with aging crew members whose landings were usually low. I asked him if anybody had tried to break the rule. "Nope," he said. In Hama, according to him, when people found out that somebody was not complying with co-op rules, that person would likely be formally or informally punished by other members. Formal punishment might be a fine and probation in fishing, as dictated in the co-op's written rules. An informal one would be destroying the violator's fishing equipment or releasing his boat from the dock overnight.

His response reminded me of Amba-sama, especially the story of Mayumi's father-in-law, who was being punished by Amba-sama for being more successful than others in his landings. In a sense, the yellow-light rule, Amba-sama, and also the octopus veto all followed a similar logic of egalitarianism. But at the same time those who were against these customary rules often claimed that they represented Hama's backward elements, which they thought should be modernized.

RESPONSIBLE SELVES

While I was living in Hama, there was one phrase that I repeatedly heard among young fishermen and also women: "We have to do something now." They often claimed that the reason they were working hard on Sundays was *not* because fisheries agents or other government officials told them to do so, but because they believed that they needed to do, emphasizing their own agency. "*We* need to do something now," they said with an emphasis on "we." They sometimes used the phrase in our interviews or during our casual conversations, but more frequently they used it among themselves during official meetings and social gatherings.

One spring afternoon, six board members of Hama's Young Fishermen's Association (YFA) gathered with Mr. Wakata, the young prefectural fisheries agent whom I mentioned earlier, in one of the co-op's warehouses to discuss an idea for a direct-sale business of surf clams (*hokkigai*, *Pseudocardium sachalinense*) to local restaurants. This business venture was originally an idea that another fisheries agent had suggested to members of Hama's YFA about a year earlier. The purpose of this business was to increase the sales value of surf clams, which had been considered as bycatch of hard clam dredging. Compared with regular hard clams, which are usually sold for 1,200 yen (approximately 12 US dollars) per kilogram, the market value of surf clams was generally low, sometimes no more than 100 yen (approximately 1 US dollar) per kilogram on average.

Among the six young fishermen, the president of Hama YFA at the time was Eiji. When I first met him, he was dressed in a clean white shirt and a pair of stone-washed blue jeans. With his neatly trimmed hair dyed light brown, he looked more like a professional surfer than a classic fisherman. He told me that it had actually been one year since the last time the board members discussed the surf clam business. In the last meeting, the board members came up with a plan with the previous fisheries agent to make some sample packages of surf clams and distribute them to selected local restaurants in order to negotiate future business possibilities. But because the busy juvenile-anchovy season was approaching at the time, they decided to wait until the fall to carry out the plan. The tanker accidents, however, that then occurred off the port of Minato and the subsequent fishing moratorium ended up further postponing the young fishermen's business exploration. That winter was impossible as well. Purse-seining was in the closed season during January and February, but because many of Hama's young fishermen work part-time jobs, mainly in construction, the venture business plan eventually had to be put off until the next spring.

In the afternoon, despite the yearlong gap from the last meeting, the young fishermen were energetic. They exchanged opinions on how to approach local restaurants, how to package clams, and their odds of success. After a while, Makoto, one of the YFA's board members, loudly exclaimed, "Let's just do it!" "We won't get any answer until we try," he added. During the spring, in order to further discuss the details of the plan, the board members held a meeting as often as once a week after work and also occasionally on the days when fishing trips were canceled. By early summer, the YFA board members and the fisheries agent had finally reached a plan on making a trial visit to a local restaurant. Mr. Wakata took the lead in doing some research on local restaurants, and at the next YFA board members' meeting, he announced to the young fishermen that he had found one restaurant that was interested in potential business deals with the YFA. After picking a date for the board members to visit the restaurant owner, they also planned to make a few product samples of packages with raw and boiled surf clams. After the president and the vice president of YFA and Mr. Wakata met with the restaurant's owner, they returned to the next meeting and reported on issues of price, total costs, and supply consistency. Ultimately, the business plan for the fish venture had to be suspended again due to the approaching early summer—the high season of young anchovies—but Eiji and Mr. Wakata both said that the meeting with the restaurant owner was a good start and that they felt confident about building something from there.

Indeed, all this enthusiasm and the cooperative attitudes of the young fishers were taken as evidence of what Mr. Wakata had once described to me as "working hard." But as with the words "We have to do something now," they were also conditioned by young fishermen's common frustrations with the current situation and their anxieties about the future. One evening at a local bar, I asked Eiji and Makoto, who had had spoken cheerfully during the YFA board meeting earlier, about their predictions about the likelihood of success for the venture business plan. Both of them said that they had no idea whether it would become successful but that they hoped that it would. Makoto continued, "Business is not easy, and we are a bunch of amateurs." "But," he added, "we've gotta do something." He was chatty that night. He emphasized how concerned he was about the future of the fishing industry and also about their families. He said that he often felt scared when he thought about his responsibilities for his wife and young children. And then he dropped his head into his hands and said, "What're we gonna do?" It was ambiguous whether he was addressing the question to somebody in particular or whether he was talking to himself. One of his friends lifted up the remote controller for the karaoke machine and responded, "Do you want to sing?" Makoto said okay and took the controller.

That evening, he might have been just a little too drunk and so acting a little more melodramatic than usual. But it was not the first time that I had heard him talking about his concerns over the declining landings and the uncertain future. Whenever I asked him about the future, he expressed the same concerns. Indeed, he seemed to be an enthusiastic go-getter, shouting things like, "Let's just try!" as he did at the YFA's board meeting. But those words also sounded, to me, like a pep talk for himself under the pressure and anxieties about the futures of himself, his family, and the fishing industry.

Those young fishermen—as well as women, as I will discuss in the next chapter—in Hama were, in fact, already working hard, as the young fisheries agent had acknowledged. In particular, through working closely with fisheries agents, they were making good efforts to follow the neoliberal policy suggestions. But in reality, the processes in which they became hardworking collaborators were complex, serving as poignant reminders of their nuanced relationships with the rhetoric of modernization. Rather than simply accepting the policy language that fisheries agents translate for them, those young fishermen and fisherwomen made their own decision to support the neoliberal policy suggestions by interpreting their challenging social and natural conditions and considering what they themselves needed to do to survive. As an unintentional consequence of their personal efforts to survive, however, they also ended up helping modernization advocates to justify their rhetoric and to survive as well.

CHAPTER 3 Mamas' Elegy

I first became aware that motherhood plays a significant role in the neoliberal futurism of survival when I learned about a women's fish-vending business in Hama during the prefecture-sponsored meeting in February 2007. That particular Sunday, more than sixty men and women of coastal fishing families from all over Ibaraki Prefecture gathered in a large conference room at a seaside resort hotel in Hama. They were dressed in clean but casual clothes, like sweatshirts and jeans. Behind the front stage, there was a large banner draped on the wall: "Fisheries Forum FY2006: Considering Business—How Should Fishers Sell Their Fish?" The event was an annual workshop that the prefecture's fisheries office organizes for members of the Young Fishermen's and Women's Associations. This year's theme was, as written on the banner, the fish sales business, particularly direct marketing strategies by fishers.

A prefectural official in a dark suit delivered the opening remarks. Then a senior economist from a fisheries consulting firm in Tokyo, wearing a slightly more casual suit, gave a keynote lecture. After he summarized the Japanese fish market system and its history, he presented his suggestions for what fishing families should do to survive in the future. He proclaimed that fishing families could no longer prosper by merely catching fish and selling them to local fish wholesalers as they had done for generations. He emphasized that, for the future of coastal fishing, fishers would have to *modernize* their business strategies by, for example, developing new marketing strategies and coming up with ideas to add or create new value for their fish. During the Q&A session after the keynote lecture, a fisheries agent who served as a moderator called on a woman in her late fifties, Akiko, to give a speech on her "case study" of developing a new marketing strategy.

Akiko stood up with a microphone in her hand and introduced herself in a strained voice, adding that she was a member of the Women's Association at the Hama fishing co-op, and one of the founding members of a seafood-vending business that they had named Fishermen's Mamas' Shop (Ryōshi no Kāchan no

Mise). In her ten-minute speech, she explained that the reason they began developing their business was because they wanted to make financial contributions to their own fishing families by marketing some of the fish that their husbands and sons catch directly to consumers instead of selling all of them to middlemen with high wholesale margins. She also mentioned that their vending project originally started with twelve members of the Women's Association more than two years earlier, when they sold local fish directly to local residents and tourists at a corner of the fish market within their fishing port in the summer of 2004. After a few more test-runs, they finally began running the fish shop regularly on Sunday mornings, except during the midsummer months due to the absence of proper cooling equipment necessary to meet food safety standards.

Akiko also mentioned that the fish they sold typically included fresh flounder as well as processed squid and young anchovies, which the women lightly boiled and sun-dried at the corner of the wharf on weekdays. All the fish they sold at their shop were locally landed in Hama and bought through auctions at the Hama fishing co-op's fish market. In other words, the fish that the shop sold was not technically the fish that those women's husbands and sons had caught. Akiko emphasized that the shop was designed to support their fishing community as a whole rather than selfishly making profits only for their own families. In her speech, she also included some stories about the challenges they had overcome—for example, obtaining the sales license and the co-op's approval, as well as locating workspace—and named a few issues that they were currently facing, among them recruitment of members, work rotation, time management, and wages. She said that, because of their limited revenues from selling fish and the many hours required for preparations, wages were low, and thus they had had difficulty attracting new members to join their business. She then concluded her speech by saying, "Although we face many challenges, we will continue trying our best."

A discussion session that followed Akiko's presentation began with commentaries given by the economist and a couple of prefectural officials, praising her and her fellow women's efforts to run their fish shop as meaningful contributions to the better future of Japanese coastal fisheries. The rest of the commentators also complimented the Hama women's venture as a ground for hope. One of them mentioned that the Hama women's efforts would improve the "rationalization of business," which would help stabilize the household income of those fishing families, who are suffering from continuously declining landings. Two fisheries officials also joined in the rally of compliments by commenting that Akiko and her fellow women would also make important contributions to the "improvement of women's participation," "promotion of seafood culture," and "revitalization of fishing villages." Obviously, their use of these particular phrases directly drawn from the fisheries policy guidelines was deliberate. It was fisheries agents' task to put the policy agenda into actual practice at local level. Thus, through transforming coastal fishing families into piscatorial entrepreneurs like those women in Hama and also through translating the meanings of the transformation for fishing families, the fisheries agents were working hard to achieve the overall policy goal of modernizing the fishing industry.

From the start, particularly given the work of the fisheries agents, it was not too surprising to find out that the women's fish-vending business in Hama was largely informed by the state's neoliberal policy rhetoric on fisheries modernization. But Akiko's speech made me wonder about her and other women's interpretations of their fish-vending business as well as their gendered roles as women of fishing families in the context of the neoliberal futurism of survival. The language of motherhood embedded in the fish-vending business was especially curious. What are women of fishing families expected to do as mothers? Why are they narrated as mothers? These questions continued to puzzle me as I carried out my fieldwork among women in Hama. Eventually I realized that it was not just women but precisely "mothers" who were expected to play the leading role in assisting coastal fishing families' future survival. Like mothers who are expected to provide unconditional love to their families, those piscatorial mothers—namely, fishermen's mamas—are now presumed to take intimate care of not only their own individual families but also their community of fishing families and, even more broadly, the nation's struggling fishing industry.

The women in Hama embody the entanglements between the survival stories of modernization and fishing families. The survival of modernization relies not only on those fishing families who struggle for survival but also, and more specifically, on their women. By asking women to act in keeping with motherhood and engage in its emotional labor, this neoliberal fisheries modernization project ends up reproducing conventional narratives of "backward" fishing communities and their idiosyncratic gender roles for women.[1]

THE MOTHERHOOD PROJECT

Akiko told me later on, although she did not mention it in her speech at the fisheries forum, that the idea of the Fishermen's Mamas' Shop originally came from fisheries agents who suggested it to her and other women. Moreover, it was actually one of the fisheries agents who wrote her speech. When I had a chance to talk to the fisheries agent later, he proudly acknowledged that it was he and his fellow fisheries agents who came up with the idea of a women's fish-vending business in order to fulfill their broader policy objectives. He also humbly patted himself on the back by mentioning how much hard work they had to put into starting the women's fish-vending business in Hama. He said that he knew that the shop would be a good market-oriented solution, making use of women's ability to cook and sell fish in order to offset the income loss from reduced catch sizes. At first, however, he and his colleagues struggled to get positive responses from fishing families. Many of them expressed skepticism about the likelihood of the project's success. But in the end, the twelve women of Hama agreed to go along with it. And the fish-vending business eventually became successful enough for Akiko to give a speech at the prefectural fisheries forum.

"Fishers have to do more than just catching fish to survive in this modern age," said Mr. Tabata, the prefecture's chief fisheries agent, to me when I visited him in his office. His statement was consistent with the central government's recent policy direction. Following the neoliberal rhetoric of "Do It Yourself" (DIY) and self-responsibility, the new policy agenda suggests that fishing families must modernize their business in order to deal with their ongoing financial struggles. But while the policy suggestions call for adapting new concepts such as entrepreneurship and women's empowerment, these "modernization" projects often largely rely on traditional gender norms, especially those surrounding motherhood. Although fisheries officials often argue that developing the fish business is intended to help fishing families to survive, ideals of motherhood are always hinted at as an important part of the project. The motherhood on which the seafood-vending project focuses is not that of just an ordinary mother, especially not the contemporary kind of mother who lives in the city. Instead, it is meant to suggest a countryside mama, or *kāchan*, who is earthy but deeply loving, and who also has strong, thick arms with which she can rescue her children if they are in trouble. But in the context of Japanese neoliberal gender politics, coastal mamas' ambiguous positionality between a dependent and independent member of a family is similar to those of women elsewhere (Alexy 2020). While they were supposed to act as independent and entrepreneurial business owners of their fish-vending business, they had to maintain their identity as "mothers" who were considered to be supportive but dependent members of their family and community.

As noted in the 2006 edition of the official annual Fisheries Agency white paper, the government claims that the Japanese fishing industry overall is facing serious trouble. Fish landings have been declining, and fewer and fewer young people are becoming commercial fishers. Fishing families are struggling due to the increasing costs of fuel and other necessary fishing expenses in the face of stagnant or even declining fish prices. The Fisheries Agency also argues that the low price of fish has been partly caused by changes in the Japanese diet, as fewer and fewer Japanese people consume seafood as meat consumption grows consistently. These troubling trends, according to these government reports, are not only an economic issue but also a cultural one: *we are what we eat*. While fish is an important part of who the Japanese are, the declining fish consumption is a crisis of Japanese culture. The white paper also narrates that modern mothers have increasingly become clueless when confronted with the slimy body of a whole fish, and many of them purportedly do not even know how to prepare simple seafood dishes, arguing that the decline of women's devotion to traditional home cooking with fish for their families is one of the major causes of the reduced seafood consumption (Fisheries Agency 2009). Therefore, Japan needs traditional coastal mamas who will devote their time and effort to saving not only their own families but also the community, the industry, and the Japanese people. Coastal mamas are expected to be mothers to all of them.

Given this kind of expectation from the government, the twelve women in Hama said that what actually helped them to start their fish-vending business was the urgent feeling of "having to do something now" for their families and fishing community. It was apparently the same phrase that young fishermen used when they explained why they were collaborating with fisheries agents to develop their own wholesale business. But women had their own version of explanation. "I can't catch fish myself," one of the twelve women told me, "but I wanted to help the household income somehow." In reality, women of fishing families have always worked very hard, as they took care of almost all of the necessary tasks involved with their family business except for actual catching of fish. In some cases, women caught fish as a deckhands and took care of the other tasks as well. But these women's hard work was often undervalued, viewed as only secondary contributions. The notion of women's supporting role was also evident in official narratives. For a long time, since the Hama Women's Association (WA) was originally established in the late 1950s, the WA had been managed and narrated as a support for the local fishing industry, while captains—who are always men—do the "main" work at sea.[2] Accordingly, the four pledges in the manifesto of the Prefectural Federation of WAs all emphasize their roles in assisting, contributing, helping:

First, we band together and help each other to build a strong community.
Second, we use these bonds of solidarity to improve our social and economic status.
Third, we work hard to plan and rationalize our livelihoods.
Fourth, we voluntarily contribute to the sound development of our fishing co-op in order to build a comfortable and affluent fishing village.

Traditionally, based on the pledges, the Hama WA's typical contributions had been limited to such activities as cleaning the fishing port, serving snacks at local festivals, and taking care of the flower beds in front of the co-op office building. In 2004, for the first time in the WA's history, the twelve members opened their fish shop in order to bring additional income to fish landings, hoping to support not only their families but also their community of fishing families.

GENDERED RULES

During the year I lived in Hama and Minato, I spent countless hours at their fishing harbors, participating in an everyday duty called *okamawari*, "land tasks." Such work takes place around (*mawari*) the land (*oka*), including unloading fish from boat decks onto the quay, carrying fish from the quay to the fish market, sorting fish by species and by sizes, scaling fish, laying fish at the auction site, uploading sold fish onto buyers' trucks, and cleaning the fish market afterward. The total time required for land tasks varies by the type of fishing activities (e.g., purse-seining or bottom-trawling), but the backbreaking duty usually starts at around 9:00 a.m. and does not end until around 3:00 p.m. The land tasks themselves were mostly similar in Hama and Minato, but their associated rules were vastly different.

In Minato, the decision of who takes care of land tasks is up to each family. Women often are in charge of land tasks, but when women are not available, men assume that responsibility. During the work itself, Minato families often help other families who are relatives or friends, but it is a matter of choice. There is no formal rule or punishment regarding the duties. In contrast, in Hama, women sometimes catch fish alongside men, but land tasks are strictly women's duty. The age range of those handling the land tasks varied widely in Hama—the youngest were in their twenties and the oldest women in their seventies—but they were invariably women. When I spoke with fishing families in both Hama and Minato, these strict gendered rules in Hama were occasionally narrated as a marker of Hama as a "classic fishing village," which often connotes patriarchal traditionalism and backwardness. In Minato, fishing families typically described their style of work as rational (*gōriteki*), as opposed to that in Hama, which they considered to be old-fashioned and "stubborn" (*atama ga katai*, more precisely translated as "hardheaded"). They also often said to me that Hama's gendered division of labor is strictly simple: "men catch fish, and women sell fish."

But in real life, women of fishing families were responsible for more than just selling fish. In fact, women of fishing families in Hama were perhaps busiest people I have ever met in my life. It was especially true for those women who ride on so-called "husband-wife boats" (*meoto bune*). In Hama, in the last few years as their annual landings were continuously declining, an increasing number of women have become commercial fishers so that their families can cut down on the cost of hiring deckhands. On those husband-wife boats, however, female fishers' work as deckhands at sea was largely considered to be an extension of unpaid domestic labor. Therefore, after they return to the harbor from a fishing trip, while their husbands only served as occasional onlookers at the fish market, many of those women continued to complete land tasks because they are strictly the duty of women, or, more specifically, of captains' wives. As I saw them every day at the harbor in Hama, those mama fishers often effortlessly jumped from the edge of the fishing boat onto the quay as soon as their husbands moored their fishing boats, and quickly began working on their land tasks by unloading fish baskets. They then kept working until all the rest of land tasks were completed.

In Hama, land tasks are not only physically demanding, but they also have their own idiosyncratic rhythm. Some one hundred women were working on land tasks on each fishing day, coordinating their movements with practiced and policed efficiency; whoever falls out of rhythm will get chewed out by others. It is calm when women chat with other women while they are awaiting their husbands' and sons' return from a fishing trip. However, it immediately heats up when fishing boats come back to the port. Handling fish requires speed and care. Women often told me that the fresher fish are, the higher prices they get. Thus, women engaged in land tasks are always on the run. In order to sell their fish for the best price, they have to be quick, and in order to be as quick as possible, they need other women's hands. Unlike the more family-based cooperation in Minato, in Hama, in order to be helped, they must reciprocate and help others when needed. Practiced women go through all the procedures quickly, smoothly, and rhythmically while keeping up a lively banter (occasionally with surprisingly ribald jokes) and laughing with each other. In order to do the work effectively, a novice must learn from experienced women how to properly engage with others.

Mayumi was one of the experienced women who taught me how land tasks work in Hama. But twenty-something years earlier, she, too, had been a novice. According to her, her first day of land tasks was a bitter experience. "I knew nothing about land tasks," she said. At the time, she was still a young "city bride" who had just married a son of a fishing family in Hama. On the morning she first encountered land tasks, she went along with her mother-in-law, as many women do on their first day. When they arrived at the harbor crowded with women on their land task duties, her mother-in-law told Mayumi to watch what she did. So she stood by her mother-in-law and tried to learn the procedures by watching. But another woman suddenly yelled at Mayumi, "Get out my way. Don't just stand there like an idiot!" She called the experience "terrifying." Other women told me similar stories about their first time performing land tasks. But through learning by watching what older women do and being yelled at by their senior counterparts, women of fishing families eventually become themselves strong coastal mamas.

In Hama, during land tasks, women often asked me the same question: "Minato wasn't like this, eh?" When they were experienced older women, the subsequent conversations usually reflected their view of Minato as being something other, and of course less authentic, than a "real" fishing town like Hama. But for many of the younger women, the uniqueness of Hama's land-task environment was often used to criticize how backward their fishing community was. In such cases, what they saw as "old-fashioned" practices were largely about the formal and informal rules governing land tasks rather than the tasks themselves. While elders claimed that the rules are necessary to maintain their sense of community and egalitarianism, younger ones argue that the rules are unnecessarily inflexible and irrational.

According to Hama's rules, all fishing families must share the labor and costs involved with land tasks. For example, for purse-seining or clam-dredging, the rules indicate that each boat must provide a woman to take care of all the necessary land tasks, including landing, scaling, and selling fish at a local fish market. If a boat does not provide a land-task woman, the owner must pay a penalty of five thousand yen (approximately fifty US dollars). The person must be a woman; a man is not allowed to be a substitute. A young woman once murmured to me

Mamas' Elegy

that she could have earned additional income for her household if she were to take a part-time job, but she had to stay at the harbor for most of the day for her land tasks. She said that her mother-in-law was too old to take care of land tasks, so she had to do the work. If she were to take a wage job elsewhere, she would have to hire somebody else to perform her land tasks or pay the fine. Either way, she would likely gain nothing.

While living in Hama, I listened to countless conversations about the co-op's rules and contesting views of them, with many of the younger generation of fishing families being particularly critical of them as a straitjacket limiting their business. But in practice, it is hard to judge whether these rules actually disadvantage any of them. Moreover, despite their complaints about the rules being backward, one might argue that the restrictions could work, even if unintentionally, as conservation methods like those idealized in descriptions of resource management by Japanese coastal fisheries. By limiting fishing pressure on marine resources, these rules might be supporting the health of the coastal environment. That said, what I want to underline here is not how these rules actually function. Rather, it was their interpretations of the rules and their self-diagnosis of their community's backwardness that helped those women to collaborate with the state's neoliberal modernization policy, even though it requires women to be traditional fishermen's mamas.

"WE HAVE TO DO SOMETHING NOW"

Akiko and her fellow members of the Fishermen's Mamas' Shop told me in interviews that, although they were told by fisheries agents that the vending business was intended to open up the new future, it would not guarantee their survival in the industry. It was hardly a perfect solution, and they understood that. The catches of the two major species that are especially important in Hama—young anchovies (*shirasu*) and hard clams (*hamaguri*)—had been declining for years, so the fish-vending business was supposed to be a solution to the reduced income caused by the decline of landings. But by working for seven or eight hours every week to prepare and sell the fish at the shop, each member was earning only ten to thirty thousand yen (approximately three hundred US dollars) per month. The result was too small to make up for the income loss that their families were facing. In addition, there were about 120 fishing families in Hama, but only twelve women initially participated in the vending business. Many other women, especially young ones, declined the invitation to join the fish-vending business. They said that they were too busy with childcare or that they preferred taking a part-time job outside, such as at a family restaurant or supermarket, because these paid better hourly wages.

So why did these twelve women choose to undertake the vending business? The answers that they gave me were along similar lines to the comment from one woman: "I felt like we had to do something now." But something about what? As I spent more days in Hama, it became clearer to me that what they were hoping to accomplish by participating in those unconventional projects was to find ways to somehow make the future less uncertain. What could fishing families do when the landings of major species that they rely on are continuously declining, and when the species themselves do not seem to be coming back? One way to deal with it is to quit fishing. But quitting fishing is usually not an easy option. Fishing families in Hama and elsewhere in Japan usually have a large amount of debt from updating and maintaining their boats, engines, and equipment, which the state has historically encouraged as a way to modernize fishing. Men and women of fishing families often told me that they could not quit fishing unless they paid off their debts. Or, as fishing families in Minato did with octopuses, another way to deal with the declining catches is to continue fishing for any available yields of their usual species for as long as they can be caught, while also going after other available species to make up for the reduced catches. But Hama's strict customary rules prevented fishing families from flexibly adjusting their fishing methods or target species—for example, the ban on octopus-potting or the rule of the yellow light—which then kept them from recouping the financial loss caused by the tanker accidents. Within their limited options, Hama fishing families struggled to find new paths to survive, as simply quitting fishing was impractical.

And so, the views of many women and young men of fishing families in Hama—that the co-op's old-fashioned traditions were overly restrictive and irrational—combined with frustrations over declining prospects led to a growing sense that backward customs were preventing them from succeeding in the modern world. Older men who were in charge of the co-op politics did not seem to be willing to change the traditions. Hence, they expressed the "need to do something now," before it was too late, and an entrepreneurial move encouraged by fisheries agents became one way to do so.

AKIKO'S MISSION

Akiko, the woman who had delivered the speech about the Fishermen's Mamas' Shop at the prefectural government-sponsored meeting, had been living in Hama since she married the son of a fishing family when she was in her twenties. Like many other members of the Hama co-op, Akiko's husband owned a fishing boat weighing close to five metric tons that conducted purse-seining and clam-dredging. Akiko and her husband had a son, but he had left the town for a nonfishing job, or "inland job" (*oka no shigoto*), as she called it. Thus, the middle-aged couple had had to hire a deckhand when her father-in-law retired a couple of years earlier.

Because Akiko's husband lives on purse-seining and clam-dredging throughout the year, her family had faced a dramatic cut in their income because of the decline in the landings of young anchovies and hard clams over the previous few years. She as well as other women often murmured that they hoped for a jump in stagnant fish prices or a break from the rapidly increasing cost of oil. One day she explained to me that the main reason she had agreed to take the leading role in opening the fish-vending business was because her family had been suffering from reduced landings. She was also concerned with her family's financial losses due to the wages they had to pay to their deckhand. She said that she had tried to become a deckhand herself—like those women in Hama who worked as crew members on so-called "husband-wife boats"—but she had to give up the idea after experiencing a few trips with severe, untreatable seasickness. But her engagement with the fish-vending business was apparently more than just about helping her household. It was an opportunity that finally allowed her to find a way to survive in the "traditional fishing village."

Akiko herself was not from Hama or any other fishing community. "An arranged marriage brought me to Hama," she explained. "And here," she added, "there is a clear difference between those women who were originally born in Hama and those who were from the outside." She said that "the originals" were strong and inherently skillful at taking care of land tasks while exchanging witty ripostes to sour jokes and sexual innuendo. In order to survive in Hama, she thought that she needed to become more like the originals. But she found that extremely difficult to achieve. Thus, while striving to fit into the idiosyncratic society of Hama fishing families, she even studied the cultural history of Hama, hoping to gain a better understanding of "the originals."

One day, when I was chatting with her at the harbor while we waited for fishing boats to return, she asked if I had done much research on the history of Hama's fishing industry. I told her that I had done some but not yet enough. She told me that I must study the history if I wanted to *really* understand the people of Hama. She then mentioned a book about Hama's history written by a historian, which she had found a few years earlier at a used bookstore. She said that after reading the book she felt like that she finally understood where Hama's idiosyncratic culture of the traditional fishing village came from. The next day, she handed me her copy of the book at the fishing harbor and told me that I should take a look at it.

The title indicates that the book is about the modern history of Hama fishing families' life during the Meiji Period (1868–1912).[3] The small-sized paperback was written by a school history teacher and released by a minor publisher as part of a book series focusing on local histories and anecdotes. Its contents on the lives of people in Hama are divided into three major categories—men, women, and lifestyles—implying that a gendered division of labor is a traditional base for Hama's culture. A chapter on "men of the shore" focuses on the structure of the fishing industry and the shaky and dangerous work environment. A chapter on "women of the shore" introduces two kinds of women in Hama: women of fishing families—who take care of everything besides the actual fishing, including selling fish, housekeeping, and child-rearing—and also those women who work for the town's sex industry. Although the sex industry largely developed as part of beach tourism, according to the book, fishing families were also associated with the industry. The chapter explained that going to a brothel was a way to celebrate good catches and also that, for poor fishing families, sending their daughters to brothels was an option to deal with their debts. A chapter on Hama's lifestyle uses historical documents to depict a generally low living standard of fishing families. Furthermore, it also claims that the poverty relates to the town's apparent lack of sophistication: fishing families lack a general sense of the economy, politics, health, education, and even morality.

In a chapter on lifestyle, the author seems to be especially concerned with a lack of financial management skills as a fundamental problem of fishing families in Hama during that period in history, but he also implies, by using the present tense, that some of the characteristics of the fishing families he describes remain unchanged today. Household incomes of fishing families fluctuate since they depend on unstable landings. There are good days when large landings bring a great deal of money, but on many other days there is no income due to bad weather and bad catch. Thus, in theory, fishing families should come up with an adequate financial management plan in order to stabilize the household income, by saving some money during good times or investing it in fishing equipment for better success in the future. Nevertheless, as the chapter claims, historical documents indicate that men of fishing families often squandered earnings on gambling, alcohol, and prostitutes when catches were going well. As a result, fishing families repeatedly suffered when bad catches brought in no revenue. In addition, the chapter mentions that many adults of fishing families were diagnosed with sexually transmitted diseases and that their children were often malnourished.

The book was, in fact, troubling because the author's historical arguments often lack supporting evidence. But it was, indeed, fascinating, especially its interpretations of the culture of Hama's fishing families. Moreover, what made me more curious while reading the book was Akiko's perception of what it offered. When I spoke with Akiko again after I finished reading the book, she told me that the idiosyncratic history narrated in the volume greatly shocked her. At the same time, she added, learning about it actually helped her to reconcile herself to the foreignness that she had consistently felt since she joined Hama. Accepting that she was an outsider, she continued to try to better fit into the fishing community. A few days later, I witnessed a moment when she was making this very effort among "the originals." In the afternoon, Akiko and I were standing by the quay in front of the fish market with other women on land-task duties. A few of us spotted a boat entering to the harbor. "Look at that boat," Akiko said in an animated tone, "It looks like they've got a good catch today. The boat is sinking!" It was obvious that she wanted to congratulate the boat and its captain's wife, who was standing right next to her. But other women laughed at her. A woman immediately said to Akiko, "What did you just say? Sinking?! That's really bad luck! *We* say, 'the bottom of the boat is dipping.' Not sinking. Sinking is bad. Dipping, not sinking, get it now?" "Oh sorry, sorry," Akiko replied, "Dipping. Okay, okay. My mistake. Sorry!"

After the conversation, Akiko emphasized that she had been trying to fit into the society of the fishing community for more than thirty years. She said that she had become accustomed to earthy jokes and occasional teasing by other women of fishing families, but she still frequently wonders about the cultural gap between the world of fishing community and that of the outside. "But, every day is learning," she then concluded; "it's the same with fishing, land tasks, or the small fish-vending business." Since she started the fish-vending business, interactions with her business partners—mostly "the originals"—had been added to her everyday life practices, gradually giving her a better sense of belonging and learning to become a real coastal mama.

CHANGES IN THE TIDE

In 2006, from Thursday through Saturday every week, Akiko and her partners devoted a few hours a day to prepare for their Fishermen's Mamas' Shop on Sundays. This preparation involved filleting, drying, boiling, packing fish in separate plastic containers, and attaching product labels for sale. Such activities were done both before and after their land tasks. While performing these preparations, they discussed issues related to the business as well as chatted about their families and fishing situations. Their usual work space was located at the corner of the fish market so that they could use the running water and other necessary equipment such as tables and knives. Their spot was about thirty meters away from where land-task women stay while waiting for boats to return, so some land-task women who were not part of the vending business occasionally stopped by at the site where preparation for the seafood stand was held. Those women typically did not help out but usually just asked general questions such as what they were doing and how the business was going. Akiko and her partners always welcomed those onlookers, hoping that some of them might join in the vending business. But recruiting new members, especially younger women, was challenging.

The average age of the twelve women of the fish-vending business was more than fifty-five years old. The youngest member was in her forties, and the oldest member was in her mid-seventies. For all twelve women, purse-seining was the main source of income for their own households, so the decline in purse-seining landings was a shared concern. Two of the women had been working as deckhands for their husbands. Although both of them became deckhands to cut the cost of hiring crews, they still had to hire a woman for their land tasks because of the co-op rule, as explained earlier, that stipulates a five-thousand-yen fine for not providing a land-task woman. They indicated that it would be too demanding to juggle the three duties by themselves: a deckhand, a land-task woman, and a fish vendor. The two oldest members in their mid-seventies, who both previously served as board members of the Hama WA, expressed that they had volunteered to join in the vending business, hoping to support the future survival of their fishing community. Both of them explained that because their sons and their wives had already succeeded in their family fishing businesses, they wanted to make contributions for the future of younger generations. But in order for the fish-vending business to become sustainable, they needed younger partners.

Thus, in order to recruit new members, they occasionally asked women to join their fish-vending business. But they had hard time receiving a positive response. "Understandable, actually," one woman said. She said that it would be difficult for young women to devote their time to the vending business while taking care of the usual land tasks at the fishing harbor in addition to child-rearing and housekeeping at home. There were also women in Hama who had part-time jobs at a local restaurants or supermarkets for Sundays and/or evenings during weekdays. A couple of women who did not join in the vending business told me that the expected income from the fish shop was lower than their part-time jobs despite the longer work hours. They said that they sympathized with the idea that the vending business would support their local fishing economy, but immediate demands had to take priority. "Thinking of the future of the fishing industry is important, for sure," one of them added, "but it's much more urgent for me to bring cash to my family now."

Bringing in family income was, indeed, a concern the women of the Fishermen's Mamas' Shop shared. The small return for the hard work made the fish-vending business look more like a volunteer project than a real business, as a woman who had previously turned down an invitation to join in the team had once said. The twelve women of the vending business distributed their surplus among themselves based on their work hours, measured both in terms of preparation and in actual work at the booth. The expenses include the cost of the fish, which they buy at the market rate, as well as other costs associated with processing and packaging. The average income from the vending business per person for each month was usually less than 30,000 yen (approximately 300 US dollars). By dividing it by forty-eight hours of work on average, an hourly income becomes slightly more than 600 yen (approximately 6 US dollars), which was 200 yen lower than the prefectural minimum wage. Unquestionably, the stipend from the Fishermen's Mamas' Shop did not come close to matching their hard work. One afternoon while preparing fish for an upcoming Sunday, Akiko said, "the income from the vending business is not so much so far, but we hope that we can improve it in the future and bring a healthier economy to Hama."

But by the spring of 2007, the tide around the Fishermen's Mamas' Shop finally began to change as a result of shared frustration and anxiety that continued to grow among Hama fishing families. At the annual meeting of the Hama WA in March, the large conference room of the co-op office had a heated discussion about the vending business for over an hour. At first, Akiko, who served as the leader of the fish-vending project, reported on the activities that she and her colleagues had worked on for the past year and also announced their agenda for next fiscal year, including a field trip that they were planning to take in order to visit and exchange knowledge with other coastal mamas who were on a similar mission.

After Akiko finished her speech, one woman stood up in the audience and said, "You say you want other people to join, but you don't tell us much about what you do. That's unfair!" Akiko looked a little confused and glanced at the fisheries agents for a second. And then she responded politely through a microphone, "I just gave my best explanation, but if you would like to know more about our business, please talk to us in person. We would love to tell you more details." The woman stood up again and added, "What about the field trip that you just mentioned? Aren't you using the WA's budget for your trip? If so, why aren't we invited, too?" A few women in the audience whispered, "She's right! Why aren't we invited?" She then looked straight at the co-op president who was sitting in front of the crowd and asked him directly, "Mr. President, are we invited?" The president quickly turned around to have a private consultation with the co-op office manager, and after a minute or so, he turned back with a microphone. "Okay," he responded, "the co-op will fully support the field trip. You all are invited." The meeting closed with everyone's applause.

A SUNDAY MORNING

On a sunny Sunday in early July 2007, the fishing port in Hama was crowded and lively. Twelve women, standing in their usual white rubber boots at the corner of the fish market, were contributing to the noise, loudly calling out to locals and tourists walking by. "Hey there, welcome! Come and try our fresh and delicious fish!" Wrapped in their matching ocean-blue aprons and bandanas around their heads, these women looked cheerful. The signboard leaning against the wall read "Fishermen's Mamas' Shop." On the folding tables were packs of fresh and prepared fish, such as sardines, young anchovies, flounder, and squid. At ten o'clock, customers started forming a line. Within just a few minutes, the line grew as long as twenty meters. Customers often asked how to best cook the fish, and the women gave them a quick recipe of their home cooking. After a couple of hours, by noon, the few dozen packages with fresh and processed fish that the women had prepared in the past few days were all gone. "Sold out!" shouted one

FIG. 5. A line of Sunday-morning customers outside the Fishermen's Mamas' Shop. Photo by author.

of the women. A few of the coastal mamas apologized to late customers as they left empty-handed. After cleaning up the spot and their equipment, the twelve women greeted each other, "Good work!" They then called to each other as they left the wharf, "See you again tomorrow."

The next day they got back together for their usual land tasks, and on Thursday they began preparing for the following Sunday. They were still the same twelve women, but they seemed optimistic and hopeful. While we were chatting at the usual corner of the harbor, one of them mentioned that their field trip with other Women's Association members had recently been scheduled for the end of the summer. Another woman said that she was hoping the field trip would help them to recruit new partners for their fish-vending business. I ask them where they were going. One of the women responded that the fisheries agents who had arranged the itinerary told them that they were going to visit a seafood restaurant run by another group of coastal mamas in the neighboring prefecture.

I had to return to the United States before the women went on their field trip. But a few months later, one of the fisheries agents emailed me that the field trip had been successful and that more women had joined the coastal mamas' business. He also mentioned that they—fisheries agents and those women—were discussing a new proposal to open up their own seafood restaurant. Subsequently, in spring 2010, they eventually celebrated the grand opening of Mamas' Restaurant built next to the fish market in Hama. The restaurant quickly became a popular spot among beach tourists, who formed long lines during weekend lunchtimes. By then as many as forty-five women had joined the restaurant business. Their success was soon to be reported in local and national newspapers alike as a story of hardworking and cheerful piscatorial women making great efforts to support the future of not only their families but also their fishing community as a whole, while also generating hope for Japan's fishing industry more broadly.

But the lively drama of coastal mamas did not end there. In March 2011, when the first anniversary of their shop's opening was just around the corner, the triple disaster struck. Although the building itself survived, the tsunami flooded the entire restaurant and destroyed all the necessary equipment. The subsequent Fukushima Daiichi nuclear accident caused additional damage by halting fish supplies and creating safety concerns for consumers due to radioactive contamination in the region's fish. But despite the serious challenges, the coastal mamas reopened their restaurant in June, only eighty-one days after the disaster, due to their hard work and financial support from state and local governments. The situation after reopening remained precarious, of course, due to the ongoing nuclear crisis and its many repercussions. The restaurant could only serve limited menus, focused on those fish species that were determined after radiation monitoring to be safe for consumption. At times, the restaurant had to temporarily close because of occasional fishing moratoriums when substantially high levels of radiation were detected in major target species. But the coastal mamas kept their restaurant open, working hard to generate additional income to make up for reduced revenues from fishing.

Eventually, as the restaurant became even more successful than before the disaster, those coastal mamas in Hama would be treated as a symbol of women's role in disaster reconstruction and difficult times in general, not only locally but also nationwide. Those women brought additional income not only to their own families with their hourly wages but also to their fishing co-op with the restaurant's profits. Even the director-general of the Fisheries Agency celebrated them in a speech, specifically citing the coastal mamas in Hama as having helped to revitalize their fishing community "with their motherly smiles and power." Indeed, emotional motherhood plays an important role in the context of neoliberal politics of survival, as it has increasingly become nearly impossible to ignore mothers' essential roles for muddling through precarious times, including a nuclear crisis (Kimura 2016) and a global pandemic (Donaldson 2020; Güney-Frahm 2020). Just as coastal women had been expected to nurture fishing communities through their acclimation to a neoliberal economic environment, they are now expected to behave as responsible mothers for reconstruction from an epochal disaster and future challenges waiting to emerge in the precarious seascape.

CHAPTER 4 The (Un)expected

On March 13, 2011, Masataka Shimizu, the president of the Tokyo Electric Power Company (TEPCO), said in a late-night news conference held in Tokyo that the main explanation for the nuclear meltdown at the Fukushima Daiichi reactors was that the magnitude of the tsunami exceeded their expectations (Fukushima Study 2016).[1] Throughout the aftermath of the Fukushima nuclear disaster, TEPCO aimed to minimize or avoid liability by emphasizing that the event had been impossible to predict—or "beyond expectations" (*soteigai*). TEPCO argued that the nuclear accident had occurred as part of a natural disaster rather than as the result of human error. Unsurprisingly, this allegation was widely criticized within and outside the country. Whatever the legitimacy of TEPCO's disclaimer of liability, the debates on what is "beyond expectations" open up an opportunity to extend our understanding of living with the precarious seascape, where natural and man-made disasters alike are both within and outside of expectations.

Expectation and anticipation are both orientations toward the future, but they differ in their relationship to the past. Expectation is built upon past experience, whereas anticipation is built upon the present and does not rely on the past (Koselleck 2004; Bryant and Knight 2019). From this perspective, the catastrophe of the Fukushima Daiichi Nuclear Power Plant was partly expectable but also not expectable, or "unimaginable" (Fisch n.d.). It was partly expectable because there had been nuclear accidents in Japan, including the one that occurred in 1999 in Tokaimura, located less than eighty miles south of the Fukushima Daiichi Nuclear Power Plant. In light of the previous experiences, the possibility of a nuclear accident was expectable. At the same time, it was not expectable because neither a quake nor a tsunami had ever triggered a nuclear accident before. In fact, although it was just a pure coincidence of nature, no major natural disasters had occurred near nuclear power plants since the first reactor in Tokaimura began its operation in 1968. Hence, because of the lack of experience, the Fukushima accident, especially its magnitude, was not expectable. Many critics, however, have argued that the possibility of the disaster should have been anticipated with the accumulated knowledge of the nation's proud community of seismologists (Clancey 2006) and the historical records of the area's seismic activities, including the 869 Jogan earthquake, which caused a tsunami of a similar magnitude to the one experienced in 2011. After all, because it is almost impossible to predict future nuclear disasters without adequate past experience, if we are to continue living with technologies that can cause future industrial disasters, we must learn to expect the unexpected (Perrow 2011).

But what is it like to live with expectations of the unexpected, and what happens when the unexpected occurs? How do people survive on such occasions? The following survival stories of fishing families—gathered in the immediate aftermath of the 2011 triple disaster of earthquake, tsunami, and nuclear accident—reveal that their responses to the disaster were largely informed by their past experiences with earlier disasters as they had been living with the highly industrialized seascape. For fishing families living on the Joban Sea, both natural and man-made disasters are "ordinary" and thus expected, although it is always hard to anticipate when they will occur and how they will affect the ocean or human lives.

HISTORICAL EXPECTATIONS

On March 11, 2011, an earthquake of magnitude 9.0 struck northeastern Japan at 2:46 p.m., followed by the first wave of tsunami, which arrived on the coast shortly thereafter. The men and women of fishing families living on the Joban Sea and elsewhere along the northeastern coast whom I interviewed told me that they had never felt a violent shake like that before. But many of them did what they had long prepared to do in the event of a major tremor, as commercial fishermen who live on the coast of a seismically active country. That is to say, expecting tsunami, they took their fishing boats offshore. Rescuing fishing boats from tsunami waves by rushing them into the open sea is called *okidashi*, which literally means "to push offshore." It is an experience-based lesson that has been handed down for generations among fishing families of modern Japan. The original history is unknown, but considering the reasons behind the practice, it is most likely a recent tradition, which developed as part of the state-led fisheries modernization. In the context of coastal fisheries, it was after the end of World War II, from the 1950s through the 1970s, that the state promoted the mechanization of fishing boats in order to increase efficiency and yields. A modern fishing boat with a powerful engine and electric equipment is an expensive property, unlike a small wooden open boat.

For coastal fishing families, their modern boats are lifelines of their business. These days, a typical five-ton coastal fishing boat fully equipped with a high-speed engine, sonar, fish-finders, GPS units, and electric net-haulers costs roughly a half million US dollars on average, approximately the same as two houses in typical fishing towns in Japan. Losing such an expensive necessity would risk a fishing family's basic survival. Thus, fishing families have been told by elder members of their community that when a big quake occurs, the first thing that they must do is to save their precious boats on the chance that a tsunami will follow. This tradition also has a gendered aspect. The actual practice of *okidashi* is usually done by men of fishing families. Men save their boats, while women, children, and elders evacuate to high ground.

On the afternoon of March 11, while many fishermen did what they were supposed to do, what was beyond expectation was that the tsunami would arrive more quickly than historical knowledge had suggested. Based on recent experiences during the past half century, it usually takes an hour or so for tsunami to arrive after a quake, but this time was an exception.[2] Among the many tsunami strikes that were recorded on that day, the first wave actually reached the shore as early as twenty minutes after the quake. Consequently, while many fishermen succeeded with their *okidashi*, others did not make it. In some cases, they were too far from their ports to get to their boats on time. In other cases, the unprecedentedly fast-moving tsunami claimed their lives during their attempts.

FOLLOWING EXPECTATIONS

In Minato, according to the municipal record, among the six tsunami waves in total that reached the shore within three hours after the quake, the largest one was more than two meters tall. When I visited Minato's harbor a month after the tsunami in early April, I spotted Hajime, a young captain in his late thirties. He was standing on the quay, but his boat was not there. He told me that he had tried to save his boat but did not succeed. When the earthquake struck at 2:46 p.m. on March 11, he was taking a break at a *pachinko* parlor after that morning's fishing trip, which he wrapped up around 1:00 p.m. The pachinko parlor was not too far from the harbor, but the postquake traffic of people trying to evacuate made it take more time than usual for him to get to the shore. After about fifteen minutes, he got to the harbor's entrance, but then he noticed the water had already receded so much that he could almost see the bottom of the harbor. He remembered that his father had told him to be cautious when water recedes; it is a sign of an imminent tsunami. He had seen tsunami a couple of times in the past, but both of them were less than twenty centimeters high. But judging by how much water had disappeared from the harbor prior to the tsunami's arrival, he immediately realized that he had to ditch his idea of saving his boat. He quickly turned around and drove away from the quay. The next day, a friend called his cell phone to report that his boat had been found washed up sideways on the sandy beach next to the harbor.

The scene of the harbor a day after the tsunami—as another captain, Daisuke, described to me—was like "the apocalypse." When Daisuke returned to the harbor in Minato after spending more than twenty-four hours offshore for his *okidashi*, waiting for the risk of further tsunami to subside, he spotted a few boats sitting on top of the quay. As he got closer, he also found a few more sunken boats underwater. As he entered the harbor, he began to spot a few cars and scooter bikes that fishermen had left on the quay before going for *okidashi*. He noticed that one of the trucks underwater was his. The surface of the water was glittering with oil spilled from sunken boats and cars. On the quay, there were piles of debris—including tangled fishnets, ropes, baskets, and other equipment that were washed away from fishermen's storerooms—which those fishermen who did not leave for *okidashi* pulled out of the water so that returning boats would be able to enter the harbor. Across the harbor's concrete floor, there were three deep cracks of as long as forty to fifty meters, as well as countless smaller ruptures and bumps everywhere.

In Hama, the tsunami's impact was greater than in Minato. The largest wave that approached the town was taller than four meters. Fortunately, there were no deaths in the town. But two captains, Mr. Matsumoto and Mr. Kitamura, were convinced that this was just by luck, or "a miracle," as Mr. Kitamura said. That afternoon, Mr. Matsumoto—who was a retired skipper and the president of the Hama fishing co-op at the time—was working at the co-op office building by the harbor. While loud sirens were repeatedly alerting coastal residents who had just been jolted by the quake itself to approaching tsunami, he told all the co-op staff to leave the office and flee to the hilltop. But he remained at the harbor in order to watch his co-op's fishermen—including his son—racing their boats offshore. The initial wave of tsunami reached the harbor as he was walking back to the entrance of the co-op's office building. "It happened so suddenly," he recollected.

FIG. 6. Deep cracks in Minato's fishing harbor caused by the 3/11 earthquake and tsunami. Photo by author.

When he realized it, the water was already covering his knees. He tried to open the building's front glass doors, but they did not budge with the water pressure. The water quickly rose to his chest, but he managed to reach the side entrance and quickly ran upstairs, where he remained until the water subsided.

Mr. Kitamura's story was more surreal. "It's like a movie," his friend said, urging Mr. Kitamura to tell me about his survival episode. Indeed, his narration was like a Hollywood disaster film. In the afternoon of March 11, he was visiting the next town with his wife for shopping. As soon as they felt the big quake, they hopped in their car and hurried back to Hama. The traffic was not bad on their side of the road because most of the drivers were heading in the opposite direction, away from the shore. "But the ride was super-choppy," he said. The road's pavement was buckling and surging like liquid, and random cracks appeared as they drove. At one point, he even had to quickly jerk his steering wheel to avoid a manhole lid that was suddenly ejected by a surging gush of water from the underground storm drains.

The (Un)expected 77

After they finally made it to their house, Mr. Kitamura dropped off his wife and headed to his fishing boat in the harbor. The water level was already low, but he jumped onto the deck anyway and immediately started the engine. He also turned on his two-way radio. He told his fellow captains who had already escaped offshore that he was about to head out of the harbor. In return, his friends kept yelling at him to hurry up. But the water was too shallow. Stuck on the bottom of the harbor, his entire boat started to tilt. But he still maintained hope that the next tsunami wave might give him enough water to escape, and thus he kept the engine running. Instead, the next wave capsized his boat, nearly trapping him along with it. "He suddenly disappeared from the radio," a friend interrupted as Mr. Kitamura told me the story, "I really thought at that moment that he was finished." "Me, too," Mr. Kitamura responded.

Luckily, he barely managed to get himself out of the captain's booth and started swimming. He was not sure which direction he was heading, but he swam as hard as he could. At one point, he put his head above the water, but could not see anything. "It was pitch black both under and above the water," he said. By the time this happened, the sun was already down, and there were no lights anywhere; the tsunami had caused blackouts up and down the coast. After a while, his hand hit a concrete wall, so he climbed up on it without knowing where he was. He looked around and up. "And there was the moon," he smiled; "it was especially beautiful that night." Suddenly, under the moonlight, he understood that he was at the far end of the harbor's seawall. He carefully walked along the top of the seawall and reached the quay. And then he headed not to his home but to the hilltop hotel that he and his wife had selected as a meeting point in a case of disaster; the hotel was one of the town's designated disaster evacuation centers. He hoped that his wife had already taken their children and his parents to the hotel. "And they were there, so we all had a sigh of relief," he said as if he was reading an ending line of a storybook.

Mr. Kimura told me this story about a month after the tsunami when we were chatting in front of the harbor with five other fishermen. His boat had been sent off for repair, whereas his friends' boats were moored by the quay, thanks to their successful *okidashi*. At that point, Ibaraki fishermen were already aware of the news from a few days earlier about the high-level radiation contamination detected in fish from the coastal water of Ibaraki. These fishermen in unison expressed their disappointment at the likelihood of a long extension of the fishing moratorium. They also mentioned their anxieties about the uncertain future. In the late morning, even though they knew that they could not go fishing, a number of fishermen were hanging out at the harbor. "You never know when another tsunami might come," one captain said. Another captain explained that, like other fellow fishermen gathering at the harbor, he was too worried to be away from his boat, thinking that there might be another tsunami. They succeeded in their *okidashi* on March 11, but ongoing aftershocks made them worry about the possibility that they would fail the next time. Additionally, just the previous evening, the largest aftershock following the quake set off a tsunami warning. Most fishing boats in Hama were immediately taken offshore. As it turned out, no tsunami came, but their recent experience with the tsunami only a month earlier triggered their quick reactions to the tsunami alert. A new expectation has been added to their historical one: tsunami can approach as soon as twenty minutes following a major earthquake, and thus *okidashi* must be carried out immediately after a tsunami alert.

REVISING EXPECTATIONS

Experiencing the unexpectedly fast-moving monster of a tsunami on March 11, many fishing families quickly revised their expectation of tsunami and also their future plans on *okidashi*. But the fishing families' revisions of expectations turned out to be different between Ibaraki and Fukushima. In Ibaraki, while those fishing families of Hama and Minato revised their expectation that tsunami may approach as soon as twenty minutes after a quake, they have largely maintained their expectation for *okidashi* as an important practice to secure their future survival. In Fukushima, on the other hand, dreadful experience with the tsunami made fishers lose their expectations for *okidashi*. In case of tsunami, as they argue, it is more important to focus on saving lives than fishing boats, no matter how valuable the property is. Fukushima fishers' lost expectation for *okidashi* provides us an opportunity to discuss an alternative relationship between expectation and the future, one that undermines the teleological expectations embedded in futurism (Ferguson 1999; Bryant and Knight 2019). The following story from Fukushima tells us about expectations of the unexpected and their relations to the future.

In Fukushima, the postdisaster situation was far grimmer than I had initially imagined. Along with some Japanese colleagues, I visited a town in northern Fukushima in May 2011. According to the official report, among the nearly five hundred deaths in the town, many of them were members of local fishing families, including twenty-four skippers. When we went to the town's harbor, we saw a number of coastal fishing boats neatly moored. But other than us, nobody was around. Behind the harbor, the fishing co-op's three-story concrete building was utterly destroyed by the tsunami. On March 11, the wave swallowed the entire building and the adjacent coastal landscape. A small open boat had evidently crashed into the top of the building and remained jammed on its top floor, with half of its body hanging in the air. Next to the co-op building were the ruins of a fish market, one of the largest ones in the prefecture. The concrete rooftop and walls had all been washed away, but a few thick concrete pillars were left standing in the air.

While visiting the town, we interviewed two fishermen, Mr. Nakajima and Mr. Tanaka, in the office at the municipal sports center. The center was one of the town's main evacuation centers, where hundreds of people—including many fishing families—had been living in its gym rooms. Next to the gym complex was the center's office building, the second floor of which had been lent to the town's fishing co-op as their temporary headquarters. We entered the building and took the stairs to the second floor. At the end of the stairway, I found a large sheet of paper posted on the wall, which had a long list of the co-op's more than four hundred members and the names of their boats. Some of the names had been crossed in red ink, and blank spaces in between names were filled with scribbles, indicating the details of their losses, such as individuals, boat, or both. The second floor was chaotic and noisy. Everybody was busy handling phone calls and working on various documents on desks covered with piles of papers and folders. Some of the co-op staff members openly expressed their irritation with us for bothering them in the midst of the ongoing disaster.

Mr. Nakajima and Mr. Tanaka, however, surprised us with their gestures of normality. After they accepted our condolences for their losses, they laughingly apologized for the chaotic temporary office. I wondered whether they were acting normal as their way to cope with their unthinkable sorrow or because they wanted to hide their real emotions from outsiders like us, who could not truly understand their pain. But I decided that it would be the best for me to go along with their seemingly normal conversational stance, awkwardness notwithstanding. After we sat down around a table, one of us asked where they were when the tsunami came. "It was completely unreal!" Mr. Tanaka said, as if he was describing something exciting. Mr. Nakajima agreed with nods and said, "It was just like the movie *The Perfect Storm*!"

According to him, when the quake struck, he and his friend were in the middle of a meeting with a fisheries agent, discussing plans for a new project to promote their local fishing. But as soon as the quake calmed, both of them immediately left the meeting and drove back to the harbor, even though they were not sure whether they were too late to rescue their boats. By the time they arrived at the harbor the tsunami was already approaching, but they still took off in order to save each of their boats. Mr. Nakajima barely made it, whereas his friend did not. "Tsunami doesn't look like a wave, do you know?" Mr. Nakajima said as he gestured a wave with his arm. "It was more like a gigantic wall of black water," he added. Turning his arm to make a right angle, he continued his story. Looking at the tall wall-like black water coming toward him, he thought that climbing straight up against the wall would flip his boat over. Switching his arm's angle to about sixty degrees, he said that he thus decided to go diagonally against it to climb over the wave. "I had a safety vest, but my knees were rattling," he continued with his animated hands and body gestures. "As I was climbing on the gigantic tsunami, I quickly turned my head over to check my friend's boat behind me," he continued, "and saw his boat just as it was being overturned."

He then added before any of us could interrupt him with expressions of sympathy or shock, "I am happy that his body has finally been found." Apparently, a number of people were still missing, but according to Mr. Nakajima, his friend's body was found because he had tied his body to the boat with a rope before he sank. "Perhaps he knew he was not going to make it, and that is why he tied his body to the boat so that he could at least return to his family's place even as a dead body," Mr. Nakajima assumed. I was intrigued by the tone of excitement that Mr. Nakajima maintained throughout his storytelling. He and his friend were even laughing at points. They narrated the deadly tsunami in the same tone of voice they used to tell their stories of big catches, something "normal." No anger or sorrow was expressed.

In reality, of course, nothing was normal. Both Mr. Nakajima and Mr. Tanaka, like many other fishing families, lost their family members as well as their homes in the tsunami. After they returned to their harbor from *okidashi* after a couple of nights, they found out that they had lost their loved ones and that the entire coastal neighborhood had disappeared, except for the foundations of houses on the ground. Since then, Mr. Tanaka had been living with his wife in one tiny corner of the sports center's basketball court. Mr. Nakajima had been living with his wife and their child in his wife's parents' house on the hillside. Their saved boats had remained tied to the quay since they returned from *okidashi*, expecting that the ongoing Fukushima nuclear crisis would continue to prevent them from going back to the sea for a long while. Without being able to go fishing, both Mr.

Nakajima and Mr. Tanaka, like most other fishermen in the town, had become day laborers. Depending on the schedule, they had been involved in debris-cleaning or construction work for fixing tsunami-devastated roads and other facilities.

Remembering that the biggest aftershock happened in the evening of April 11, I asked them whether they did their *okidashi* again when the tsunami alert went off that evening. "No," they responded together quietly. I wondered whether they had lost their sense of urgency to save their boats because of the uncertain future caused by the ongoing Fukushima nuclear crisis. I hesitated to ask the exact question, so I simply asked them why. Their response was different from my guess. They both indicated that it was not worth risking their lives. A boat is replaceable, they both said, but a life is not. As long as we live, there is always a future. The future is unpredictable, but the unexpected does not necessarily mean doom and gloom. There might be a chance that the capricious ocean brings hope, like the emergence of dominant year class of clams and octopuses that helped fishing families in Minato to survive in the aftermath of the tanker accidents.

"Incidentally," Mr. Nakajima said, "I heard that flounder caught for [radiation] monitoring were all big and full." He argued that the disaster caused a lot of harm to humans but has given the ocean a chance to recuperate from damages caused by humans while humans were too busy dealing with the disaster to harm the ocean. "By the next year," he added, "our sea will be filled with swarming fish, I bet!" I nodded slightly hesitantly, wondering whether he was actually expecting that commercial fishing would reopen as early as the next year. At the time, even an optimistic estimation indicated that the fishing moratorium in Fukushima would continue for at least a couple of years. But I eventually realized that Mr. Nakajima was only talking about the possible changes in the ocean. In fact, he never indicated that he was anticipating that he might be able to catch a school of large flounder in the next year. Perhaps he wished that he could, but that was not what he said. He was pointing to the ironic alignment between the damages of the dreadful disaster for humans and the improvement of the marine ecology. After all, as experienced commercial fishers like Mr. Nakajima and his friends know, the ocean is expected to be the unexpected. It frequently acts beyond humans' expectations.

EXPERIENCES WITH RADIATION

In the aftermath of the nuclear meltdown, among numerous challenges that the Fukushima nuclear accident has caused, perhaps radioactive contamination of the ocean was the most unexpected. In the history of Japan's nuclear accidents, the Fukushima disaster was the first to cause accidental leakage of radioactive isotopes into the ocean. Moreover, the amount of radioactive substances that the crippled reactors in Fukushima have released into the ocean was easily the largest among all the nuclear accidents that have ever occurred in the world's history (Pacchioli 2013). Similar to the occurrence of the nuclear accident, aftereffects on the ocean in case of a nuclear accident, as many have argued, should also have been anticipatable, especially considering that all the nuclear power plants in Japan are built by the sea in order to use the seawater for the coolant systems. Prior to the Fukushima accident, however, the consequences for the ocean had been not only unexpected but also largely assumed to be insignificant.

For decades before the Fukushima disaster, the Japanese government's disaster management plans in case of nuclear accident indicated that radioactive isotopes would simply disperse and be diluted once they were released into the ocean, so that radioactive contamination per square miles of seawater would not be enough to harm humans or the marine ecosystem. In the wake of the Fukushima accident, this estimation turns out to have been wrong. Because of their prior assumptions, however, the government had never considered setting any radiation safety standard for fish, and it did not even monitor the radiation contamination of fish until almost a month after the nuclear meltdown occurred, when commercial fishers questioned their false assumption. It was Ibaraki fishers who initially questioned the official projections and demanded that the government carry out radiation monitoring for fish caught in their coastal water. Those fishers argued that if the government claims that fish in the ocean are safe, it has to provide scientific evidence for that claim.

In Ibaraki, nearly three weeks after the tsunami, those fishers whose boats were saved were ready to go back to work at sea. But they were understandably worried about the radioactive contamination of fish, anticipating the possibility that the government's claim that the fish were safe could be false. Moreover, their fish wholesalers had stipulated that they would not purchase any fish landed in any harbor in Ibaraki or Fukushima until fish safety had been officially determined. For those wholesalers, it was an unavoidable decision because they assumed that they would not be able to sell their clients fish from Ibaraki, especially fishmongers at Tsukiji Fish Market in Tokyo. Therefore, it was crucial for Ibaraki fishers to demand that the government undertake radiation monitoring of their fish in order to find out how contaminated the fish were and whether they were safe to consume. A negative result would provide official evidence of the safety of fish from Ibaraki. If the result were positive, they would be able to file lawsuits against TEPCO for compensation.

Indeed, having lived with the repeatedly ruined seascape, Ibaraki fishers were highly acquainted with necessary legal procedures for dealing with natural and industrial disasters alike. As an experienced fisherman who has experienced multiple disasters in the past, Hiroshi, the fisherman in Minato whom I introduced in the prologue, once gave me a minilecture on the legal procedures in case of disaster. He explained that when a natural disaster affects your business, fishers claim compensation from their insurance provider and also submit paperwork to the government in order to receive whatever disaster relief funds for which they might be eligible. "But," he emphasized, "when a man-made disaster causes any damage to your business, whoever is responsible for the cause is supposed to compensate you for your loss," adding, "but you can't just wait for the money. You gotta fight for it. For that, there are two important things that you have to have." One is a good lawyer, and the other one is "the numbers."

While holding up a two-inch-thick binder of his landing records in front of my face, he explained that, in order to show evidence of the economic losses caused by a man-made disaster, each boat owner had to submit detailed daily landing data from the previous five years, listing the weight and the sale price for each fish species. Based on the past landing records, a daily compensation amount would be calculated for each boat owner. For those days that a man-made disaster caused the cancellation of fishing, each boat's expected income per day would be compensated. Hiroshi also explained how to fight for compensation when fish are officially determined to be safe but fish prices turn out to be considerably lower than usual due to consumers' safety concerns about their fish. He said that when it happens, fishers could file lawsuits against the company that caused the man-made disaster for reputational damage. In case of reputational damage as well, he emphasized that having detailed landing records is critical in order to present sufficient evidence for the damage, by showing the difference between the expected and the actual values that they received for their landings.

In early April, while both the government and TEPCO were still insisting that fish in Ibaraki waters were safe from radiation pollution, there were two options left for Ibaraki fishers. The first option was to reopen fishing—even though wholesalers had already told them that they would refuse to buy fish from them—and then file a lawsuit against TEPCO for economic damages caused by the nuclear accident. This was, of course, not ideal because it would require time, effort, and money in order to collect sufficient evidence by catching fish that no wholesaler would purchase. The second and their preferred option was to extend their moratorium and demand compensation for those extra days of fishing closure. But in order to go with the latter choice, they needed official evidence, showing that fish in Ibaraki waters were, in fact, contaminated with high-level radiative substances.

For fishers, the second option was not only financially reasonable, but it also matched their expectations. Based on their experience-based oceanographic knowledge, fishermen in Ibaraki were certain that radioactive substances had traveled southward from the crippled reactors in central Fukushima to Ibaraki waters along the familiar nearshore current. Therefore, as some fishers told me, they were actually flabbergasted by the government's anticipation that radioactive isotopes had been dispersed into the ocean and become safely diffuse. "So stupid," one exasperated fisherman said. He added, "Do they think the ocean is one big swimming pool or something?" Every fisher knows that the marine environment is highly complex, consisting of the complicated topography of the seafloor and multidirectional water currents. One fisherman sarcastically laughed, "Even my elementary-school kids know basic science like that!"

After the Ibaraki fishers' urgent request, the government finally agreed that the Ministry of Health, Labor, and Welfare would conduct a monitoring test on fish caught in Ibaraki waters. On April 4, fishermen in a northern town in Ibaraki went out to the adjacent water for the first time since the tsunami and brought back a basket of *kōnago*, or Japanese sand lance (*Ammodytes personatus*) for radiation monitoring. In the evening, the test result was announced. As Ibaraki fishers rightfully assumed, the Ministry reported that a high level of radiation was detected in the fish. The detected iodine 131 in *kōnago* fish was 4,080 becquerel per kilogram (Bq/kg), and the cesium was 526 Bq/kg. Ibaraki fishers shortly thereafter made the official announcement on the extension of their fishing moratorium, not only for *kōnago* but also for all the other fish species within the entire waters of Ibaraki Prefecture.

The next day, the Ministry also announced that they had added fish to the list of food items for the tentative radiation safety standard, and that the thresholds for acceptable fish were determined as 2,000 Bq/kg for iodine and 500 Bq/kg for cesium. This announcement soon provoked impassioned public debates that also engaged the fishers themselves, especially regarding the tentativeness of the safety standard. According to the Ministry, the standard was officially considered to be tentative because it was decided without necessary policy-making procedures due to emergency circumstances. The Ministry also explained that, due to the nation's lack of experience with nuclear crisis, it determined the safety standard based on the guidelines that the Nuclear Safety Commission had established back in 1980 (Ministry of Health, Labor, and Welfare 2011). Moreover, because the 1980 guidelines did not even include seafood products due to their anticipation that radioactive isotopes would safely disperse at sea, the safety threshold numbers for fish species were provisionally borrowed from the tentative safety standard, which had been used for vegetables, crops, meat, and eggs since the immediate aftermath of the nuclear meltdown. For consumers and fishers alike, this double tentativeness was especially alarming. The legitimacy of the tentative safety standard for any food items was doubtful enough, and many people also were skeptical of the idea of using the same standard for both agricultural and fisheries products, given that radioactive substances seem to accumulate differently in plants, land animals, and fish. Despite these public concerns, however, the Ministry repeatedly proclaimed that as long as food products met its announced standards, they would be officially considered safe to sell and eat. The government hoped that this standard would provide consumers with a sense of safety. But to the contrary, many consumers avoided buying fish from Fukushima or Ibaraki, classifying *any* fish from the region as risky.

For fishing families living on the Joban Sea, living with the highly industrialized seascape means living with not only natural but also man-made disasters. Having experienced a series of disasters, they have learned how to survive in the aftermaths. The magnitude of the 2011 triple disaster was indeed exceptional, but fishing families muddled through by following their experience-based knowledge of survival. Thus, from local fishers' perspectives, the outcome of the nuclear meltdown was within expectations. They remember their experiences with consumers' hesitancy to purchase their fish in the wake of previous industrial disasters including the 1999 Tokaimura nuclear accident and the 2006 tanker accidents. Remembering their past experiences, they hoped that they would be able to survive again this time. In addition, although the amount of nuclear contamination in the ocean this time is incomparable, they still wished for the ocean's speedy recovery. At the same time, though, they also expected that the actual future trajectories ahead of them would have to involve unexpected pathways.

As we will see, local fishing families continued muddling through to survive with the yet-again ruined seascape during the first few months after the Fukushima nuclear disaster. Their response to the nuclear contamination of the ocean and its risk was influenced by the fact that it was impossible to know in the present how risk would unfold in the future.

CHAPTER 5 Fourfold Pain

On a warm late afternoon in early June 2011, more than eighty fishermen from all over Ibaraki gathered in a community center adjacent to one of the prefecture's largest fishing harbors. It had been three months since the triple disaster—the earthquakes, the tsunami, and the nuclear meltdown—had devastated the long coast of northeastern Japan, and the immediate consequences were still ongoing. By the side of the door to the conference room, there was a white signboard with the day's theme written in black: "An Assembly to Talk about the Future of Ibaraki."[1] But as it turned out, nobody actually spoke about the future during the entire event, at least not in a straightforward sense.

In fact, the main objective of the event was to offer Ibaraki fishermen an opportunity to articulate their challenges in the midst of the ongoing multifold disaster to two bureaucrats of the Fisheries Agency of the Ministry of Agriculture, Forestry, and Fisheries who had been invited from Tokyo. The participants were mostly young fishermen, ranging in age from their twenties to their early fifties. At 3:30 p.m., the large room was already crowded. All the chairs had been occupied by the time the meeting started at 4:00 p.m., and a few fishermen who had come in late were standing by the doors. At the front, there was a long table where the two bureaucrats, both dressed in dark suits with plain ties, sat with two fishermen. One of the fishers was Mr. Hashimoto, an experienced bottom-trawler in his sixties, who had organized the day's meeting, and the other was the president of the prefectural federation of Young Fishermen's Associations, whom Mr. Hashimoto had asked to serve as the meeting's chairperson.

This event was atypical as far as fisheries-related meetings go, which signified the magnitude of the disaster's consequences. Conventionally, when official meetings take place between government representatives and fishers, it is almost always the prefectural fisheries officers who come up with plans and organize such events, and they usually have to beg fishers to actually participate in those meetings. But this time, it was fishers themselves who planned the meeting; Mr. Hashimoto had even taken the dramatic step of negotiating in person with one of the Fisheries Agency's office chiefs to send somebody from his office to Ibaraki in order to listen to fishermen's voices at the town meeting. Mr. Hashimoto explained to me later that he thought that it would have taken too much time to organize a meeting like this if he had had to go through the prefectural fisheries office. "Too much bureaucracy," he said. In the afternoon, I actually saw two prefectural fisheries agents sitting at a reception desk right outside of the conference room. One of them murmured, "We were completely bypassed.... We didn't even know about this event until just a few days ago, but we can't just do nothing, you know, so we decided to give ourselves a job as receptionists." He then added, "But I'm impressed by Mr. Hashimoto for having pulled off such a special meeting in the midst of the lingering disaster." When an announcement informed us that the event was about to begin, I took a seat next to a group of Minato fishermen. The two fisheries agents remained at the reception desk.

At 4:00 p.m. the meeting began with Mr. Hashimoto's opening speech. He briefly introduced the two bureaucrats and told the audience that they were here to listen to voices of Ibaraki fishers. "So" he added, "please tell them your honest stories about the challenges you are currently facing." Mr. Hashimoto then called one fisherman at a time over to the front of the room and asked each of them to talk about the damage the disaster caused to his co-op and his own work, as well as about challenges that his co-op or that he personally was facing. Each fisherman spoke for about two to three minutes, directly facing the two bureaucrats. The first speaker was a fisherman from a town located at the north end of Ibaraki. He complained that neither the state or the media had paid sufficient attention to his hometown, even though the situation of his co-op—considering the wreckage from the tsunami and the radioactive contamination of fish in his fishing grounds—was basically the same as that in southern Fukushima, directly to his north. Another fisherman from the middle of Ibaraki said with a shaky voice, "I have no idea how to get out of this situation." The tsunami had badly damaged his boat, on which he still owed many years of loan payments. He would now need to add debt for loans to fix his boat to those associated with the boat's purchase in the first place.

The next fisherman pointed out that the special low-interest loan that the Fisheries Agency implemented for supporting the reconstruction of disaster-affected fishers was ineffective. He explained that, because of the extensive conditions of the loan program, he could not use it to cover the significant and necessary costs, such as salaries for his crew. In turn, Mr. Hashimoto asked the two bureaucrats to comment on these concerns. The older official took the microphone. His highly bureaucratic responses were broad and unspecific. He said with apparent sincerity that the fishermen's speeches made him realize that there were some discrepancies between the Fisheries Agency's relief efforts and local needs. He then said, a bit ruefully, "Changing the rules, if necessary, would have to be discussed at the Diet," placing the responsibility for a fix with legislators in Japan's parliament. Listening to this comment, a fisherman next me murmured to his friend, "He sure is a bureaucrat."

The second half of the meeting focused on radiation issues caused by the nuclear accident on the adjacent Fukushima coast. A young fisherman from the southern Ibaraki shore grumbled that fish prices had been consistently terrible because of consumers' fear of radiation contamination, even though their fishing grounds had reopened about two weeks earlier, after the government's declaration of safety. Three other fishermen from the southern region also mentioned the declining fish prices and the damaged reputation of their fish. Another young fisherman questioned the legitimacy of the radiation safety standard that the government had implemented for fish in early April. He also mentioned that, although fishing had already reopened in their southern waters, he and his father had made a family decision not to resume fishing until they felt that their fish were actually safe. He explained that he had to make the decision, even though it would make his family unable to request compensation from TEPCO because it was technically their personal decision not to catch fish despite the official permission to reopen fishing. He said that he did not feel safe enough to feed his fish to his own kids. "I have small children," he said, "and they love eating fish from our coast." "Our fish will eventually be delivered to many other families' tables," he continued, "and I just can't sell fish that I won't even let my kids eat."

At the end, a fisherman named Kenji read his brief closing remark: "Like Fukushima, we are suffering from both the natural and man-made disasters. We are in 'fourfold pain.'" He then listed the four kinds of challenges that are causing the pain: the earthquake, the tsunami, the nuclear disaster, and "damage by rumor." "Damage by rumor" (*fūhyō higai*) is a term that is usually used to describe the economic loss to producers of a commodity whose price is reduced due to consumers' hesitancy to purchase it because they want to avoid the risk associated with the commodity. For fishing families—and farmers—affected by the Fukushima nuclear disaster, "damage by rumor" is also a legal term used to claim damage compensation against TEPCO when their products are given unusually lower prices even though they meet the government food safety standard. But many people, including a number of fishing families, questioned whether or not "damage by rumor" was an appropriate term for describing the consequences of consumers' avoidance of food items with low-level radioactive contaminants. Is consuming fish with low-level radiation actually safe? Is it legitimate to identify anxieties about the health risks of seafood hauled from the waters near Fukushima as groundless rumors? But regardless of the legitimacy of the term itself, "damage by rumor" has been one of the major obstacles and a source of pain for fishing families who try to survive on the Joban Sea after the nuclear accident. Kenji concluded his speech, "All we want is to catch fish from a clean ocean. Please help us to make our wish come true."

Ten years later, Kenji's wish would remain unfulfilled, despite the ocean's gradual recovery from radioactive contamination. Unlike the situation for freshwater fish or terrestrial animals, plants, insects, and fungi, radiocesium contaminants in seawater, sediments, and fish bodies in the Joban Sea continuously decreased during the first decade after the disaster, thanks to the open and continuously diffused marine environments (Wada 2021). Nevertheless, the precarity of coastal fishing families persisted due to widely held and contested views of the radiation risk sustained by the ocean and in marine life. Therefore, a long battle for coastal fishing families in Ibaraki and Fukushima arose over the issue of so-called "damage by rumor." Caught between conflicting narratives on radiation risk, fishing families living in the precarious seascape wonder what will unfold next as they imagine and reimagine their future there.

The following stories tell us about everyday lives of coastal fishing families who tried to survive in the midst of what Ulrich Beck has famously called "anthropological shock" (Beck 1987) during the immediate aftermath of the nuclear catastrophe. In particular, the stories of fishing families highlight their struggles as producers of contested commodities, namely fish with low-level radioactive contaminants, that trigger forms of pain and sorrow distinct from those among consumers (Kimura 2016; Sternsdorff-Cisterna 2018). In order to survive as fishing families, they have to catch and sell fish when fish are declared safe for consumption according to the government radiation safety standard. But fishing families often find themselves mired in fissures created by the politics of low-level radioactive contamination, in which government officials, scientists, and consumers evince diverse views of safety and risk and behave accordingly and differently. In such a postmeltdown "risk society" (Beck 1992), the economy of fishing is as precarious as the ocean itself. Nevertheless, fishing families continue muddling through to stay alive in this once-again ruined seascape.

DAMAGE BY RUMOR

Looking at the immediate aftermaths of the Fukushima nuclear meltdown was like watching what Ulrich Beck wrote in "Anthropological Shock" (Beck 1987) unfold right in front of us. In particular, Beck's description regarding social confusion and disintegration over conflicting information on radiation risk and security, which he wrote in the wake of the 1986 Chernobyl nuclear accident, felt almost like a prophecy. Like those German mothers whom Beck observed in 1986, many consumers in post-Fukushima Japan devoted substantial time and effort to learning how to avoid foodstuffs with a probable risk of radiation contamination and to search for safe foods for their children (Kimura 2016). But besides the striking similarities, ethnographic details also tell us idiosyncratic survival stories of people in both cases.[2] Among such particularities, so-called "damage by rumor" and related debates about the risk and safety of low-level radioactive contamination remained the constant backdrop for coastal fishing families in the years following the Fukushima disaster. But "damage by rumor" is not a new concept that developed in the context of post-Fukushima Japan. In fact, for those fishing families who live with industrialized seascapes in Japan, it is rather a familiar one because it has repeatedly emerged and coexisted with modern disasters.

According to the sociologist Naoya Sekiya, based on his analysis of various "damage by rumor" cases in the past fifty-plus years, the term refers to "economic damage caused by anxiety about risk, through media coverage, resulting in consumers' restrained purchasing of commodities that are *supposedly* 'safe'" (Sekiya 2011, 12, emphasis added). The case in which the term was used for the first time in history was the *Lucky Dragon* incident in 1954, when the Japanese tuna fishing boat *Lucky Dragon Five* (Daigo Fukuryū Maru), along with its twenty-three crew members on board, were exposed to radiation fallout caused by the US testing of a hydrogen bomb over Bikini Atoll (Sekiya 2011). The incident, which killed one of the crew members who succumbed to radiation illness within months, was immediately followed by the proliferation of nationwide "nuclear panic," which led to consumers' excessive fear regarding the nuclear contamination of fish. It consequently caused a severe decline in demand for not only tuna but also other fish species landed in Yaizu, the home port of the exposed fishing boat, even though the official monitoring results asserted their safety. After the incident and subsequent disputes, the economic damage that fishers suffered from the declined demand for supposedly safe fish was called "damage by rumor" and officially recognized as a condition for compensation by the US and Japanese governments.

Thereafter, as a number of industrial disasters—such as chemical spills, tanker accidents, and nuclear accidents—have occurred from coast to coast in Japan, "damage by rumor" has become a nearly inevitable form of secondary damage. For fishing families, there is even a standard procedure in cases of industrial disaster. As soon as a disaster happens, local fishing cooperatives immediately cancel fishing activities in the affected coastal waters, and the fishing moratorium continues until the government confirms that it is safe to fish. When fishing reopens, fishing cooperatives, on behalf of their members, claim compensation for the income loss caused during the moratorium against whoever is responsible for the disaster. But prolonged consumer concerns about potential risks posed by the industrial contamination typically delay any recovery of fish prices. Thus, when industrial accidents occur, fishing cooperatives also claim compensation for the lost income from depressed fish prices as an actionable "damage by rumor." On the Joban Sea, fishing cooperatives and their members followed the same procedures in the wake of the 1999 Tokaimura nuclear accident, the 2006 tanker accidents I described in chapter 1, and the 2011 Fukushima nuclear accident.

But even for those experienced Joban fishing families, the aftermath of the Fukushima nuclear disaster has been distinctive, especially due to the magnitude of the damage as well as the ambiguous boundary between so-called "actual damage" and "damage by rumor." Unlike the Tokaimura nuclear accident, which did not leak radioactive contaminants outside of the facilities, the Fukushima nuclear meltdown released historic amounts of radioisotopes into the air and the ocean, similar to the volume produced by the catastrophic 1986 Chernobyl accident. As a result, debates over the boundary between "actual damage" and "damage by rumor" have become a long-term conundrum. On the one hand, the government straightforwardly distinguishes between safe and risky products by evaluating the results of monitoring according to the government's radiation safety standard. Officials claim that the official standard provides sufficient scientific information on food safety measures, emphasizing that the risk of consuming low-level radiation in food products is negligible. On the other hand, no matter how much the government affirms the safety of products with low-level radioactive contamination, many consumers still find them risky, especially in regard to their potential, largely still unknown consequences for their future health. In addition, some consumers point to the partial nature of regular radiation monitoring, testing for and assessing levels of radioactive cesium but possibly not for other radioisotopes that might evade detection and thus pose acute risks to consumers. Many consumers making their own judgments of food safety therefore consider information on the location of food production to be a more straightforward and trustworthy indicator than the government's radiation safety standard. As a result, regardless of the government's safety claims, a considerable number of consumers end up avoiding food products from Fukushima or neighboring prefectures like Ibaraki and purchase produce from elsewhere instead.

Because of widespread consumer preference to avoid products from Fukushima and neighboring regions, the government has widely proclaimed that citizens in Japan must combat the "damage by rumor" and help the economy of the disaster zone. In doing so, the government also emphasized the importance of behaving based on scientific facts rather than unscientific rumor, or "junk science." But consumers' concerns about safety are frequently based on data on radiation risk that they gathered as "citizen scientists," not just on groundless rumors (Kimura 2016). In their own scientific investigations, these consumers often show notable sophistication by, for example, setting a more distant time horizon for their projections and questions than the government considers for its own risk assessments. They are, in this sense, aware of living in a "risk society" in which "risks accumulate slowly, are not limited in time and space, affect future generations, and are often testable only after the fact" (Fischer 2009, 127; see also Beck 1992).

The particular dimensions of "damage by rumor" following the Fukushima nuclear disaster offer a reminder of the implications of living in a risk society, in which our relationships with uncertain risk become dynamic through our active engagement with incomplete knowledge about it. Since the Fukushima accident, government officials, scientists, and laypeople alike have gained a great deal of knowledge about radiation risk, but at the same time they also have encountered additional forms of uncertainty. Their relationships with radiation risk in post-Fukushima Japan, therefore, are constantly animated by the ambiguous boundary between certainty and uncertainty. Living with invisible radionuclides in post-Fukushima Japan, risk and safety alike are, in fact, both certain and uncertain. It is true that radiation particles themselves are invisible to human eyes without a mechanical aid like a Geiger counter. Although some new advanced technologies—such as "autoradiography" (Mori and Kagaya 2015) or a gamma-ray camera[3]— have been used to visualize radiation substances after the Fukushima incident, the human eye alone cannot identify radioactive particles. Nevertheless, in post-Fukushima Japan, radioactive contamination has become largely "visible," thanks to various representations of radiation information available on public displays, in the news media, and various online sources. Aspects of radiation therefore become certain, presented in different ways to citizens, readers, and consumers, even as the implications remain unclear and contested. These partial relationships with certain and uncertain risk are especially evident in the narratives of low-level radioactive contamination.

Some experts argue that there is no harm in consuming or being exposed to a limited amount of radiation, whereas others warn that the accumulation of low-dose exposure will result in cancer, congenital conditions, or other health problems. In fact, there is no existing scientific consensus on whether low-dose radiation exposure causes health issues in the long run, but the Japanese government has largely supported the theory of its relative harmlessness over other interpretations, emphasizing the limited risks of low-level exposure. For example, based on the government's radiation food safety standard, food items that contain a lower level of radiation than the official limit are considered to be "safe" to consume and sell. Thus, in order to spread the word and to demonstrate the legitimate safety of consuming low-level radiation, prime ministers, cabinet members, and other politicians all have engaged in familiar performances in front of media groups. Just as they did in previous cases that were allegedly considered as "damage by rumor," they appear on television to chow down on vegetables and fish from Fukushima and Ibaraki with exaggerated smiles, saying, "Umm, so delicious!" as if food's tastiness testifies to its harmlessness.

But in reality, as our knowledge of "low-level" radioactive contamination remains incomplete, the ambiguous definition of what is determined to be "low" continues to serve as a source of social frictions and a subject of public debate (Weston 2014). Given consumers' partial knowledge, their responses to the government's rhetoric on "combatting damage by rumor" have indeed been diverse. A majority of consumers avoided food items from Fukushima and near there. But there were also consumers who actually made the voluntary, active decision to purchase and eat food items from those areas in order to support the struggling producers in the disaster zone. Encountering consumers with diverse perspectives on radiation risk, fishing families, too, tried to survive the immediate aftermath of the accident by exploring ways to keep their businesses alive with supposedly safe fish featuring only low-level radioactive contamination.

BUY, EAT, AND SUPPORT!

On an early, sunny Sunday morning in May 2011, four fishermen from Hama—Yukio, Hiroki, Mamoru, and Atsushi—were visiting Tokyo's Tsukiji Fish Market. The world's most famous fish market was already filled with booth tents and people who came to the day's special disaster reconstruction event. The event's title was, "Buy, Eat, and Support in Tsukiji!"[4] The main objective, as written on the event's banner, was "to support the disaster zone and eradicate 'damage by rumor.'" At the beginning of the event, the president of the Tsukiji Fish Market Association made some opening remarks, appealing to the audience for their help. He said that the profits of the event would be donated to funds for disaster relief. He also emphasized that, by purchasing fish and agricultural products from the disaster zone and beyond, especially those suffering "damage by rumor," visitors could support the people of the disaster zone and their reconstruction.

The fair at Tsukiji was one of many reconstruction events that had been organized since the March 11 disaster, following a slogan promoted by the Ministry of Agriculture, Forestry, and Fisheries: "Eat and Support!"[5] The ambience that morning was cheerful, more like a state fair than a disaster reconstruction event. Many visitors were families with children. They hopped from one booth tent to another to check each vendor's special food items. Visitors with their plates filled with freshly cooked food, such as fried noodles, grilled squid, and fish on a stick, occupied a large eating space with folding tables and chairs. Dozens of others who could not find spots at the folding tables stood against one of the walls, cradling their plates with one hand and holding chopsticks in the other.

The four fishermen from Hama had their booth tent right in front of the dining area. When I showed up a few minutes before 9:00 a.m., they were setting up a table in front of their booth. They told me that they were the only fishermen from the disaster zone who were able to bring local fish to sell at the event. Within the large disaster zone, from Aomori Prefecture at the northern top to Ibaraki Prefecture at the southern end, only a few regions in the northern and the southern ends had reopened their fishing activities at the time. In addition, considering the distance to Tokyo, the only fishers who could relatively easily show up for the event were those who lived in Ibaraki. In Hama, young anchovy fishing had finally been approved for reopening by the Ministry of Health, Labor, and Welfare two weeks earlier after a series of radiation monitoring results indicated acceptably low-level radiation. Commercial fishers in Hama were excited about finally being able to return to work at sea after the two-month-long moratorium since

Fourfold Pain

FIG. 7. A fisherman handing out boiled young anchovies at the post-Fukushima "combatting damage by rumor" event at Tokyo's Tsukiji Fish Market. Photo by author.

the nuclear meltdown.[6] The price for young anchovies from Ibaraki had remained unusually low. The fishers had expected it but were disappointed nonetheless. The low price of fish from Ibaraki was obviously a reflection of consumers' anxiety over low-level radiation and their suspicion of the legitimacy of the government's safety standard. However, since fish from Ibaraki were officially designated as safe, the low price could only be recognized as an effect of "damage by rumor," not actual damage caused by nuclear contamination. In this context, the blame was directed to those consumers who maintained their "unreasonable" fear of low-level radiation. Moreover, commercial fishers in the disaster zone were also expected to act as "front-line soldiers" in the war on "rumor" by demonstrating the safety of their fish directly to consumers. Thus, on the day of the event in Tsukiji, the four fishermen from Hama represented commercial fishers of the disaster zone in the fight against damaging rumor.

"Look at these beautiful young anchovies!" said Hiroki cheerfully, while making a white mountain of the fish like a pile of fresh snow on a large bamboo basket. In fact, a young anchovy is a tiny fish of less than two centimeters, and a freshly boiled body turns a delightful white like a snowflake. As he was handing me a blue jacket to match theirs, Hiroki told me that they had caught those young anchovies in Ibaraki just three days earlier. Then he explained step-by-step the procedures we needed to follow for the event. They were simple and straightforward. We were going to pick a couple of pinches of the tiny fishes from the big pile onto a small plastic plate and then hand out each to as many people as possible. "Like this!" Yukio showed me how to make a sample and handed one to me: "Here you go!" This unexpected offering made me quietly panicked. But after a second of hesitation, I quickly popped a few boiled young anchovies into my mouth. "Yummy, isn't it!?" asked Yukio. I nodded. It was, indeed, delicious just like the fresh young anchovies that I used to enjoy when I lived in Hama four years back. But I was nervous. It was actually the first time that I had eaten something that I knew to be contaminated by radiation, even if its level allegedly was safely low.

To tell the truth, although I did not confess this to the four fishermen, I, too, had been one of those consumers criticized in the press and by the government for causing "damage by rumor." Since the Fukushima meltdown, I had been avoiding any food products from either Fukushima or Ibaraki. Whenever I went grocery shopping, I picked food products, labeled by the prefecture of their harvest or landing, that were made somewhere far from the disaster region. The farther away the location was, the safer I felt. On that day, though, I tried to put faith in the notion that the level of radiation contained in their young anchovies must be low. I knew that, if not, the fish could have not been served even at the reconstruction fair. I was also aware that there were radiation specialists who had argued that consuming low-dose radiation does not cause a health risk. But I was still anxious about how safe it was to eat those young anchovies, knowing that scientific knowledge is always incomplete, particularly with concerns as novel as the effects of nuclear disasters on human health. Like other consumers, a series of questions went through my mind: What if the experts' projections turned out to be wrong? What if low-dose consumption could actually cause some health issues in the future? Is there any potential risk in relation to future pregnancy? But I also knew that I could not possibly share any of these questions with the four fishermen. So I remained cheerful and tried my best to hide my anxieties from them or anybody else at the fair.

"Please, try our fresh and tasty young anchovies!" The four fishermen and I yelled repeatedly. And we handed out the tiny fish on a plate to whomever was willing to try. As he was giving one sample to a young family with a small boy, Hiroki said to them with a kind smile that he and his fellow fishermen caught these young anchovies only three days ago. The mother seemed pleased and passed one sample to her young boy. "Yummy?" the mother asked. "Yup," the boy nodded. "Thank you very much!" Hiroki and I said to the mother and the child. "Good luck and hang in there," the mother replied with a smile along with a casual bow, expressing her sympathy and support for the fishermen from the disaster zone. For about two and a half hours, without any break, we kept calling out to people walking by our table. Many people stopped, took our samples, and gave us warm greetings.

The majority of the people who came to our table were young families with young children. Small children particularly loved those familiar, salty, little young anchovies. A couple of boys who appeared to be five or six years old, came back to our table and asked for refills. "More, please!" the boys shouted as they held their empty plates in front of their little faces with beaming smiles. "You got it! Here you go, big boy!" Hiroki gave them a bigger pile of boiled young anchovies on each of their small plastic plates. They came back two more times. The four fishermen and I laughed as we watched the boys giggling and running back and forth between their eating table and our booth. There were also a couple of women who looked unmistakably pregnant. I was shocked that they were there at the reconstruction event, especially given the theme of buying and eating potentially risky food. I silently hoped that they would not ask for a fish sample. As soon as I spotted them, I stopped calling out loud. But both of them stepped toward me and asked for a sample. After chowing down the young anchovies, they, too, thanked us and gave us a warm greeting.

Before noon, all the boiled young anchovies that the Hama fishermen had brought from their hometown were gone. I was too busy to count how many samples we actually gave away, but the total was close to a couple of hundred, possibly more. Given the nature of the fair as a reconstruction event, it was understandable that visitors were there in order to support the disaster victims, especially those farmers and fishers who were trying to rebuild livelihoods damaged by the triple disaster. Their purpose was, as the slogan suggested, buying and eating foods from the disaster zone. But I was actually intrigued by the fact that, among all the many people who came to our table, nobody mentioned or even hinted at concerns about radiation, except for two senior citizens. One old man expressed his sympathies and support for disaster victims and told me that he was seventy-five years old so that he was not afraid of radiation because he was too old to be affected by it. "It takes thirty years for radiation to cause a cancer, I heard, but I will be dead way before then," he laughed. It was, in fact, one of the widespread "rumors" in post-Fukushima Japan that radiation takes thirty years to start causing harm in bodies. The other occasion was when an older woman asked a straightforward question: "Is the fish safe?" While I hesitated, a prefectural fisheries officer who was standing next to me responded, "Yes, they are safe." "That's good," she replied, and left without any further question.

Looking back at the event, my interactions with the visitors made me wonder what made them decide to actively consume low-level radiation and what radiation risk or safety actually means to them. Based on the rhetoric of "combatting damage by rumor," they are considered "good citizens" who support disaster victims and behave based on scientifically sound information. But, while it was clear that the idea of supporting disaster victims played an important role for visitors, I remembered how little scientific information on safety—or risk—I was able to spot during the event. At the fishermen's booth and elsewhere within the event space on the day in Tsukiji, safety was largely presumed. As far as I observed, there was no written information on safety, and nobody—neither producers nor consumers—seemed willing to openly discuss or share scientific information on safety. When I asked about the result of radiation monitoring on young anchovies, Hiroki told me that all the test results were available on the website. But the information was not shared at the fishermen's booth, and I did not meet a single visitor who asked for it. I asked the fisheries official from the prefectural office why they did not display the information. His response was that he was worried that providing the information would make consumers suspicious of the safety of fish rather than help them to feel safe.

After I returned home that day, I visited the Ibaraki Prefecture's website in order to investigate the record on radiation monitoring for young anchovies. According to the record, the most recent radiation monitoring of young anchovies had been done five days earlier. The result was 3 Bq/kg for radioactive cesium. A few days after the event, another test result came out. This time the finding was higher: 67 Bq/kg. Both results fell far below the government-sanctioned radiation hazard threshold of 500 Bq/kg, suggesting that the radiation level was low on both days and thus that the fish was *safe*. But the fact that there was little information on the radiation level at the Tsukiji event—or at any of the other events designed to combat "damage by rumor" that I have attended—suggests an ambiguous relationship between feeling safe and the sciences of safety (Sternsdorff-Cisterna 2018). It also suggests that accepting the government's safety standard does not necessarily mean that the person gained a feeling of safety based on careful consideration of the science behind the safety standard. For many visitors, feeling safe was a commitment as a citizen of the country that was undergoing a devastating nuclear disaster rather than a scientifically sound decision.[7]

For some visitors, feelings of guilt no doubt played a part in their decisions to voluntarily buy and eat low-level radiation in the food products from the disaster zone. The crippled Fukushima Daiichi Nuclear Power Plant was built in the first place for the purpose of producing cheap and abundant electricity for companies and households in Tokyo and neighboring cities. It is true that it was a national project and that the power plant provided employment in rural Fukushima. But it is also true that most people in the Tokyo Metropolitan Area did not make even the slightest effort to imagine where their electricity was produced or to worry about the risk that was produced along with the energy. If low-dose radiation is supposedly safe or safe enough to consume, people thought that taking uncertain risk by buying vegetables and fish from Fukushima and Ibaraki was the least they could do to make up for their sins.

That said, there were—and are still—many other consumers who kept away from products from Fukushima and Ibaraki, or any regions where radiation had been detected. Some of them said that they felt guilty for playing a role in spreading damage by rumor, but some others expressed anger at being labeled "bad citizens." They asked why supporting disaster victims should mean purchasing risky food for themselves and their families?

"IT'S JUST THE REALITY"

In late July 2011, as the nuclear disaster's effects lingered, I visited a town in Ibaraki in order to attend a daylong seminar on how to promote businesses using the town's local fish. It was part of a nine-seminar series that the municipal office and the town's Chamber of Commerce and Industry had co-organized and planned before the disaster, funding it through a government subsidy. The seminar series was originally scheduled for the spring, but due to the March 11 disaster, they had delayed it until July. At the time, while commercial fishing remained entirely banned in Fukushima, it was partly reopened in Ibaraki for limited fish species that had been officially approved safe, such as young anchovies and a few mollusk species. But other species including flounder and sea bass remained excluded due to high radiation levels detected through monitoring.

In a medium-sized conference room in the city's largest hotel, tables and chairs were set facing the podium, which stood atop a platform. The room was sultry, as were many other places in Japan at the time. In order to obey a nationwide request for energy conservation due to the shutdown of all of the country's nuclear power plants for safety checks following the meltdown, school and office buildings maintained their room temperature around 28°C (approx. 80°F). One member of the city office's staff took note of the sparse crowd and murmured that turnout for that day's seminar was not as high as the organizers had hoped. In addition to three people from the city hall and the Chamber of Commerce, four local fishermen, a wholesaler, and a processing company owner showed up in the morning, but a couple of fishermen left before lunchtime. More than half of the chairs remained empty throughout the day.

That day's keynote speaker was an entrepreneur with an MBA from an American university who introduced herself as a mother of three sons. Despite the seminar's seemingly uncontroversial objective—to promote businesses using local fish—she did not hesitate to be contentious. She said flat-out to the attendees that fish-related businesses in general have good potential in a fish-eating country like Japan, but consumers like herself would never buy fish coming from either Fukushima or Ibaraki. Showing a PowerPoint slide with a picture from *The Late Show with David Letterman*, she explained that the man sitting next to the famous talk-show host was Dr. Michio Kaku, a well-known American professor of theoretical physics, who appeared on the show as a guest. According to her, when Letterman asked the professor how long it would take for the nuclear crisis in Japan to be contained, he responded that it would take at least ten years. And she repeated, "He said, optimistically speaking, ten years!" She continued, "My three boys drink three packs of milk a day. Because they consume so much, I check where it is produced, and avoid products containing milk from Chiba or anywhere near Fukushima. It is very unfortunate, but this is how housewives' consumer behavior works. Nothing can be done about it. And you just need to accept that." She emphasized, "From a marketing point of view, it's all up to consumers to judge whether the radiation numbers indicate that something is dangerous or safe. I am sorry to say this, but it's just the reality."

After the seminar ended, Mr. Nishikawa, an owner of a local fish processing company, murmured to me, "producers [namely fishers] have no sense of crisis." He then turned around and said to his friend, a fisherman, "See, didn't I tell you?" "Huh?" the fisherman responded. Mr. Nishikawa added, "I told you. What she [the speaker] just said is the true voice of consumers." The fisherman just said, "Ah." A few minutes later at a postseminar party, I asked Mr. Nishikawa what he meant by fishers having no sense of crisis. In response, he criticized fishermen for seemingly believing that things would get better if the media stopped spreading the "rumor." He continued, "As the speaker said earlier, we need to show the [radiation] numbers. Only consumers can make a decision [whether their fish is safe or not]. So, we need to do rigorous monitoring and keep making public announcement on the results. The situation won't get better if we don't come forward."

In reality, fishers' views on radiation monitoring and the information disclosure were more nuanced and diverse than Mr. Nishikawa suggested. Some fishers were worried that actively announcing the information to the public might lead to further perpetuation of the bad rumor. Others felt much as Mr. Nishikawa did about the importance of transparency. But, in fact, none of the fishers I interviewed disagreed with the government's radiation monitoring of fish or the disclosure of the results on the prefectural or the national government's websites. They seemed to think that governmental monitoring was adequately carried out, and no further effort—for example, independent monitoring at the co-op level—was necessary, considering the expensive monitoring equipment and additional manpower required to handle the testing. A few fishers claimed that the government should do more rigorous testing.

One of the fishermen I interviewed in Hama questioned whether the government's lack of explanation of the results might be contributing to the spread of rumor. "Think about it for a second," he said. "You catch different types of fish for radiation monitoring from the same location at sea. And then, let's say, the test result of a pelagic fish from the upper layers of the water comes out safe, but a demersal fish from the bottom of the sea of the same location comes out not safe. Would you eat the pelagic fish?" I hesitated, not wishing to answer the question directly. "You see?" he added. "I don't blame people for not trusting the test results." Another fisherman asked me whether I was aware that the head, bones, and guts are removed before a fish is tested in the monitoring device. I said yes. He asked me if I knew why. I had read on Ibaraki Prefecture's website that it was because people do not usually eat those parts. "But we sometimes do!" he said. "A sardine and a saury, you eat the guts, right? Why don't they include them?"

According to the website, each fish species is tested in a way that matches with how people usually consume it. As part of the prefecture's webpage, entitled "The Fukushima Daiichi Nuclear Power Plant Accident's Effects on This Prefecture's Fisheries Products," there is a section for frequently asked questions (Ibaraki Prefecture n.d.). The third question asks, "Aren't you removing guts in order to lower the radiation number of the test result?" Below the question, the provided answer explains that they test the whole fish for small fish such as sand lance (*kōnago*) or young anchovies (*shirasu*) that are usually consumed whole, and they test only the meat part for those larger fish whose bones and innards are usually not consumed by people, except for some particular species, like angler fish (*ankō*), whose innards are likely to be consumed. In addition, it also states that radioactive cesium is usually contained more in muscle tissues than innards, so removing innards would not reduce radiation numbers. The next question asks, "How extensive exactly are the effects on a human body?" The answer makes an effort to provide complicated "scientific" measurements in an "understandable" manner for laypeople. The explanation does not tell you whether or not it is safe but suggests instead what levels of radiation are considered "normal."

Reading these official explanations and the numbers, some consumers interpret them as a sign of safety, whereas others continue to express concern about the potential health risks of consuming low-dose radiation. As the speaker said during her speech at the local fish seminar: it is indeed up to consumers how they interpret scientific information and how they turn that interpretation into action, buying or avoiding those fish with low-level radiation. There seems to be no quick solution to getting rid of "damage by rumor." All fishers can do is to keep selling their supposedly safe fish, hoping that more consumers will trust in its safety sometime in the future. Nobody knows when that time will come, but as the speaker of the workshop phrased it, "that's just the reality."

After the meeting of "An Assembly to Talk about the Future of Ibaraki," Mr. Hashimoto, who was the event's organizer and an experienced bottom-trawler, invited a few of us out to dinner at a nearby restaurant known for serving local produce—fresh fish and vegetables in addition to fine sake. The group included two bureaucrats from the Fisheries Agency; a fisheries official from the prefectural government; Kenji, the fisherman who had discussed "fourfold pain" in his concluding remarks; and me. During the dinner the bureaucrats, especially the older one, were chatty and laughed a lot, whereas Kenji remained mostly quiet.

As I was pouring sake into his cup, the older bureaucrat said, "To tell the truth, we were actually worried about getting beaten black-and-blue today. But we were relieved that Ibaraki fishers were calm and gentle," he continued. "When we visited fishermen in Fukushima the other day, we were totally beaten to a pulp, right?" He chuckled and called on his younger colleague. "Miserably," the younger one quietly laughed. Neither Mr. Hashimoto nor Kenji responded. After the dinner, Mr. Hashimoto invited Kenji and me to his home to chat for a little longer. In his car on the way to his home, Mr. Hashimoto emphasized how important it is for fishers to get to know and work well with the bureaucrats. "We fishers today can't just fish, you know," he said, "We have to play politics."

About three weeks after the meeting with the bureaucrats in Ibaraki, on June 28, the Fisheries Agency announced its "Fisheries Restoration Master Plan." The thirty-page pledge provided detailed plans on not only how to rebuild the disaster-devastated fisheries industry but also on how to build a better future for the industry. And the master plan's grand strategy for accomplishing the goals was, yet again, modernization. The master plan stated that, in order to rebuild the devastated fisheries in the disaster zone, old structures would have to be reformed. Furthermore, it insisted that reconstruction should not be about reconstructing the pretsunami conditions but about building the new future. In order to build the new future, it said, the declining, backward industry would have to be modernized. Three objectives for achieving modernization were listed in the plan: (1) to promote energy- and cost-efficiency; (2) to promote the rationalization of the distribution system of fisheries commodities; and (3) to open the coastal waters for private businesses.

Ulrich Beck, in his interview with a Japanese newspaper during the immediate aftermath of the triple disaster, described post-Fukushima Japan as a quintessential example of a risk society, in which people must deal with uncertain risk that they had previously produced through earlier modernization efforts (Ohno 2011). In the aftermath of the nuclear meltdown, the government officials, scientific experts, and laypeople alike newly learned a great deal about radioactive contamination about which they had previously been uncertain. But no matter how much new knowledge we gain about radiation risk, uncertain risk remains uncertain. In the post-Fukushima risk society, certainty of radiation risk is like a mirage: we feel we might be able to grasp it, but it always recedes as we try to move closer. In order to survive in this risk society, the Japanese government called, once again, for further modernization.

Modernization apparently works like an addiction (Pels 2015). Modernization efforts produce uncertain risks, and in order to deal with such risks, modernization advocates call for further modernization. Moreover, in this cycle of addition, disasters play an important role as an enabler. In the name of disaster reconstruction, further modernization is legitimated as a method for surviving the very challenges that were caused by earlier modernization. For commercial fishing families, living in a seascape already marked by environmental precarity within a larger risk society has meant responding to and living with the government's addictive relationship with modernization.

CHAPTER 6 Fukushima FORWARD

In Japan, 2013 was a strange year. Two years after the tsunami and the Fukushima meltdown in 2011, it seemed that a sense of normality had come back, even though the disaster was still ongoing. When I returned to Tokyo from the United States during the summer, most people in the city seemed to be busy at work or school just like they had been before the disaster. Although the disaster had clearly altered everyday life, the changes had seemingly become part of a new normal. At least, that was how it felt in Tokyo. For example, with all of the nation's fifty-four nuclear power plants remaining shut down pending security and safety checks, enforced energy conservation (*setsuden*) became part of everyday life. Thanks to this new custom, unlike in the summers before the disaster, I did not have to complain about overly chilly office buildings or the trains made nearly arctic by aggressive air conditioners.

In contrast, in Fukushima as well as other disaster-affected areas, normality seemed to reside in the distant future, barely perceptible. Two years after the disaster, thousands of people were still living in temporary housing units, and those Fukushima residents who had been displaced from the nuclear evacuation zones were still unable to return to their hometowns (Gill 2013). The sea was hardly normal either. Radioactive wastewater from the crippled reactors had been continuously leaking and deliberately dumped into the ocean without anyone's consent, as TEPCO had belatedly admitted to the public. In Fukushima, all the commercial fishing activities had been suspended except for limited pilot operations. In Ibaraki, while some species remained banned, commercial fishing had been reopened for those species the government had determined to be safe. But market prices for fish from Ibaraki remained low due to consumers' fears about radiation risk. Thus, fishing families in Fukushima and Ibaraki were still living largely on compensation payments from TEPCO, without knowing how long it might take for fishing to return to normal.

In 2013, despite the highly precarious marine environment and acute anxieties among fishing families, a bright future literally sprouted out off the coast of Fukushima. That is to say, the initial turbine of the world's first floating wind farm—named "Fukushima Future"—was built off the southern Fukushima coast, right outside of the "no-admission zone," the twenty-kilometer radius from the crippled Fukushima Daiichi Nuclear Power Plant. When the floating windmill made its sensational media debut in June, this brand-new energy infrastructure of the future looked strikingly gigantic. Equipped with eighty-meter-long blades, the turbine was as tall as 105 meters above the water surface, taller than a thirty-story skyscraper popping out of the Pacific Ocean. On the side of the bright-yellow platform, the windmill's name was inscribed in a large font with black paint. In addition to celebrating the coming of the new future for Fukushima, referring to the windmill's iconic name, the media also reported enthusiastically that, after the initial three-year demonstration phase for testing three varieties of floating wind turbines with different capacities and power generation systems, the next grand plan would be to build the world's largest floating wind farm with an additional hundred turbines across the offshore area of Fukushima.

Given the name of the initial turbine, the floating wind farm project's strong will to build the future was unmistakable, but it had also been apparent from the outset, ever since the Ministry of Economy, Trade, and Industry (METI) entrusted the "pilot project" to the Fukushima Offshore Wind Power Consortium in November 2011. The consortium called the pilot project "Fukushima FORWARD" as a nickname, assembled from some of the letters in the official title, "Fukushima Floating Offshore Wind Farm Demonstration Project." The project's budget was 25 billion yen (a little over $300 million), allocated from the Japanese Diet's supplementary budget of 11 trillion yen (nearly $150 billion at the time) for disaster reconstruction efforts. The consortium explicitly proposed two futures that the project would advance: one for Japan, and another for Fukushima.[1]

In fact, Fukushima Future was not the only futurity that emerged in postdisaster Fukushima. The wind energy project was actually set in motion as part of the postdisaster futurism that emerged and began to accelerate roughly a year after the historic catastrophe. On March 11, 2012, the first anniversary of the disaster, Fukushima's prefectural government announced a new official slogan, both in Japanese and English. The Japanese version reads, "Fukushima Kara Hajimeyou," which could be translated as "Let's Start from Fukushima." The English version of the slogan says, "Future from Fukushima." On Fukushima Prefecture's official website, a statement titled "The Slogan Says It All" reads, "Without doubt, Fukushima Prefecture will recover from the great catastrophe and the nuclear disaster. Fukushima's reconstruction will demonstrate new possibilities of society.

FIG. 8. Fukushima Prefecture's official logo, "Future from Fukushima." Courtesy of Fukushima Prefecture.

We would like to create new flows from Fukushima. 'Let's Start from Fukushima' is a slogan of our will to begin the future."[2] In addition to the slogan, the prefectural government also introduced an official logo accompanying the message. Along with the slogan in the both languages, the logo features a white egg with the shape of Fukushima Prefecture printed in light grassy green at its center. The egg's shadow, as well as the letters of the slogan, are printed in darker green, like leaves on a tree. The logo embodies Fukushima's wish for a rebirth with a clean environment and also its declaration of strong commitments to rebuilding a sustainable future for the prefecture and its residents.[3]

Indeed, the narratives of the future attached to Fukushima Future and "Future from Fukushima" were all hopeful. The news on the emergence of the new renewable energy project provided a sense of hope to those who wish for a more sustainable future, which felt like a utopia emerging amid the ruins of the Fukushima nuclear crisis (see also Morris-Suzuki 2017).[4] In addition, given the ongoing struggles resulting from the nuclear disaster in Fukushima, the project's orientation toward the future reminded me of hope in the Blochean sense, which exists in the "not-yet" consciousness. At the same time, though, I also recognized a gap between the discussion of hope in the Blochean sense and the discourse of hope involved with the building of Fukushima Future. That is the orientation toward the present. For Bloch, hope derives from the darkness of the now (Bloch 1995, 288–289; see also Miyazaki 2004). But in the discourses of hope among those who are in charge of building Fukushima Future, the darkness of the present in Fukushima was largely missing. In this context, hope derives from the brightness of the future, closely associating with a capitalist image of utopia generated through futurism (see also Thompson and Žižek 2013; and Morris-Suzuki 2017).[5] In addition, as I looked further into post-Fukushima futurity, it became apparent that the future is not simply a horizon newly imagined in the wake of a meltdown. Although all those "future" projects suggest that they are designed to build a new future for postdisaster Fukushima, they are actually not new at all. In fact, the main objectives of all the postdisaster "future" projects had already been introduced before the 2011 disaster. Although these projects' goals gaze at the future, they were also built on old dreams, yearning to achieve further capitalistic progress yet again.

But while plans based on this "yet-again" kind of futurism were proceeding, how did coastal fishing families in Fukushima actually respond to the positive futurity that the Fukushima FORWARD consortium presented? What did they think of the future in general, and how did they envision it? As it turns out, while encountering nostalgic futurism embedded in the Fukushima FORWARD project, fishers' views on the futurism project were in fact varied. Some fishers actively opposed the project, while others enthusiastically supported or sneered at it. But besides their diverse responses to the project, their perspectives on the future were more similar than different. Their observations on the future reside in the present, whereas their hope remains somewhere in between the "not-yet" and the "yet-again."[6]

DISASTER FUTURISM

In *The Politics of Survival*, the political anthropologist Marc Abélès argues that at the end of the World War II—or, more precisely, after the dropping of the atomic bombs on Hiroshima and Nagasaki—people around the world shared the belief that tomorrow would be better than today (Abélès 2010, 1). Despite problems such as wars, poverty, discrimination, etc., they believed in utopia and thought that they could overcome challenges by making progress. But Abélès also claims that such a world no longer exists; the world is now preoccupied with anxieties about surviving in the troubled future, with utopias buried or unimaginable. Considering the growing concerns that he discusses in relation to globalization, climate change, and terrorism, I have no trouble seeing what he sees in current political discourses that are intimately linked to images of a precarious future. At the same time, however, by thinking of the futurism that emerged yet again in Fukushima, I find it hard to ignore the utopian future that remains alive—vividly and persistently—in the present world. Therefore, though Abélès implies that "the politics of survival" operates through the imagination of a futureless dystopia, the politics of the future—at least in Japan but perhaps elsewhere as well—is built upon not only anxieties but also ongoing nostalgic aspirations for "the brilliance that the future will bring" (Abélès 2010, 1).

Given the consortium's enthusiasm for producing the new futures, it was not particularly surprising that they chose the name they did for the first turbine. But at the same time, the name itself is intriguingly strange. "Fukushima Future" might be catchy in English, but it is more awkward in Japanese. The awkwardness comes from the fact that nothing syntactically links the two words—Fukushima and *mirai* (the future)—meaning that there is no indication of the relationship between them. Looking at the phrase, one might wonder what it is actually supposed to mean. What is the relationship between Fukushima and the future? Are we supposed to read the phrase as "Fukushima's future"? Or is it "Fukushima *as* the future"? If so, the future of whom? Of the people of Fukushima, or of Japan as a whole? Perhaps, from the government's and the consortium's perspectives, their answers would be yes to all of these questions. "Fukushima Future," as they have claimed, opens the future not only for Fukushima and Japan but also for Japanese fisheries.

In terms of building Japan's future, the consortium suggested that creating the world's first offshore floating wind farm would develop technology and knowledge that would eventually help to ensure the development of the country's new and internationally marketable energy industry. The consortium itself emphasized that it was an *all-Japan* team, consisting of eleven of the nation's megacorporations and its most highly rated university. The Fukushima floating wind farm project "opens up the nation's future," as the team leader from the trading conglomerate Marubeni Corporation emphasized on his company's website (Marubeni n.d.).[7] Additionally, by carrying out this national project in Fukushima, the consortium also claimed that the offshore wind farm would open up a new future for Fukushima. If the pilot project succeeded, the consortium planned to build a hundred additional offshore turbines all along the Fukushima coast. Although the turbines for the pilot project would have to be assembled at dockyards outside Fukushima, the future turbines, according to the consortium and METI, would all be built locally, and the energy produced by the wind farm would be consumed locally. Hence, this would promote a kind of "local food movement" (*chisan chishō*) for energy. By building new dockyards for assembling turbines in Fukushima, this future energy industry would also generate local employment in Fukushima and invite population growth from outside. The future community would draw in not only those people employed in dockyard businesses but those working in the schools, supermarkets, hospitals, and so forth that will cater to workers and their families. Just as nuclear power plants had once produced their company towns—the so-called nuclear castle towns (*genpatsu jōka machi*)—these alternative energy industries would support the region in a new, environmentally and financially sound future.

In addition to the national technological future and local economic future that the consortium would ostensibly create, Professor Takeshi Ishihara—the project leader of Fukushima FORWARD and one of the nation's leading wind power engineering experts—argued that the offshore wind farm would also open up a new future for Japan's fishing industry. In an online article entitled "Tomorrow's Wind Blows at Sea," Ishihara states that one of the major challenges the project faces is the issue of coexistence between the wind farm and the fishing industry. Ishihara acknowledges considerable opposition from commercial fishers of Fukushima, who were reluctant to give up access to fishing grounds that the massive structures would occupy. But he says that there is a solution. His proposal is to build an "ocean farm" (*kaiyō bokujō*) by converting the windmill platforms into "artificial reefs," which will increase the density of wild fish stocks, just as real reefs do.

As he told me in a personal interview, the wind power and ocean farms would not only produce energy and increase fish population, but they also would promote the evolutionary transition of the energy and fishing industries from backward "hunter-gatherers" to era-appropriate "farmers."[8] While we chatted, Ishihara explained his theory on why these industries need to be transformed. "Humankind once consisted of hunter-gatherers, but we first achieved our current progress through 'farmerization' (*nōkō-ka*)," he said. "Similarly," he continued, "petroleum is hunter-gatherer-like energy. You dig a hole and extract oil until it dries up, and then you dig another hole. That's too random and inefficient. Fishing, too, has been hunter-gatherer-like. Fishing based on intuitions and experience can't provide a stable supply (of fish). We need a new, farm-like fishing industry." He underlined that farmerization is required for the future of humankind. "Human societies prosper after shifting from hunter-gatherers to farmers," he emphasized, "that's a solid historical truth." Hence, by "farmerizing" both energy and fishing industries, he claimed that they could "co-exist and co-prosper" (*kyōzon kyōei*).

Despite the novelty of the offshore wind technology, Professor Ishihara's narratives on the relationship between windmills and fisheries sounded awfully familiar to me, resembling the ways in which people used to talk about the symbiosis between the nuclear power plants and fisheries. In fact, the phrase *co-existence and co-prosperity* was exactly the same as the one that had been used in the earlier discussions of nuclear energy. While Professor Ishihara used the phrase to describe the symbiosis between the wind farm and fisheries that an ocean farm would accomplish, the fisheries official of Fukushima Prefecture, as mentioned in the introduction, used it in his postdisaster interview with a newspaper to emphasize the intimate relationship that had existed between the nuclear power plant and fisheries prior to the nuclear disaster. Their resemblance, of course, is not an accident. The ideas of the ocean farm and the nuclear hatchery both stem from the same past of Japan's modernist ambition to accomplish a sustainable future for the ocean.

The concept of "ocean farms" is, moreover, hardly a new idea. It was originally introduced in Japan during the 1970s by the nation's marine scientists as a modernist vision of how humans and the marine environment would become increasingly intertwined to mutual benefit. Often marked both by hypermodern technology and environmentalism, the iconic futuristic imagery of ocean farms—displayed in international expos and science textbooks—soon became popular among Japanese children and adults alike, who enjoyed visions of technological improvement in the midst of the nation's miracle-like economic growth. For those technocrats who worked for continuous Japanese modernization through eco-development, the idea of ocean farms was brilliant. It allowed people to imagine Japan's bright future as a modern nation that would simultaneously accomplish continuous industrial progress as well as marine sustainability. By the late 1970s, however, Japan shelved the "ocean farms" idea, adopting another proposal for building the nation's modernist sustainable future—namely, nuclear fish hatcheries.

Over the course of the next few years in the 1980s, eleven marine fish hatcheries—including the one that I visited in 2004 next to the Fukushima Daiichi Nuclear Power Plant—were built adjacent to nuclear power reactors around Japan. In the aftermath of the Fukushima meltdown in 2011, all the nuclear reactors of the nation were shut down (with some having tentatively reopened), and adjoining hatcheries have been struggling to survive without the thermal discharge that the plants had supplied for all those years. And now in postdisaster Fukushima, after a half century, the idea of ocean farms has been reintroduced as a strategy to rebuild Japan, redeeming the failure of its earlier modernization project, specifically in the moment of the nuclear meltdown. At the end of the day, the narratives of the Fukushima FORWARD make the project a perfect example of both "disaster capitalism" (Klein 2007) as well as "disaster nationalism" (Choi 2015). Or, considering the enthusiastic employment of futurity, it might be more appropriate to describe "disaster futurism," which points to the way preexisting dreams of modernization gain political support for being put into practice in the context of disaster reconstruction by employing utopian languages of the future (see also Morris-Suzuki 2017).

THE DISTANCE TO THE FUTURE

In July 2014, I revisited Mr. Tanaka, a coastal fisherman in northern Fukushima (see chapter 4), with my coresearcher.[9] The last time I had seen him was in May 2011, two months after the tsunami and nuclear meltdown. At that time, I had met him at the town's municipal sports complex, which was being used as an evacuation facility. Their home had been washed away by the tsunami, so Mr. Tanaka and his wife had been living on a tiny spot barely larger than ten square feet within one of the gymnasiums being used as temporary shelters. This time, I met him in his apartment within the town's large temporary housing camp. They had been living there for about three years since they moved from the municipal gymnasium. Prior to our visit on the hot summer day, Mr. Tanaka had warned us that a GPS unit would be useless to find their location. The large camp itself was hard to miss once we reached the hilltop neighborhood, but it was quite a bit harder to locate a particular unit among more than a thousand prefabricated longhouse-like buildings. The large camp had nine subdivisions, so we first looked for the one that held Mr. Tanaka's unit. After a few minutes driving around the camp, we finally found his division. In front of the entrance to the division, Mr. Tanaka was standing, pointing to a large open space to let us know where to park our car. "Did you find us okay?" he asked as we were walking to his building.

Mr. Tanaka's own cell was located in the middle of the building. The inside had a single room of 80 square feet in addition to a small cooking space. Walking through the narrow kitchen, he welcomed my coresearcher and me into the main and only room, which Mr. Tanaka and his wife used as a living room/sleeping space. There, two younger fellow fishermen who worked with Mr. Tanaka, Satoshi and Kenta, were waiting for us. After quick greetings, five of us found our own positions directly on the floor, seated around a small, low table placed in the middle of the room. As we were sitting down, the floorboards squeaked. Looking down, I spotted a few green-headed thumbtacks pinned onto the floor, which made me realize that there was actually a thin carpet between me and the floorboards. Looking around the room, I saw one corner occupied by folded futon mats, and the other by cardboard boxes and other belongings. As he was turning on his air conditioner, Mr. Tanaka apologized to us for the room's stuffiness. He said that he had hardly used the air conditioner when he used to live in his old coastal home, thanks to seaside winds always breezing through windows. "A temporary housing unit," he grumbled, "makes a hot summer hotter and a cold winter colder." With his temporary home having exceeded its recommended duration of two years, his ceiling had more than handful of rain stains.

For the more than three years since the tsunami and the Fukushima meltdown, three fishermen had been working almost every day as construction workers to fix various elements of the tsunami-damaged infrastructure, such as seawalls, highways, and railroads. Mr. Tanaka apologized on behalf of another friend of his, who had hoped to join us but could not that day. He said that his friend had to go to decontamination work: the tasks included removing highly radioactive topsoil, packing it in special bags, and storing them in designated lots. Then Mr. Tanaka laughed that his construction work made his skin even darker than when he used to spend every day on his fishing boat. Indeed, these three fishermen's faces and arms were deeply dark, even though they had been away from fishing trips for more than three years. Satoshi said that although he had been back at sea for occasional "test fishing" and for traffic-patrolling duties in the water around the new offshore floating wind energy farm, most of the sunlight that their skin had absorbed was from construction work.

"What do you think of the wind farm?" my coresearcher asked the three fishermen, segueing into the topic of the floating wind farm project. "We don't have much interest in it around here. But those bottom-trawlers might have," Satoshi responded. Mr. Tanaka explained that small boats like theirs—which operate purse-seining and gill-netting alike—in northern Fukushima rarely make the long trip down to the southern waters of Fukushima, where the wind farm's pilot project is located. "Will you feel the same even when the wind farm project is being expanded?" my coresearcher asked. In fact, the wind farm consortium had announced their ambition in the beginning of the project: once the pilot period ended and pending further approval, they hoped to build a hundred of those floating windmills all along the Fukushima waters. "Well," Mr. Tanaka continued after a pause of a couple of seconds, "if I picture it, that many mills lining up in a huge row across the entire offshore, that'd be creepy." I asked, "So, what do you *really* think of the wind farm?" But Mr. Tanaka's response was the same as it had been earlier; he does not think of the wind farm that much. "Plus," he said, "in our town, bottom-trawlers hold most of the decision-making power. They oppose the wind farm, so we have to oppose it, too." He added, "But the south is different," explaining that fishers in southern Fukushima had been enthusiastic supporters of the wind farm project.

"So, what are your plans for the future?" I asked. I was curious to understand what these fishermen were planning to do in the future given that their ocean, fish, and reputations are all polluted by radiation, and nobody seemed to know when the contamination would be cleaned up. If they were not interested in the wind farm as a new way to gain income besides fishing, as the consortium had suggested, I wondered what they were planning to do for the future and how he envisioned the time ahead. When I asked the question, I expected to hear a sense of despair vis-à-vis the highly precarious future, or, even worse, their futurelessness. But they expressed not only despair but also hope.

Mr. Tanaka's immediate response to my question was, "I know the fish [population] is growing. But even if we could have a good catch, we can't sell the fish." Indeed, given the ongoing restrictions on fishing and consumers' fears about Fukushima fish, it was hard to imagine that commercial fishing would be reopened anytime soon. "In addition," Mr. Tanaka continued, "fish wholesalers have moved their business to other areas outside of Fukushima and haven't come back." Indeed, without wholesalers nearby, reopening fishing in Fukushima would be extremely difficult. Nonetheless, despite the difficulties that Fukushima fisheries would continue to face in the future, Satoshi emphasized that he and other fishers were all prepared for the moment it would happen in the future. He told us that Fukushima fishers had already resumed their fish-stocking programs in order to enhance the growth of the fish population in the prefecture's coastal waters. The fish hatchery adjacent to the Fukushima Daiichi Nuclear Power Plant had been washed away by the 2011 tsunami, but according to Satoshi, for the previous two years, the Fukushima prefectural government had been buying flounder juveniles from Niigata (a neighboring prefecture with a coast on the Japan Sea side of Honshu, the central Japanese island), and Fukushima fishers had been releasing them into their local waters. "It's important to keep on releasing juveniles, I hear." Mr. Tanaka said, and Satoshi agreed.

"Oh, by the way," Mr. Tanaka said, with a smile. He announced to us that he had just received the news of an official approval for building new homes on a hillside for those fishing families who had lost their coastal homes in the tsunami. He also said that the construction of those new homes would be completed in two to three years. "Finally," he said and looked around the room of his temporary housing. I followed his gesture and noticed their neighbor's voice coming through the thin wall. I also realized that, if everything goes well, they would be moving into their new homes in two to three more years, but this would also mean that Mr. Tanaka and his wife would need to continue living in this temporary home until that time. But he did not mention the next two to three years of their extended life in the temporary housing. I wondered whether it was because he did not want to ruin the hopeful news by referring to the extra time in the temporary housing, or whether it was because the prospect of the new future made him too happy to worry about the immediate burden. Feeling it would be insensitive to ask, I swallowed the questions.

As we moved on to the next topic of conversation, their hopeful attitude toward the future remained. "How many of your fellow fishermen have decided to give up the idea of returning to the sea?" I asked. "None," Kenta responded, "at least among young ones, as far as I know." He said that fishermen in their twenties and thirties had not lost hope of returning to fishing in the future. As they explained, their fishing co-op in northern Fukushima has one of the largest fishing populations in the northern region of Japan. The number of young fishermen in their co-op is particularly high—approximately sixty fishermen younger than forty years old—especially compared to other aging coastal towns in the northern region, where there are rarely enough sons eager to take over family fishing businesses. But the situation is different, according to Mr. Tanaka, among senior fishermen above the age of sixty. He said, "Those old folks without a son seem to have given up already. They don't take good care of their boats anymore." Although the old fishermen's despair was understandable, I was surprised that the younger ones had maintained their hope for the future comeback. I had imagined that the highly anguished future would have encouraged young fishers to give up their hope of fishing and to consider changing careers sooner than later.

Puzzled by their attitude toward the future, I asked them straightforwardly, "Do you have hope for the future?" All three of them said neither yes nor no. Instead, they responded that they could not think of hope for the future yet. Kenta explained that uncertainty about radiation contamination is the main reason. He said, "The contaminated groundwater underneath the nuclear power plant is continuously leaking into the ocean. It's hopeless as long as consumers have a feeling that there is something in our fish." "But," he added, "I still want to continue fishing." My coresearcher asked, "How long will you be able to maintain that hope?" "That might be an issue," the three fishermen responded. I wondered what this meant, so I asked, "What do you imagine when you hear the terms, 'the near future' and 'the distant future'?" Satoshi said, "Perhaps, the near future is in five years. The distant future is ten to twenty years ahead." The other two nodded. Mr. Tanaka mentioned that their new fishing co-op's building would be completed in one or two years. "Without successfully stopping TEPCO's underwater leakage, nothing can be started," Satoshi said, "but, within five years, we might be able to *prepare* for standing on the starting line. That's our hope." He added, "Without that, we can't think of the time beyond then." Mr. Tanaka joined, "A lot of us are gill-netters here. Without the reopening of gill-netting in sight, we can't envision the longer-term future." But for gill-netting to reopen, they need healthy flounder. Flounder was the main commercial fish species in Fukushima. Until the 2011 disaster, Fukushima's total landing volume of flounder had been the top in the country. Since the Fukushima meltdown, however, flounder is one of the few species that has not witnessed any appreciable drop in its level of radioactive cesium contents, unlike many other species. Marine biologists at the prefectural fisheries experimental station had been trying to figure out why that was the case, but to that point it had been a huge mystery.

Intrigued by their views on the future, I asked one last question before we ran out of our time for our interview: What do you think of the windmill's name, Fukushima Future? "Fukushima what?" Satoshi asked back. It turned out that none of the fishermen actually knew that the windmill had a name. I was surprised by their response, and they themselves seemed surprised that they had not noticed the name. It was especially surprising because only a few minutes earlier we had been talking about their occasional work as patrolmen of offshore traffic around the wind turbine, with them reflecting on how gigantic the whole windmill looked. The inscription of the name in a large font size, Fukushima Future, on the platform should have been immediately noticeable. But the fishermen did not know about the name or did not notice it even when they were looking at the very building from just a few meters away. Having newly learned the name of the initial windmill, Kenta laughed, "Only a facade!" "Even kids don't think Fukushima has much of a future," Mr. Tanaka said. "I don't think that Fukushima Future is about Fukushima's future," he added. "Fukushima Future makes no sense," Satoshi said in a sarcastic tone, "but wouldn't it be more realistic to name it 'Fukushima No Future'?" The rest of us burst into laughter.

These fishermen's narrations on their ambiguous views on the future and hope were intriguing. They say that they are very anxious about the future of pollution and also that they are unable to imagine the distant future. They did not even see the future—literally and metaphorically—in Fukushima Future. And yet, they simultaneously expressed hope for the future comeback of fishing, despite that such a prospect existed only in the hazy, distant future. On one hand, by maintaining hope for the distant future while looking at the darkness of the present, their attitude toward the future reminded us of Ernst Bloch's sense of hope (see also Miyazaki 2004; and Allison 2013). But on the other hand, even as they themselves dismissed the new futurity of the floating wind farm project, their comments about the rebuilding of the fish co-op facility and the fish hatchery—namely, the infrastructure of the past's futurism demolished by the tsunami—and its connection to their own hopes also suggest that these attitudes cannot easily be separated from futurism. Interested in further exploring hope's ambiguous relationship with the past, the present, and the future, I traveled next to the southern region with my coresearcher to visit another group of Fukushima fishermen who were known as strong supporters of the floating wind farm project.

KEEPING THE LIGHT OF FISHING ALIVE

Inside the tin-roof barn it felt like a large sauna. On a hot summer afternoon in August 2014, my coresearcher, his graduate student, and I visited three fishermen—Mr. Yajima, Mr. Mizuno, and Mr. Nakano—in a coastal town of southern Fukushima. These active middle-aged captains in their fifties were known to be the backbone of the next generation of their town's commercial fishing. The seaside barn in which we had gathered was their "office," which they rebuilt as a workplace for abalone and sea-urchin fishers after the old one had been washed away by the tsunami in 2011. Above a window frame, there was a new-looking miniature Shinto shrine (*kamidana*), and the next wall was covered by a large nautical map of the coastal waters of southern Fukushima as well as a large dry-erasable planning board filled with their schedules for that month. On the planner, more than half of the month was dedicated to debris cleaning and seawater and fish sampling for nuclear monitoring.

Among the three fishermen, Mr. Yajima was the most vocal and enthusiastic advocate of the offshore wind farm project. He was an experienced coastal fisherman—in his early fifties at the time—who had been catching fish in the now-infamous sea of Fukushima since he was a teenager, for more than thirty-five years. He said that he was skeptical of the wind farm project at first, like many other fishermen in all of Fukushima, but as he had more conversations with the consortium members, he gradually gained hope for prospects. He especially liked the idea of the "ocean farm." He said that the ocean farm would provide fishing families an option to survive as fishing families. In saying that, he was not in denial about radiation contamination. It was the opposite. He suspected that it would take an uncertain number of years—a couple of decades or possibly more—for Fukushima fishing to recover. In his account, the consequences of the nuclear accident had been more severe in the coastal water of the south than the north in Fukushima because of the flow of the ocean currents directing radiation substances southward. "That is why," he emphasized, "we have to try something new like wind power in order to keep the light of fishing alive."

Because of the long duration of radiation contamination, Mr. Yajima worried that there might be no fishing families left when the sea is finally reopened for commercial fishing in the future. In order for fishing families to survive as fishing families, they need to keep fishing. In order to promote this goal, Mr. Yajima found his hope in wind power and ocean farms. He explained that, in his generation, they could maintain their family fishing businesses by catching small amounts of fish for radiation monitoring, using their boats for recreational fishing, or the like, while waiting for the ocean to recuperate and for the radiation "rumors" among consumers to fade away. He also suggested the possibilities of earning wages from work related to maintaining ocean farms or to ecotourism involving the floating wind farm. And then, he said, he hoped that in the future, when commercial fishing is finally reopened, his children or grandchildren will still be there to catch fish.

And so he viewed the wind farm as a hopeful solution for disaster reconstruction. But in fact, he and other fishermen in his town had been worried since before the disaster about losing their prospects for fishing. Unlike the northern town of Fukushima with many young fishermen, many fishing families in the south had already been grappling with the lack of successors. As a result, at the time of the interview in 2014, about one-third of the roughly ninety fishing captains were seventy or older. Mr. Yajima's and Mr. Mizuno's families both faced the same issue. Mr. Yajima has an adult son who used to work with him on their family's boat. But he had left fishing for another job with a more stable income. In Mr. Mizuno's case, he has only daughters, and neither of his sons-in-law was planning to take over the family's fishing business. Thus, since his father retired from fishing, Mr. Mizuno's wife had been his work partner on their boat. Given his and his wife's age—both in their fifties—Mr. Mizuno had been worried about how many more years they could continue working together. He doubted that they would be able to do for another twenty or thirty years. "But," he said, "I could handle it by myself if it were a recreational fishing boat. So if the wind farm could attract recreational fishers, that wouldn't be bad at all."

For these fishermen who had been anxious since long before the disaster about the future survival of their fishing industry, the futurity of the wind farm appeared to be a source of hope. And this hope helped them to "see" not the near future but the distant one. "Do you know the first turbine's name, Fukushima Future?" I asked. Mr. Yajima quickly responded, "Of course! It's so big, you can't miss it!" These southern Fukushima fishers' views of the future were opposite from those of the group of the northerners, who saw the near future but not the distant one and also were unaware of the name of Fukushima Future or the label on the turbine's platform. These southerners not only had known the name but also had seen and admired the label. Mr. Yajima told me that, when he first saw the floating windmill, he was worried that it would be knocked off by a typhoon. In fact, in the previous fall they had one of the strongest typhoons in the recent years. After the storm, he took his boat to the offshore wind farm to check on it. "And then, there it was, still standing up firmly right in front of me!" He admired the incredibility of "human power." He also mentioned that, looking at the windmill standing strong after the typhoon, it even made him hopeful for the future. "We could do many different things from now on," he said. "Considering the children's future," he continued, "even if a windmill breaks, it wouldn't hurt anybody, unlike a nuclear power plant. In the long run, [the answer is] natural energy, I think." "What about the near future?" I asked. "The near future is uncertain," Yajima answered, "the windmill might stop working next year, but the potential is infinite."

As I was listening to Yajima and his friends' cheerful accounts of the Fukushima offshore wind farm, I was actually happy to hear that they had found some hope for their future survival. I was also intrigued by the power of futurism. The southern Fukushima fishers' narratives on the new infrastructure, indeed, tell us a great deal about aspirations for and anticipations and imaginations of the future (see Appadurai 2013). Infrastructure is a powerful apparatus for generating optimism, as we see in the earlier history of Japan's surviving modernization. But at the same time, I could not help but also wonder about what would come next. The futurism of the wind farm project seemed to have succeeded in allowing those southern Fukushima fishers to cultivate a sense of optimism within themselves. But obviously, the wind farm project itself would not change at all the actual condition of radiation pollution that makes the very future itself extremely precarious. While futurism implies infinite potential, nobody knows the future of futurism in advance. As I would find out in the following summer and as Mr. Yajima himself suggested, the near future is indeed uncertain.

CHAPTER 7 In Limbo

In summer 2015, my coresearcher and I revisited Mr. Yajima in southern Fukushima. Our original plan was that he would take us on a boat tour to see the actual Fukushima Future windmill floating offshore. But about a week prior to our visit, Mr. Yajima called to tell us that our boat trip had to be canceled due to an upcoming typhoon. The news was disappointing, but my coresearcher and I decided that we would still visit him to ask about updates. I arrived in the coastal town in southern Fukushima the day before our appointment with Mr. Yajima in order to observe a special exhibition designed by the Fukushima Offshore Wind Farm Consortium, which was installed within the town's seaside tourist center. The two-story building was like a shopping mall, which included a few fresh seafood stores and sushi/seafood restaurants, where visitors can enjoy tasty local fish, in addition to souvenir shops on the first floor and some more seafood restaurants and public event spaces on the second floor.

When I arrived at the tourist center, the large parking lot was almost empty. I was unsure whether it was deserted because it was an afternoon in the middle of week or if it was usually that way because of the ongoing aftermath of the nuclear disaster. Remembering the news stories about Fukushima's struggling tourism industry since the meltdown, I assumed that the absence of cars had much to do with the disaster. But I also wanted to believe that some tourists had come back, especially for weekends. I thought about asking one of the fishmongers at the mostly empty fish stores on the first floor, as they seemed to have time on their hands. But I did not have the courage to do so, worrying that my question might come across as insensitive. I eventually went straight to the second floor, where the wind farm's special exhibition was located. The exhibition room was empty too. Above the entrance door was a sign, "Fukushima Offshore Wind Power Communication Center." Their brochure explained that the consortium opened the special exhibition to inform local residents and experts in related fields about the project's objectives and progress.

In its four-hundred-square-foot space, the exhibition looked like a booth built for an industrial expo. In addition to three glass cases enclosing dioramas of offshore windmills, the walls were covered by a dozen panel posters and a large TV monitor, endlessly looping the consortium's promotional video. All the information displayed there was identical to what I had already read on the consortium's website. I nevertheless examined each item carefully, but it did not take more than twenty minutes to finish. As one of the poster panels explained, the consortium's pilot project was originally designed to be completed by 2015 after the installation of three windmills of different sizes. But it was already the summer of 2015, and though the second wind turbine had been assembled, it had not yet been installed offshore. The third, and final, turbine was not yet even under construction. But the special exhibition did not acknowledge the delay in the project's progress or explain any changes in their original grand plan. To tell the truth, the fact that the exhibition did not touch on the change in the project's original plan was not entirely surprising. I left the exhibition room feeling disappointed at and unsettled by the seemingly hazy future of the offshore wind farm project.

Across the hallway from the exhibition entrance, I found a glass door to a deck. It looked like a good spot to meditate on what I had just observed in the exhibition room. Below the deck, a few young women with small children were sitting on a bench along the boardwalk chatting and laughing. The deck was peaceful. The panoramic view of the port was spectacular. The sky was mostly covered by thick clouds, but the west side was glowing in the light of a setting sun. In that direction, on the wharf at the other end of the port, there was a local aquarium, which looked like a large spaceship made out of glass. To its left, there was a gigantic bridge still under construction. Back toward the port, there was a large, mostly empty space that looked like it was set aside for the construction of a major building, perhaps a shopping complex. Next to this apparent construction site was the city's new commercial fish market, which was built behind the tourist center and had just opened that summer.

I looked around the deck, trying to find a place to sit down, but instead found a signboard of the port area, which had two pictures. One was an aerial photograph of the port, and the other was a map of the port with names of buildings. Above the pictures was the title "Aquamarine Park" followed by another line that read, "The wharf redevelopment project that opens the dream gate to the future." Imagining the future completion of the port surrounded by an aquarium and a number of shopping sites, the picture reminded me of the gentrified waterfront of Baltimore. According to the city's official website, the redevelopment project of the port area had been one of the city's major plans since before the disaster in 2011, making it another example of what I call "disaster futurism."

But by 2015, even as many of the postdisaster projects of future-building were still unfinished, the utopian image of the future that emerged in the aftermath of the Fukushima nuclear meltdown had already begun to recede. Like the temporary nature of "disaster utopianism" (Solnit 2010; see also Morris-Suzuki 2017), it turns out that disaster futurism also has a short life span. But unlike disaster utopias that emerge through grassroots movements, the temporary life of disaster futurism is preconditioned by government bureaucracy. Allocating annual budgets for each project, officials might gesture toward a long-term or undefined future but plan for a shorter period of fixed budgeting. Thus, the utopia of an individual futurism project is assured of survival only within its budgeted period. Its life span might be extended through budget renewal, but the temporary nature of the bureaucratic system remains the same. In 2015, the final year of the original planned budget, the utopian hope of the Fukushima offshore floating wind farm was particularly fragile. As the consortium was busy readjusting the original plan due to the delays, Mr. Yajima and other fishermen were also spending their own time in limbo, muddling through to survive in the precarious present while wondering whether or not the floating wind farm would coexist with them in the future.

The temporality of suspension is evident in the interactions between the Fukushima offshore floating wind farm and local fishermen. In his discussion of the temporality of infrastructure, Akhil Gupta has argued: "Suspension, then, instead of being a temporary phase between the start of a project and its (successful) conclusion, needs to be theorized as its own condition of being. The temporality of suspension is not between past and future, between beginning and end, but constitutes its own ontic condition just as surely as does completion" (Gupta 2015). Gupta's observations on human and nonhuman beings who live with infrastructure in suspension are useful in examining how Mr. Yajima and his fellow fishermen responded to the floating wind farm and its receding utopian image, and also how they still retained hope that they could survive in the highly uncertain seascape.

CHANGES IN THE TIDE

At 8:40 a.m. the next day, unlike the quiet tourism center the previous afternoon, the brand-new fish market was already crowded with a few dozen people. The market facility was drastically different from the old one, which had been abandoned after the disaster in 2011. The old one was a traditional-style landing fish market, which is typically one large open-air space with a concrete floor and rooftop. In a traditional setting, like their old one or the ones in Minato and Hama, a fish market floor is usually crowded with whomever and whatever is involved with fish trading—fish, fishers, women of fishing families, wholesalers, auction managers, trucks, buckets, Styrofoam boxes, and so forth. All of them move or are moved from one corner to another in a seemingly chaotic and yet orderly and practiced manner. Besides fish auctions, a traditional open-air fish market also provides an important communal space for fishing families—especially women—to mingle while waiting for their families' boats, having a break over snacks, or fixing fishnets. The new fish market, however, was completely different.

The new fish market looked like a modern food processing factory building. Everything was designed to be orderly and efficient. Unlike the old ones, this new fish market is strictly used only for fish trading, and only those wholesalers and fishers with special permission are permitted to enter the actual building. According to their manager, the new one is the most modern fish market in Japan, equipped with not only the latest sanitation system but also radiation detection devices. The facility is divided into separate rooms, and both fish and people can only move one way from one room to another. The first room is an auction section, where fish are brought in and put in Styrofoam boxes after sorting, scaling, and bidding. Then boxes of fish are placed on a conveyor belt that runs into the next room through a narrow window. In the next room, fish boxes are labeled and stored in a temperature-controlled environment until fish traders are ready to pick them up at another section beyond the storage room. While I was fascinated by the new, modern facility, one man in the crowd said to another man, "This up-to-date facility makes traditional ones look like the third world, but this is actually standard in Norway or other European countries." As I was listening to him, I remembered a fish expert who had long argued that Japanese fisheries must be modernized and that Japanese fish markets must be updated to resemble European ones (Komatsu 2016). In the name of reconstruction, disaster futurism has made the dream of modernization advocates come true.

Within the auction room of the new fish market, Mr. Yajima was in his bright-blue wading pants and a white T-shirt, affixing a tag to each of his abalones. This morning the first auction for abalones since the disaster was being held. After repeated radiation monitoring tests for more than four years, abalones had finally been added to the list of safe species for the "pilot fishing" program. In order to be on time for that first auction, Mr. Yajima and his fellow fishers had gone diving the previous day when the ocean was calm. All the abalones at the auction were large. Perhaps because no humans had disturbed them for these few years, the abalones seemed to have grown not only in their overall population size but also in their physical dimensions. But the lingering concerns among consumers over radiation contamination would continue to present a difficult challenge for those fishers. During the auction, Mr. Yajima smiled occasionally while chatting with other fishermen and wholesalers. But for a good chunk of the time, he kept a stern face with his arms tightly crossed in front of his chest.

That morning, Mr. Yajima's frame of mind offered a stark contrast to the cheery attitude that he had shown us a year earlier. He seemed frustrated. When the auction was completed, he told us to wait in a lounge space in the new fish market building. When we got there, he was already waiting for us, unsmiling, on a couch. My coresearcher asked him how things were going. He said that many of the major species for local fisheries had been added to the list of safe species for the "pilot fishing" program, naming especially sea urchins (*uni*), abalones (*awabi*), young anchovies (*shirasu*), and flounder (*hirame*). Despite the good news, his tone of voice remained low. He then told us that, although the pilot fishing had started for those major species, yields were tightly restricted. He explained that the upper limits were so low that individual captains were allowed to go fishing only a few times each month. On top of that, he added, fish prices for all species continued to be substantially lower than before the disaster.

In fact, the price given for the large-size abalones that morning was only a 150 yen per kilogram, approximately seventy-five cents per pound. Before the disaster, an average price for abalones was ten times higher, about 1,500 yen. But according to Mr. Yajima, even though the amounts that wholesalers pay to fishers are tiny, the wholesalers sell those abalones to fishmongers at Tsukiji Fish Market for a similar price as before the disaster. "That threw cold water on my enthusiasm," he said. He also said that he had once overheard a wholesaler telling another wholesaler that he does not need to bid high because fishers could still survive with compensation money from TEPCO. "That pissed me off," he added, "but I did not say anything to them." He recognized, he said, the fact that wholesalers could not receive any compensation money from TEPCO for their losses caused by the nuclear accident, and that they, too, needed to survive for their families and also for fisheries. If wholesalers go bankrupt, it also would make fishers' lives difficult because they would have to sell all of their fish by themselves. Mr. Yajima understood that. Nevertheless, the situation frustrated him a great deal.

His exasperation remained when I asked him about the offshore floating wind farm. He squinted his eyes and sighed. "The second machine hasn't even been installed, you know?" said Mr. Yajima. According to the original plan for the demonstration project, all three turbines should have already been completed by that time. The project was apparently facing not only delays but also a substantial budget cut. As a result, although the consortium had originally claimed the demonstration project would turn into an ambitious plan of building the world's largest floating wind farm in Fukushima, they had recently decided to make significant changes in the proposal. The consortium had originally suggested that they would build a hundred more floating turbines along the whole Fukushima water, but the revised proposal indicated only ten.

The biggest factor responsible for this change in the plan was politics. The offshore wind farm project was originally supported by the government when the Democratic Party of Japan (DPJ) was the ruling party (2009–12). But the budget for alternative energy projects had been substantially reduced after the Liberal Democratic Party of Japan (LDP) regained its control of the government in 2012. The LDP is a conservative party that had been almost continuously in power since 1955—except between 1993 and 1994 and also 2009 through 2012—and was also a main political power that supported the development of Japan's nuclear energy industry. Since the LDP regained political power in 2012, especially under the administration of the avowed nuclear-energy advocate Shinzo Abe, the government has proposed policies aiming to revive the nation's nuclear energy industry. Just like that, the future of the offshore wind farm project risked fading away. Accordingly, the dream future that Mr. Yajima pictured based on the wind farm project was also diminishing.

"What happens to the plan of building symbiosis between the wind farm and fisheries?" I asked. Mr. Yajima gave me no response. I told him that I had heard from Professor Ishihara, who was the consortium's project leader, that no actual research had yet been done for the idea of ocean farm. Mr. Yajima sighed. Apparently he had given the consortium multiple proposals for carrying out test operations of different aquaculture methods, but he had never heard a positive response. Some of his ideas were low cost and required little maintenance, but the consortium's response was the same. "They just weren't going to do anything about it," he said, a bit more loudly than he had been speaking until then. Up to this point, he had shown us no gesture of optimism or hope as he had the previous summer. Given the drastic changes in the future possibilities, his mood was not surprising. But now that he knew that his previously imagined future would not come to pass, what did the future mean for him? I told him that I had noticed a drastic change in his attitude toward the future of Fukushima Future, and I wondered what he thought of the future at this moment. "Well, yeah, it's a real bummer," he said as he rubbed his face with his right hand. "At first," he added, "I thought things were going in a good direction, so I devoted my time and efforts [to the wind farm project]."

Ever since the wind farm project was proposed to local fishermen, Mr. Yajima had worked closely with the consortium. He not only participated in the meetings to discuss means for the wind farm and fisheries to coexist, but he also attended the consortium's study trips to Denmark, Norway, and Okinawa. He said that he learned a great deal from those tours, which gave him some ideas for how to create an ocean farm as part of a wind farm in Fukushima. Accordingly, he had shared his ideas at the consortium meetings. He thought that he was building the future together with the consortium. But he had started skipping the meetings in the past few months. He said that he had been attending roughly one-third of the meetings, explaining that the consortium's recent attitude had been passive, and whenever he made suggestions regarding an ocean farm, they complained about their budget cuts. "After all," Mr. Yajima said, "I was working for a dream, but the plan has now changed." He understood that plans could change. But what he found most frustrating was the fact that the consortium no longer seemed interested in coming up with a plan to maintain the wind farm project in Fukushima. At the time, although the consortium changed its plan for building additional windmills, reducing the number from one hundred to ten, its members still seemed intent on carrying out the proposal to build at least ten windmills after the demonstration phase had been completed. But Mr. Yajima suspected that the number might be further revised down to zero. "You know what?" he said. "Removing one costs a huge amount of money. I wonder if they're just going to leave all the windmills abandoned at sea."

Mr. Yajima's comment conjured a picture of the future of Fukushima Future. In the middle of the blue ocean, three abandoned windmills are floating. The tall posts and long blades are covered with brown patches of rust. The windmills' yellow platforms are also badly corroded. On the side of one platform, the partially peeled-off black paint barely traces the sign that reads "Fukushima Future." This could be the future of Fukushima Future.[1] But it is just one way to imagine the future. There are multiple ways to imagine the future.

FISHING IN THE FUTURE'S RUINS

In 2017, the Fukushima offshore floating wind farm was still residing in the temporality of suspension. That October, I accompanied Mr. Yajima and his fellow fishermen on their research fishing trip to observe the condition of the fish habitat around the floating energy infrastructure. This research fishing trip was my first time to see the actual floating wind farm. I had been waiting for the opportunity over the last three years, and it finally happened on my fourth attempt. The ocean is, in fact, always precarious, and thus coordinating participant observation at sea is indeed not easy. Perhaps scheduling a field trip might have been much easier if the windmills had been located on the shore. But since the wind farm is built twenty-three kilometers off the coastline, observing it required a boat trip, which also meant that it had to be coordinated with the changing nature of the marine environment.

Mr. Yajima had originally promised me to take me on a boat trip to observe the offshore wind farm when we first met one other back in 2014, and we had planned it for August 2015. But the first attempt failed due to the typhoon. Our second attempt in summer 2017 did not work out either, yet again because of a typhoon. Hence we planned our third attempt for September, but this trip was also scuttled due to foul weather. Finally, at the beginning of October, the weather cooperated with us. If anything, the delay turned out to be especially lucky because I was also given the opportunity to observe not only the wind farm but also Mr. Yajima and his fellow fishers fishing around the wind farm as part of the research fishing trip entrusted by the project consortium.

But because of the previous unlucky cancellations, I could not help worrying about the weather until right before the fishing trip. When I arrived at a train station in southern Fukushima the evening before the boat trip, the sky was clear, and the wind was calm. I called Mr. Yajima just to confirm the next day's fishing trip, and he told me that the trip would be carried out as planned. Preparing for the next morning in my hotel room, I found myself feeling nervous because it had been almost ten years since the last time I had been on a real fishing trip. Although I had rarely been seasick in the past, I packed some motion sickness pills just in case. In addition, I stopped drinking liquids by 8:00 p.m. in order to avoid needing to use a bathroom during the fishing trip in the next morning. Mr. Yajima had already warned me that his boat—like most other small-scale coastal fishing boats—had no toilet installed. While feeling a little anxious, I was also excited about the boat trip, especially considering the opportunity to take a close look at the actual floating wind turbines and also to observe Mr. Yajima's direct interactions with the ocean as well the wind farm.

At the time, the Fukushima FORWARD project had already finished building all three wind turbines and a substation. After installing the first turbine, Fukushima Future, in 2013, the second one—which was named Fukushima New-Wind (Fukushima Shinpu)—was set up in 2015, a few months after Mr. Yajima had expressed his concerns about it. The first two wind turbines had been up and running for more than two years since, but the last one—named Fukushima Shore-Wind (Fukushima Hamakaze)—had just recently begun its operation a few months earlier in May of that year. Originally, the demonstration project was planned to be completed in three years, by 2015, but its duration had been extended. According to an announcement released in April 2016 by the Ministry of Economy, Trade, and Industry (METI), allocations from the national budget were guaranteed for entrusting the project to the consortium for an additional three years, from 2016 through 2018.[2] Thus, at that time, in the fall of 2017, it was possible to predict that the demonstration project would continue at least until the end of fiscal year 2018. But what would happen with the project beyond then was up in the air. Nevertheless, in the same report, METI also claimed that the three extra years would help the project expand the existing wind farm to a large-scale operation. It also proclaimed that the success of the project would not only create a new energy industry and new employment for people of Fukushima but also allow Japan to become the world's leader in the field of floating wind farms.

At 4:20 a.m. on an early-autumn day, the sky was still dark and full of stars. The wind was calm, and so was the sea. As soon as I got out of a rental car, I tapped my cell phone screen to call Mr. Yajima and asked where I could find him. He told me on the phone to just enter the fishing dock and I would find his boat with no problem. Sure enough, it did not take much time to spot the only boat with a running engine. Within the quiet wharf, the noise of Mr. Yajima's fishing boat sounded especially loud. His boat was a typical small-scale coastal fishing vessel slightly under five tons, common on the coast of Fukushima and neighboring prefectures.

When I showed up at the quay, Mr. Yajima and his two fellow fishermen, in addition to an observer from a private maritime research firm, were already set for the voyage. The morning's fishing trip was part of a special mission requested by the Fukushima FORWARD consortium, with the goal of collecting data in order to find out whether the floating wind turbines could in fact perform as "artificial reefs" and increase the density of wild fish habitat, which were the possibilities suggested by existing studies on offshore wind farms. In the morning, the observer's role was to gather data on fish habitat around three turbines of the floating wind farm, and Mr. Yajima and his fellow fishermen's role was to catch fish for the data collection.

As soon as I got onto the boat deck, Mr. Yajima called out to the other three and told them that it was time for departure. The two fishermen and the observer found their own spots on the deck and sat down. Mr. Yajima told me to take a seat on a ledge at the corner within his small captain's booth, which was a little less than three by six feet. When the boat went out of the wharf, Mr. Yajima picked up speed, and louder engine noise filled the captain's booth. As he was moving his boat forward, he constantly checked the screens of his fish-finder and GPS plotter while looking over the outside through the front and side windows and occasionally chatting with his friends through his two-way radio. Mr. Yajima looked too busy to bother, and the engine noise sounded too loud to carry on conversations. So I remained sitting still at the corner of the captain's booth, quietly observing his moves and the screens of various fish-finding devices.

After about an hour had passed since we left the wharf, I caught a sight of a skinny pole-like object sticking out of the ocean ahead on the horizon. "That's the wind turbine," Mr. Yajima said, "still far ahead though." It seemed to grow larger as we continued to approach for the next half hour. Although I had seen images of the turbines in photographs and videos online, the actual windmill looked far more enormous than I expected. It was so mountainous that I had trouble keeping the entire above-water structure in one camera frame. Mr. Yajima slowed down and idled his boat about a hundred meters away from Fukushima New-Wind. Quickly, the other two fishermen moved to the back of the boat and attached two long poles (or outriggers) on both sides of the boat for trawling. At the same time, the observer from the maritime research firm stuck his head into the captain's booth and jotted down on his clipboard the temperature and depth of the water that Mr. Yajima read on his GPS screen. Mr. Yajima then confirmed that all the gears were set, and he started trawling around Fukushima New-Wind. After that, he moved to Fukushima Shore-Wind and then to Fukushima Future in order to trawl around each of the three windmills.

In the middle of turbine-hopping, Mr. Yajima pointed his finger at a building on the coast and told me that it was the crippled Fukushima Daiichi Nuclear

FIG. 9. Fishermen hauling a longline during a research fishing trip to monitor fish habitats around the floating wind farm. Photo by author.

Power Plant. In fact, standing twenty kilometers offshore, we could see a complete view of Fukushima's long shoreline. Along the coast, we saw that Fukushima Daiichi (Number 1) and Daini (Number 2) Nuclear Power Plants and also the Hirono Thermal Power Plant, standing at similar distances from each other. For a couple of minutes, everybody quietly looked at the coastline. I wondered what the others were thinking while looking at the crippled plant, but I struggled to come up with an appropriate way to ask the question so that I would not sound inconsiderate. "What a panoramic view," I said eventually. "Yes," responded Mr. Yajima, but he said nothing further. Then the observer abruptly said, "One of my colleagues designed the marine hatchery that used to exist next to the [ruined] nuclear power plant," adding, "but it's all washed away except for the rooftop." I told him that I had been to the hatchery myself back in 2004. "They used the thermal discharge from the nuclear power plant, didn't they?" I asked. The observer seemed a little surprised and responded evasively. Mr. Yajima then returned to his captain's booth, and the boat started moving to the next windmill.

The next spot was finally Fukushima Future. When we got close to the turbine,

I asked one of Mr. Yajima's fellow fishermen what he thought of the windmill's name. "Not much," he said simply. I changed the question, asking him what he thought about the future. He seemed uninterested in directly answering my question about the future, but at the same time, he did not seem to mind sharing his own thoughts. He said that commercial fishing would not be able to fully reopen until radioactive wastewater from the crippled power plant had stopped spilling into the ocean. He also said that, if commercial fishing reopened before resolving the wastewater spillage, it would prolong consumers' reluctance to purchase fish from Fukushima and would definitely make their fish a tenuous bet at best. He concluded that, without knowing when the wastewater problem would be fixed, he and his family were just trying to get by in an uncertain present. Before the 2011 nuclear accident, according to him, he used to work with his two sons. But both of them had been working for private companies since the disaster. His older son still worked as an occasional crew member when his turn for test fishing came around. But his younger son had completely quit fishing. He also said that he and his wife had been working part-time jobs because the nuclear disaster compensation from TEPCO was not enough to pay for their house and boat mortgages and living expenses and, moreover, because they began feeling depressed by staying at home day after day after the disaster. While we were chatting, I noticed that he kept a broad smile on his face for the entire time. I asked him why he did not seem angry despite the unnervingly difficult situation in the present. "Because being angry won't do anything," he said with a grin.

In the end, that morning's catch was rather unsuccessful. While trawling for two hours, we only got three small dolphinfish (*shiira*) and two small bonitos (*katsuo*). If we were to sell the catch, the fuel for the trip would cost significantly more than a yield. But since it was part of the wind farm's research project, the fuel cost was paid by the consortium, and the fish were returned to the ocean after the observer recorded their names, weight, and length. At 8:00 a.m., they got another bonito, and again it was small. This time, the observer threw the fish back in the water without weighing it and told Mr. Yajima to wrap up the research fishing for that morning. "Let's go home then," Mr. Yajima yelled; "the game is over, let's call it a day." The other two fishermen started putting away the fishing gear and cleaning up the deck. Did the poor catch that morning mean that the floating wind farm had not helped to increase wild fish population, like artificial reefs, as the consortium originally expected it would do? "We don't know the answer yet," the observer responded, "but I am certain that there are fish around the wind farm." He said that his previous research fishing trip was busy with scaling as many as twenty dolphinfish. The older fisherman said that this morning's catch was poor because the ocean was too calm. "Trawling is usually successful when a strong wind blows from the north," he explained. Mr. Yajima and the other fisherman nodded. But the unsuccessful result still seemed to be disappointing for the fishermen, especially for Mr. Yajima.

Nevertheless, or maybe because of that, Mr. Yajima did not give up his search for fish. On the way back to his home port, he adjusted the setting of his fish-finder unit in order to capture young anchovies (*shirasu*) and continue checking the display during the entire return trip. That time in the early fall was, indeed, the beginning of the high season for young anchovies. While occasionally pushing buttons to switch from one monitor screen to another as he searched for a school of fish, he exchanged the information on the fish-finder with another captain through his two-way radio, but I could not hear the details of the conversation due to the engine noise. At one point, though, Mr. Yajima told me that he had detected a few good-sized schools of young anchovies. When we got close to his wharf, he called his friend into his captain's booth with an animated tone of voice. Tapping on the screen of the fish-finder with his thick index finger, Mr. Yajima told his friend, "This must be a school of anchovy juveniles!" "You should take your boat to catch it as soon as we return," he added jokingly. "Nah," his friend quickly laughed.

After we returned to the harbor, Mr. Yajima agreed to let me interview him for a few more minutes. Mr. Yajima and I went to his fishing co-op's barn and sat down on benches. I asked him the same questions I had asked him in the past two summers, in 2014 and 2015. How had he been doing? Were there any changes in the prospects for reopening of commercial fishing? What did he think of the future? Mr. Yajima sighed at first and then told me his concerns. He said that, while he looked forward to commercial fishing fully reopening, he was feeling anxious about whether he would be able to maintain enough of a yield to keep his business going. Nuclear compensation would be discontinued when commercial fishing becomes reopened, which means in practice that in order to maintain a decent yield he would need solid catches and good values for the fish. But there was no guarantee that fish prices would ever recover to the predisaster levels, especially considering the ongoing nuclear wastewater issue, in addition to the capricious nature of fishing, which means that catches are always uncertain depending on weather and other oceanographic conditions.

"These days," Mr. Yajima murmured, "every night when I try to go sleep, I can't help but think about the future and get overwhelmed by anxiety." He said that, because of having spent such uneasy nights, he was hoping that he would have a successful outcome during the research fishing trip that morning. If he could catch a lot of fish, he thought that that might reduce his worries. The discouraging result, however, was unlikely to do so. Before the nuclear accident, an unsuccessful fishing trip like this would have been seen as just another familiar frustrating experience. But, for Mr. Yajima, who was living with the ongoing nuclear crisis, even one poor catch was enough to turn his hope about the future into anxiety. Nevertheless, Mr. Yajima also demonstrated that he was not completely defeated by it. He retained hope in the precarious seascape.

A few minutes into the interview after the research fishing trip, Mr. Yajima stood up and told me that he had to go somewhere. I asked him if he had to go home. "No," he replied quietly. "Going back to catch the anchovy juveniles?" I asked, referring to the school of young anchovies that his fish-finder had captured earlier right outside of the wharf. "Maybe," he smiled, and started walking toward his storage unit in order to get his special fishnet for catching young anchovies. There was no guarantee that the school of young anchovies would still be there at the same spot. It was highly possible that the school of anchovies would have already moved to another spot by the time he returned with his fishnet. The chance that Mr. Yajima would actually be able to catch the young anchovies might have been slim, so going back to the sea might have resulted in yet another disappointment. Nonetheless, for Mr. Yajima, the image of young anchovies on his fish-finder screen was a sign of hope in the midst of acute anxieties. The futures of the floating wind farm, the radioactive ocean, and commercial fishing were all daunting. But the existence of young anchovies was a certainty, even though catching them was at that point a game of chance.

―

Mr. Yajima's back, heading back to the sea for young anchovies, reminded me that hope and anxiety and certainty and uncertainty all coexist in the troubled seascape. The sea is, by and large, unpredictable. As it depends on the uncertain sea, fishing is, by its nature, precarious. There are good catches and bad catches as a matter of course. Each outcome is the result of a combination of all sorts of conditions. Fish behave differently, depending on season, weather, water temperature, tidal flows, wind currents, and so forth. And besides the unpredictability of the fish themselves, fish value changes depending on the market, which is also highly unpredictable. Experienced commercial fishers chase after fish, mobilizing all their experience-based knowledge stored both in their own brain and their GPS units. Many fishers, including Mr. Yajima and his fellow fishers, have told me that they like fishing because it is difficult to predict. In addition, disasters—natural and man-made alike—also contribute to the precarious nature of fishing. In Fukushima and the neighboring regions, where the coastal areas are highly industrialized, not only seasonal storms but also man-made disasters—such as tanker accidents and water pollution, not to mention nuclear accidents—have historically affected commercial fishing.

Since the 2011 Fukushima nuclear meltdown, newly unpredictable factors have been part of the historically precarious seascape. In 2017, nobody yet knew how long radioactive substances at sea would take to decay, when radioactive wastewater at the damaged reactors would stop accidentally leaking or being systematically dumped into the ocean, when commercial fishing in Fukushima would be able to reopen, when consumers would start feeling safe enough to buy fish from Fukushima and neighboring waters, or how long it would take for fishing businesses to come back to what they once were, or, indeed, if that is possible at all. Mr. Yajima and his fellow fishermen understood that it would take time for all these concerns to be resolved. And yet, while battling acute anxiety over the future, they still retain their hope that they can live their life as commercial fishers in Fukushima, and they also maintain a sense of hope in possibilities for the future. Living with the troubled sea is simultaneously daunting and hopeful.

FUKUSHIMA IN CONTEMPLATION

A catastrophe changes human-nature relations. But how much and to what extent? Surely, earthquakes, tsunami, hurricanes, nuclear meltdowns, and alike significantly alter the physical landscape as well as the everyday lives of the people who dwell in it. Besides numerous challenges, a disaster may also bring new possibilities to the ruined terrain. But the Joban seascape forces us to question how much the Fukushima nuclear crisis has actually changed the ways in which people interact with the ocean. In the immediate postdisaster period, Fukushima fishing families faced profound challenges as well as new utopian hopes for dealing with the precarious future. One such hope was the government-sponsored project of the world's largest offshore wind farm in the region, which was alleged to be a platform for a new sustainable future. But like many other imagined utopias that emerged in the midst of ruins of the disasters, this particular utopia of eco-futurism was short-lived.

In his essay "After Fukushima," the French philosopher Jean-Luc Nancy expresses his hope for the emergence of a new, more democratic and sustainable world in the wake of the terrible disaster (Nancy 2014). He suggests that adopting alternative energy sources would not be a solution in itself but would offer a way to enter this new "After Fukushima" world, departing from the modernization-oriented "Before Fukushima." According to Nancy, post-Fukushima and "After Fukushima" are not the same. Moreover, he also emphasizes the importance of critically thinking about what the word *after* actually means. In "After Fukushima," he differentiates *after* from the *post* prefix, which implies succession from a *pre-* condition. For example, he argues that *post-modern* succeeds *modern*, the time of *before* when the future is constantly anticipated in the name of futurism. But he argues that the *after* in "After Fukushima" "stems on the contrary not from succession but from rupture, and less from anticipation than from suspense, even stupor. It is an 'after' that means: Is there an after? Is there anything that follows? Are we still headed somewhere?" (Nancy 2014, 15).

Nancy also insists that, although it is true that "After Fukushima" is built upon multiple *befores*, "After Fukushima" must not simply succeed "Before Fukushima." According to him, the multiple *befores* are by and large designed by modernization, and *after* cannot simply be the next similar *before*. Nancy further argues that after the experience of the Fukushima meltdown, a genuine "After Fukushima" might have begun in Japan through the development of sustainable energy alternatives to nuclear power. But globally speaking, he sees that it will still take many more years—perhaps several decades or a couple of centuries—because "After Fukushima" requires fundamental changes in culture more than just shifting from one energy source to another (Nancy 2012, 6–9).[3] Similar to Nancy's hopeful perspective on post-Fukushima Japan, the renowned Japanese political historian Takashi Mikuriya (2011, 27) wrote in a popular weekly magazine published a month after the catastrophe, "at last the long era of 'postwar' comes to an end, and we are entering the beginning of the new era, which we might call 'post-disaster.'" In the essay, Mikuriya explains that Japan's postwar era is represented by modernization (*kindaika*), which he refers to "development of scientific technology, population growth, and high economic growth" (2011, 28). By arguing that the 2011 disaster brought a transformation from the era of "postwar" to that of "postdisaster," he implies that modernization also has come to end. But based on the observations of the Fukushima offshore floating wind farm, both "postwar" and modernization survived the disaster. This does not mean that nothing has changed since before the disaster, but it also does not mean that everything has changed.

At present, we are living in the temporality of suspension, which I call "With Fukushima," floating somewhere related to, yet distinct from, "Before Fukushima" or "After Fukushima." Mr. Yajima and his fellow fishermen showed me a series of successive "presents," all conditioned both by the pasts they had followed and the futures they ostensibly aimed toward. They muddled through to stay alive together with the ever-precarious seascape. They reminded me that the present is always in limbo and that remembering it is especially important to survive in a post-Fukushima world. "In fact, staying with the trouble requires learning to be truly present," as Donna Haraway has stated, "not as a vanishing pivot between awful or endemic pasts and apocalyptic or salvific futures, but as mortal critters entwined in myriad unfinished configurations of place, times, matters, meanings" (Haraway 2016, 1).

But learning to be truly present does not necessarily mean that we stop thinking about the future. To the contrary, it is important now to critically think of the future as we gaze at the present, especially considering the popular discourses of ominous and utopian futures that have emerged in the ruins of the Fukushima nuclear disaster. For this reason, the suspension of Fukushima Future actually offers a sense of hope, by providing us an opportunity to finally talk about what it means to live with the seascape repeatedly ruined by unending modernization. Moreover, the suspension of the offshore energy infrastructure also allows us to take a moment to meditate on our preoccupation with futurism. As anthropologists Timothy Choy and Jerry Zee have written, "Suspension is an opening—not a portal nor an exit that trades the ground for that above it, but a becoming-open" (Choy and Zee 2015, 217). No matter how much we, as humans, harm or try to save the environment through modernization, there are always uncertain consequences that cannot be controlled by anthropogenic powers. Suspension, therefore, implies neither good nor bad futures but possibilities of multiple stories to weave. Staying alive with the troubled ocean is by no means easy. But as Mr. Yajima found hope in the school of young anchovies that appeared on his fish-finder screen, possibilities of collaborative survival remain in the precarious seascape.

EPILOGUE The Return of the Octopuses

Coastal fishing families in and near Fukushima before and after the nuclear meltdown in 2011 have lived with a seascape that has been repeatedly ruined by disasters, both natural and man-made. This story illustrates two major characteristics of the Anthropocene in the context of Japan. First, the Anthropocene has historically been shaped not only through recurring disasters but also through the nation's surviving modernization, which has been used as an apparatus for reconstructing distressed areas whenever a disaster happens. For this modernization, the concept of futurism has played an especially important role. Although repeatedly aimed at creating a better, brighter future, postwar Japan's modernization-oriented policies for disaster reconstruction have historically produced the present conditions of the post-Fukushima landscape and seascape.

Second, conditions of the Anthropocene in Japan—like other cases in Australia (Rose 2011) and the United States (Swanson 2017)—have, by and large, remained ordinary, at times even banal. One of the problems with the Anthropocene is its banality, as anthropologist Heather Swanson has pointed out in her analysis of the damaged landscape of Iowa (Swanson 2017). The historical modernization of agriculture has left a number of marks on the rural landscape, ranging from the polluted water by fertilizers to the drastically disappeared marshes. Nonetheless, both residents as well as visitors to America's Heartland often fail to pay attention to the ruined landscape. As of 2022, with more than ten years having passed, while there are many efforts to remember the disaster, the Joban seascape is becoming increasingly ordinary, especially in the imaginations of those of us who do not directly live and work in the blasted landscape and seascape. In order to change people's blindness toward the Anthropocene and see the connections between humans and nonhumans, Swanson calls for the importance of curiosity (see also Haraway 2008; and Haraway 2016). But how can we make people stay curious about their connections to the landscape and the seascape? This question of how presents a particular conundrum in the case of Fukushima.[1]

Before the nuclear meltdown, Fukushima was in some ways similar to Iowa. Located in what might be considered Japan's heartland, Tohoku, Fukushima was loosely imagined to be a fertile, green agricultural countryside: nothing more, nothing less. For many decades, people—both within and outside Fukushima— barely worried about the landscape and the seascape even though they had been drastically transformed in the name of modernization. But when the 2011 disaster made Fukushima suddenly infamous worldwide, it also instantaneously made people see what they did not used to see. Likewise, the disaster made the Fukushima Daiichi Nuclear Power Plant "visible" once again after spending the "invisible" period as ordinary energy infrastructure (see Star and Ruhleder 1996). Simultaneously, the disaster also enabled people to see the historically entangled relationship between the nuclear power plants and Fukushima's landscape and seascape. During the first couple of years or so after the 2011 disaster, the exposed landscape—and seascape—was referred to as both a hell and a paradise, on which people actively debated dystopian and utopian futures.

But as more time has passed, the post-Fukushima sensation has gradually become dull. People—especially those who live outside of the disaster-affected area—have increasingly lost their sense of connection with Fukushima. At the end of the day, a disaster does not necessarily guarantee that people will remain curious about problems. Even in Japan, where people encountered a catastrophic wake-up call like the Fukushima nuclear meltdown, the Anthropocene largely remains ordinary in many people's imaginations, except for the very short period of time in the immediate aftermath of the disaster. Fishing families living on the Joban Sea are continuously muddling through to survive, as they maintain hope in the ruined seascape while knowing that the toxic substances will likely stay with them for the next few decades or more.

Obviously, there is no way to talk conclusively about the ongoing post-Fukushima world. Thus, as a way to conclude this book, I share a story on the return of octopuses and hard clams, which I learned through my email exchanges with Hiroshi, whom I mentioned in the prologue. In doing so, my aim is to point out that the precarious Joban seascape is not only a symptom of Japan's surviving modernization but also a space that helps us to imagine directions into "more livable futures" (Haraway 2016) with an open-ended gaze on hereafter.[2]

On October 26, 2018, the Ministry of Economy, Trade, and Industry made an official announcement on the Fukushima offshore floating wind farm project: one of the three turbines had been slated for removal. They explained that, based on the report submitted by the project's review committee, the 7-MW turbine named Fukushima New-Wind had yielded only a poor economic performance because of machinery malfunctions.[3] Additionally, the Ministry indicated that, though it had allocated a budget for maintaining the other two turbines—Fukushima Future (2 MW) and Fukushima Shore-Wind (5 MW)—for another fiscal year, their removal was also under consideration.[4] Nevertheless, the Ministry still maintained its position that the Fukushima FORWARD project would continue to support the future development of floating wind farms in Fukushima and in Japan, more broadly.[5]

As of 2018, the future of the Fukushima FORWARD project remained in suspension. Likewise, commercial fishing families in Fukushima continued living in limbo. While the so-called "pilot fishing" program had further expanded as more fish species were added to the safety list, nobody yet knew when the fishing moratorium might officially end. In Ibaraki, most commercial fishing had been reopened, except for a few fish species. But they, too, had endured a number of challenges in the years after the tsunami. According to the government reports, the radioactive substances detected in the ocean water as well as in fish species had been substantially reduced since 2011.[6] But despite the government's official determination on the safety of the fish species that had been reopened or included for the pilot operations, consumers had lingering safety concerns about fish landed in Fukushima and Ibaraki, suspecting the possibility of future cancers and other health effects (Sternsdorff-Cisterna 2019). Of course, once toxic materials are released, people who are exposed to the poisons themselves exist in a kind of limbo, living in the present even as their bodies contain the possibilities of future health complications (Petryna 2014; Fortun 2015). But in the case of the Joban Sea, the radioactive materials from the damaged reactors have not even yet been fully contained, and exposure is likely to be prolonged by the ocean dumping of wastewater that the government and TEPCO have proposed. Given these present conditions, whenever I asked coastal fishers in Ibaraki and Fukushima about their thoughts on the future, almost all of them responded that the situations were too uncertain for them to even imagine it.

But in the midst of the unnerving time in 2018, I received two hopeful email messages from Hiroshi, the commercial fisherman in Ibaraki who had joked, as I noted in the prologue, that I might not be able to finish my book. In a message in the early spring, he wrote that a dominant year class of octopuses had appeared for the first time since I lived in his hometown, Minato, eleven years earlier. He also emphasized that the size of the dominant year class this time seemed to be even bigger than it had been back then. On top of that, he added, the population of hard clams—which had been in continuous decline for more than a decade—was gradually coming back as well. Given the fact that hard clams are an octopus's favorite prey, the double comeback might be related. For a while, the clam population had reportedly been jeopardized by the changes in tidal flows and sea bottoms due to coastal industrialization, despite local fishing families' conservation attempts in addition to the fish stocking program; their conservation efforts might have paid off. But since the emergence of dominant year class is related to the ever-changing climate and marine conditions as well as equally capricious human interventions, the detailed mechanisms were unknown.

That October, Hiroshi dropped me another email message. He wrote: "The recovery of the hard clam population has made further progress. Satsuki, you might have anticipated that we would continuously struggle with declining resources, but perhaps you won't be able to see us in such a despair again until the distant future.... These days our harbor is teeming with life like we used to see before the disaster." "So please," he concluded, "come visit us when you have a chance." Given Hiroshi's messages, it was clear that the news of the dominant year class of both octopuses and hard clams encouraged him greatly. But I could not tell from his writing how much the return of octopuses and hard clams had changed his perspective on the future. In reality, the issue of the contaminated wastewater from the damaged reactors had not yet been resolved, which means the highly uncertain situations with the seascape as well as consumers' safety concerns would continue. Considering the uninterrupted existence of radioactive substances in the seascape, the future of the Joban Sea seems, as always, highly precarious.

But by the same token, precarity does not mean hopelessness, as the multiple survival stories of the Joban seascape showed us. Possibilities of survival stay alive in a repeatedly ruined seascape. Hope may emerge even in the radioactive ruins. What is more, the survival stories of the precarious seascape also allow us to see ruination as not an end but a beginning of regeneration. As the Joban Sea was repeatedly ruined, it continuously regenerated through reconfiguring its "partial connections" (Strathern 2004) with humans and nonhumans. Such a reconfiguration is by no means healthy but alive. As humans historically engineered and ruined the sea in the name of modernization, natural and man-made things have not simply become coexistent or become a hybrid, but they configure all the species living as part of the seascape. It is impossible to separate natural from man-made, and vice versa. Whether we like it or not, finding ways to live together with the ruined seascape is what we have left, as scholars of multispecies ethnography have suggested (Kirksey, Shapiro, and Brodine 2014; Tsing 2015; Haraway 2016; Tsing et al. 2017). The future of survival is not optimistic, but possible and lively.

Possibilities of survival remain alive even in the radioactive seascape. According to marine biologists based on their studies before and after the Fukushima nuclear accident, octopuses and hard clams, like other species of mollusks, accumulate fewer radioactive substances and also discharge them from their bodies much faster than do other species (Yoshikawa, Yagi, and Kurokura 2014). Other marine biologists also suggest that radionuclides accumulate differently depending on body parts of each species (Honda 2001). The edible muscle parts of octopuses and hard clams like "legs" and "arms," for example, contain substantially fewer radionuclides than their guts or shells. Overall, the detailed mechanisms regarding the radioactive metabolism of marine organisms are yet to be learned. But the fact that radionuclides have uneven relationships with different oceanic species implies a possibility of collective survival in the ruined seascape.

In the meantime, marine scientists continue searching for answers to the questions remaining in the precarious seascape. How do radionuclides affect marine species over time when they remain in their body parts? Where do they go after being flushed out of the bodies of marine livings? What happens to radionuclides after marine species die or are eaten by other species? Many scientists assume that much of the radioactive material ends up being disposed of at the bottom of the deep sea, after being washed away by ocean currents. But what does that mean? How do the radioactive sediments in the seabed behave until they no longer emit radiation? In particular, how do they coexist with those deep-sea microbes that oceanographers have recently discovered (Helmreich 2009), or what happens to radioactive sediments when future seismic movements shake the bottom of the deep sea? Indeed, questions are numerous, and the future is opaque but also open-ended.

NOTES

FOREWORD

1. Japan has a considerable literature on the environmental consequences of rapid industrialization. See, for instance, Kirby 2011. One of the best discussions of the industrial heritage of ruined environments and human suffering in Japan, to which this work speaks, is Walker 2011. On precarity in Japan, see Allison 2013.
2. For a useful consideration of the wide-ranging engagement with the Anthropocene analytic that goes beyond deep pessimism for the human future on this planet, see Matthews 2020.
3. In that regard she provides a wonderful examination of technoscience and risk in the spirit of work like that of Murphy 2006. See also Nading 2020; and Paredes 2021.
4. Like other studies in Japan, this work provides a situated account of emerging exigent expertise in risk management in local communities. Compare Sternsdorff-Cisterna 2018.

PROLOGUE

1. All the names of individuals in this book are pseudonyms, except for public figures. Regardless of gender, I use family names for elderly and senior members of fishing families and government officials and given names for younger members of fishing families, as was the norm in my conversations with them. In these conversations, I used the polite postfix "san" for all of them, but to make it simpler for readers, I use "Mr." and "Ms." for those whom I call by their family names but have omitted them for those I call by their given names.
2. Hama and Minato, the two coastal towns in Ibaraki, are pseudonyms.

INTRODUCTION

1. I use the modified Hepburn system with macrons, using the Roman alphabet with italics, when I introduce the original Japanese names and terms in (e.g., Jōban

Oki), but otherwise, to render them less obtrusive, I render them without macrons or italics (e.g., the Joban Sea, Tokyo, Tokaimura).

2. Since its opening in 1935, the Tokyo's Tsukiji Fish Market has played an important role in setting fish values (see Bestor 2004). In 2018, Tokyo's central fish market was relocated from Tsukiji to Toyosu.

3. Thinking of the processes of disasters requires us to extend our analytical sights and imaginations both to the past and also to the future. Disasters, when they happen, reveal preexisting social conditions that accumulated in history. Uneven distribution of damages among racial, religious, or gender minorities do not happen without their preexisting vulnerability (Gamburd 2013). In the case of industrial disasters, pollutants are produced through previous efforts of modernization in the past (Beck 1992; Hecht 1998; Fortun 2001). In turn, disasters can also cause future vulnerability. When toxic materials—such as gas, oil, and radioactive isotopes—are released by a disaster, their effects on the environment and the human and nonhuman bodies that are exposed carry on into the future (Fortun 2015).

4. Charles Perrow (1984) argues that complex technological systems make industrial accidents "normal." Given the repeated nuclear accidents and tanker accidents, normal accidents are ordinary in the Joban Sea.

5. In the immediate aftermath of the Fukushima nuclear accident, the United States Nuclear Regulatory Commission (NRC) recommended that American citizens avoid the area within fifty miles (eighty kilometers) of the Fukushima Daiichi Nuclear Power Plant. Following the guideline, the National Science Foundation (NSF) did not allow their funded researchers to travel to the area of concern in Japan, except for those who had already been in Japan when the disaster occurred. Therefore, I was eligible to conduct my research in Ibaraki and Fukushima with the generous support provided by NSF's Rapid Response Research (RAPID) program. I would like to express special gratitude to NSF as well as Laura Ahearn and Bonnie McCay, who provided kind encouragement and support for me to carry out the immediate postdisaster research.

6. The survival stories in this book share the insights of animated intimacies that Kath Weston discusses in *Animate Planet* (2017). She discusses how intimacies between human beings, nonhumans, and their surroundings became animated through their interactions with the environments damaged by technological modernization.

7. This cycle of fish population is called a dominant year class. See chapter 1 for more detailed explanations.

8. Symbiosis is often mistakenly assumed to be always mutual. But symbiotic relations may be positive (mutualism), negative (parasitism), or neutral (mutualism).

9. Although this book mainly focuses on Japan, what I call "surviving modernization" may speak to other places, especially those non-Western countries in which industrial modernization has already been accomplished to a large degree. One example is

the idea and practices of "ecological modernization" that Amy Zhang (2020) discusses based on her research of the new biological waste management program in China.

10. Anna Tsing points out that, while the concepts of progress and modernization have begun to feel archaic, our current lives are still deeply associated with their categories and assumptions of improvement (Tsing 2015, 20).

11. In Japanese popular narratives, Japan's modernization began with the Meiji Restoration in 1868, or, for some, a few years earlier in 1854, when Japan officially opened up to Western nations after more than two centuries of a formal (if incomplete) policy of national isolation. As historians have demonstrated, the Meiji government's aggressive modernization policies rapidly expanded its capitalistic industrialization and transformed not only the landscape but also people's and animals' lives (Fujitani 1998; Gluck 1985; Walker 2008). Eventually, Japan's modernization project continued expanding through the violence of empire-building and in a series of wars—the Sino-Japanese War (1894–95), the Russo-Japanese war (1904-5), World War I (1914–18), the Second Sino-Japanese War (1937–38), and World War II. The empire was ultimately lost at the end of World War II in 1945, but the nation's obsession with modernization remained largely intact. In fact, the defeat in World War II—with the world's first uses of atomic bombs in Hiroshima and Nagasaki—led to a recommitment to a rhetoric of modernization that became as lively as before, and perhaps more pronounced than ever. In the name of the nation's reconstruction from the devastation caused during the war, the state launched several development projects. And these projects would eventually become the engine for the rapid economic growth from the 1950s through the 1970s, which is also referred to as the "Japanese miracle." By calling attention to Japan's industrial policy of consistently targeting modernization and development as the key agenda, the noted political scientist Chalmers Johnson famously characterized Japan as a "developmental state" (Johnson 1994).

12. Hirokazu Miyazaki presents a similar argument and emphasizes the multitemporal aspect of futurism in his commentary on Peter Pels's article on "modern times" (Miyazaki 2015, 790; see also Pels 2015).

13. The billboard was later taken down by the municipal office after the Fukushima nuclear accident occurred, and the town was enclosed due to the government's evacuation order in 2011. But some townspeople, including the person who originally came up with the slogan when he was a sixth-grade student, protested, arguing that the billboard should be maintained so people could remember and critically reflect on the town's history. The billboard eventually became part of an exhibition at the memorial museum of the Fukushima disaster, which opened in 2021 (Rikimaru 2021).

14. Thermal discharge is hazardous due to its high temperature, but it is free of radioactive materials because coolant water is conveyed through a pipe system separate from that of the radioactive wastewater.

CHAPTER 1. TANKERS, CLAMS, AND OCTOPUSES

1. Among many other scholars, Nobel Laureate Elinor Ostrom and her colleagues played leading roles in the promotion of community-based natural resource management (Ostrom 1990; Feeny et al. 1990; Ostrom et al. 2002).

2. Ibaraki Prefecture's marine fish hatchery is not built next to a nuclear power plant.

CHAPTER 2. SURVIVAL CONDITIONS

1. Shiho Satsuka (2015) also highlights the affective aspects of translation in her stories of Japanese nature tour guides in the Canadian Rockies. She depicts personal narratives of Japanese guides who grapple with meanings of self and life as they interact with the spectacular landscape and learn about it in Canadian contexts, while translating it for themselves and their visitors from Japan.

2. These larger offshore vessels eventually disappeared after the consecutive oil crises and the closure of the foreign waters due to the establishment of the EEZ in the 1970s. But Hama's coastal fishing continued to flourish by adopting modern fishing equipment.

3. In Japanese folklore studies, "religion" (*shinkō*) and "ritual" (*gishiki* or *shikitari*) are often subjects that appear in discourses about "traditionalism" and "ruralism." In the context of Japanese fishing villages, "fishfolk's religion" (*gyomin shinkō*) often refers to ritualistic practices among fishing families. Although there is some regional variety, such rituals typically celebrate god(s) or goddess(es) of the sea, those who control the weather and precious marine resources (Omori 1987). At the same time, as many anthropologists of Japan have noted (Ivy 1995; Kelly 1990; Martinez 2004; Schnell 1999), religion and rituals comprise an arena that complicates notions of "tradition" and its relationship to modernity. They argue that, although traditions are often imagined as something premodern, many of them are actually products of modernization. In the case of Hama—the so-called "traditional fishing village"—the story of the Amba-sama sea goddess reflects a similar paradox. In fact, the "traditional" ritual was something (re)invented through the technological modernization of Hama's fisheries, especially as a way to deal with sharply increased competition among fishers due to their advanced ability to catch fish.

CHAPTER 3. MAMAS' ELEGY

1. The pattern here resembles one pertaining to motherhood identified by the feminist anthropologist Carla Freeman in her study of Barbadian neoliberalism. She

argues that entrepreneurialism represents "not simply a survival strategy but also an aspirational and officially mandated path, not only a means of a livelihood but also a life*style* and way of being" (Freeman 2014, 24, italics in original). Similarly in Hama, entrepreneurialism is also narrated as an element of coastal mamas' lifestyle and way of being, although it is primarily presented as a survival strategy in support of families' livelihoods.

2. The Hama Women's Association was originally established in the late 1950s in the same year as the Young Fishermen's Association (YFA). Similar to the YFAs, the basic idea of the WAs was borrowed from the women's association of the Farmers' Co-operatives, and the establishment was suggested by prefectural officials.

3. I omit the title of the book in order to protect the anonymity of my field site and informants.

CHAPTER 4. THE (UN)EXPECTED

1. Fukushima Study is a website run by a team of scholars in Japan, which aims to provide public access to a collection of the transcripts of various press conferences given by the Japanese government and TEPCO during the immediate aftermath of the Fukushima Daiichi Nuclear Power Plant accident. http://fukushimastudy.org/t0313_1953/.

2. According to maritime civil engineering experts, in March 2011 the tsunami reached the shore unusually fast not only because of the magnitude of the quake but also because of the site of the quake's epicenter, which was located in very deep water. According to their theory of wave physics, the speed of a tsunami wave increases with the square of the depth of water. Moreover, coincidentally, on the afternoon of March 11, when the unprecedented magnitude of the quake occurred in very deep water, the sea was at high tide. Hence, the tidal energy, multiplied by the depth and the amount of water, produced an incredibly violent force as it struck the long coastline, though the tsunami's impact varied from spot to spot, depending on the distance and the angle from the offshore epicenter as well as local topographical features.

CHAPTER 5. FOURFOLD PAIN

1. The original Japanese title for the event was Ibaraki no Mirai o Katarau Kai.

2. For the case of the Chernobyl nuclear accident, see the ethnographies written by Adriana Petryna (2002) and Sarah Phillips (2002, 2004). For the case of the Fukushima nuclear accident, see those by Nicolas Sternsdorff-Cisterna (2018) and Ryo Morimoto (2022).

3. The Japan Aerospace Exploration Agency (JAXA) announced on November

15, 2012, that their research team had invented a prototype of ASTROCAM 7000, a gamma-ray camera that visualizes captured radioactive substances. The press release is available on the JAXA's official website, https://www.jaxa.jp/press/2012/11/20121115 _compton_j.html.

4. The original Japanese for "Buy, Eat, and Support in Tsukiji!" is "Katte, Tabete, Ouen Shiyo! in Tsukiji."

5. In original Japanese, Tabete Ouen Shiyou!

6. At the time, based on the rule that the Ministry of Health, Labor, and Welfare released on April 4, 2011, in order to commercially catch and sell any fish species that had been detected to have higher level of radiation than the safety standard, fishers had to ask their municipal office to submit an official letter requesting approval to the Ministry along with radiation monitoring results that demonstrate that results were lower than the safety standard for the previous three consecutive weeks. A little more than two months later, on June 27, the Ministry revised the rule and announced that approval of reopening cannot be given unless weekly radiation monitoring results show that radiation level were lower than the safety standard for the previous month.

7. Disasters often provide an opportunity for forming a new sense of citizenship. Based on her ethnographic research on post-Chernobyl Ukraine, Adriana Petryna has described a sense of belonging that disaster victims gained through their political and medical negotiations over effects of radiation exposure as "biological citizenship" (Petryna 2002). Following Petryna's discussion, Nicolas Sternsdorff-Cisterna (2018) has argued that "scientific citizenship" has been formed in the aftermath of the Fukushima nuclear disaster among "citizen scientists" who try to better understand radiation risk (see also Kimura 2016). In the case of the visitors at the Tsukiji event, a sense of belonging among those people who voluntarily consumed low-level radiation would be better described as "disaster citizenship" than as "scientific citizenship."

CHAPTER 6. FUKUSHIMA FORWARD

1. The Fukushima FORWARD project's narrative on the building of the future for Japan might be viewed as an example of what Vivian Choi (2015) has called "disaster nationalism," which she develops from Naomi Klein's "disaster capitalism" (2017). Based on her ethnographic observation of national reconstruction efforts in Sri Lanka amid the ruins of both the civil war and the Indian Ocean tsunami, Choi reveals how politicians used the disasters in order to gain popularity.

2. "The Slogan Says It All" (Surōgan Ni Kometa 'Omoi') on the Fukushima prefectural website is available at https://www.nga.gr.jp/pref_info/tembo/2012/05/post_1771 .html (translation by the author).

3. In line with this gesture toward a hopeful future, Fukushima's prefectural gov-

ernment has also launched a wide variety of new projects, targeting new agricultural business, women's empowerment, elderly care, education reforms, alternative energy, and so forth. "Fukushima Future" was, in fact, developed as part of these ambitions. And like "Fukushima Future," most of the government-sponsored projects have been given official names, including the language of the future in one way or another. The postdisaster projects in Fukushima that are named using the language of the future (*mirai*), among many, include Futaba Future Junior and High Schools, Fukushima Future Agricultural Cooperative, Fukushima Future Center at Fukushima University, and Fukushima Prefecture's official film *The Future 2061* (Mirai 2061). For other cases, too, the word *mirai* (the future) is often included as part of a project slogan or description.

4. Among many who supported and protected a utopian picture of the floating wind energy project in Fukushima, Norio Akasaka—a Japanese folklorist and a public intellectual—actually helped to generate tailwind for the green energy project. On April 30, 2011, Akasaka made a presentation as an appointed core member at one of the meetings of the government's Reconstruction Design Council, claiming that renewable energy is the answer for reconstructing the ruined landscape and seascape. "By building wind and solar energy generators throughout the nuclear devastated coastline," Akasaka stated, "we can clean up our negative reputation, and create a new image for Fukushima, fighting against the difficult challenges that mankind is facing." He also explained that, by switching from nuclear to natural energy, Fukushima would be able to break new ground to bring about a "civilizational shift" (*bunmeiron-teki na henkan*). "When that happens," he continued, "Fukushima will overturn the world's history from its very foundations, and become the land of the beginning, yielding hope for the future" (translation by the author). The original proceedings of the meeting in Japanese are available online at https://www.cas.go.jp/jp/fukkou/pdf/kousou3/akasaka.pdf.

5. The emergence of positive futurity with intimate relations to the past was also seen in the aftermath of the 1986 Chernobyl disaster. Through analyzing symbolism in academic and popular discourse, literature, and museums in post-Chernobyl Ukraine, Sarah Phillips has written, "Chernobyl is interpreted not only as a warning from the past, but as an omen for the future" (Phillips 2004, 174). Besides futurism, cultural anthropologist Adriana Petryna has pointed out other similarities between the two world's worst nuclear disasters, such as the depiction of cleanup workers as heroes, an emerging biopolitics of risk, and also a domestication of risk (Petryna 2014; see also Phillips 2011). Petryna also talks about the similarities between the aftermaths of the Chernobyl and Fukushima accidents in her special introduction to the Japanese translation of *Life Exposed* (2002), published in 2016.

6. In using Walter Benjamin's work (1969) to extend anthropological debates on time, Nancy Munn reminds us of importance of the present in thinking of the future. She writes, "A [specific] past [becomes] charged with the time of the now, which also

implies that it is charged with the expectancies or 'possible futures' entailed in the 'now'" (Munn 1992, 113; see also Benjamin 1969, 261).

7. In the interview article on the Marubeni's website, the team leader proclaims that his company's mission is to produce a new age and pledges that he would like to make Japan an energy nation of the next generation. His online interview article is available at http://www.marubeni.co.jp/business/project_story/wind/index.html.

8. I conducted this telephone interview with Professor Takeshi Ishihara on July 15, 2015.

9. I thank Professor Osamu Baba for helping me arrange the field trip for visiting Mr. Tanaka in Fukushima and also for coming along on it.

CHAPTER 7. IN LIMBO

1. I thank Edwin Eberhart, who asked me a question about the future of Fukushima Future when I presented a paper at a workshop in UCLA in January 2015.

2. METI, as well as all the other ministries, annually provides public access to so-called "administrative project review sheets" of each of their project, which includes a project overview and budget allocations. The PDF version of the Administrative Project Review Sheet of FY 2018 for the Fukushima Floating Wind Farm Consignment Project was available online at https://www.meti.go.jp/information_2/publicoffer/review2016/saishupdf/28003400METI.pdf.

3. Jean-Luc Nancy makes this claim in his interview with the Japanese translator, which is included in the Japanese version of his book.

EPILOGUE

1. In the wake of the triple disaster, a review essay that the eminent Japanese philosopher Kojin Karatani (2011a) wrote for the Japanese translation of Rebecca Solnit's *Paradise Built in Hell* (2010) in the newspaper *Asahi*—which was published on February 6, 2011, about a month prior to the catastrophe—received much public attention by being recirculated widely through social media. In his essay, Karatani concluded with his thoughts on the conundrum of how to perpetuate a paradise that emerged in a disaster. Karatani also published an essay in the intellectual magazine *Gendai Shiso* (Karatani 2011b), in which he discussed the examples of paradise that emerged and then disappeared in the wakes of past disasters in Japanese history. The English version of the essay, translated by Seiji M. Lippit, is available on Karatani's official website at http://www.kojinkaratani.com/en/article/earthquake-and-japan.html. My question about the issue of short-lived paradise extends Karatani's thoughts by incorporating the discussions of how to live in the Anthropocene.

2. In describing how to build more livable futures, Donna Haraway prefers the term *Chthulucene* to the *Anthropocene* to identify the new epoch (Haraway 2016). Unlike the Anthropocene, in which both problems and solutions are imagined in human-centric ways, in the Chthulucene, Haraway argues, humans and nonhumans are inextricably linked in tentacular practices. In addition, whereas stories in the Anthropocene tend to imply an ending with apocalyptic or salvific futures, those in the Chthulucene are always ongoing with the futures remaining open-ended.

3. The report released by the review committee for the Fukushima offshore floating wind farm project is available online at https://www.enecho.meti.go.jp/category/saving_and_new/new/information/180824a/pdf/report_2018.pdf.

4. According to the Ministry of Economy, Trade, and Industry (METI), they invited applicants from corporations to manage the project of removing the three turbines from Fukushima's offshore waters. In the application guidelines (see the link below), METI indicates that the 7-MW turbine was expected to be removed by 2021 and that the other two turbines (2-MW and 5-MW ones) were also being considered for future removal (see https://www.enecho.meti.go.jp/appli/public_offer/1903/190311a/pdf/1.pdf).

5. The METI's summary of the entrustment budget for the Fukushima floating wind farm for the fiscal year of 2019 is available at https://www.meti.go.jp/main/yosangaisan/fy2019/pr/en/shoshin_taka_20.pdf.

6. The archived data of radiation monitoring is available on the website of Japan's Fisheries Agency at https://www.jfa.maff.go.jp/j/housyanou/kekka.html.

WORKS CITED

Abélès, Marc. 2010. *The Politics of Survival*. Translated by Julie Kleinman. Durham, NC: Duke University Press.
Agrawal, Arun. 2005. *Environmentality: Technology of Government and the Making of Subjects*. Durham, NC: Duke University Press.
Alexy, Allison. 2020. *Intimate Disconnections: Divorce and the Romance of Independence in Contemporary Japan*. Chicago: University of Chicago Press.
Allison, Anne. 2013. *Precarious Japan*. Durham, NC: Duke University Press.
Appadurai, Arjun. 2013. *The Future as Cultural Fact: Essays on the Global Condition*. New York: Verso.
Barnes, Jessica, ed. 2016. "Environmental Futures." Special issue, *Journal of the Royal Anthropological Institute* 22 (S1).
Beck, Ulrich. 1987. "The Anthropological Shock: Chernobyl and the Contours of the Risk Society." *Berkeley Journal of Sociology* 32: 153–165.
———. 1992. *Risk Society: Towards a New Modernity*. London: SAGE.
Benjamin, Walter. 1969. *Illuminations*. New York: Schocken.
Bestor, Theodore C. 2004. *Tsukiji: The Fish Market at the Center of the World*. Berkeley: University of California Press.
Bloch, Ernst. 1995. *The Principle of Hope*. Vol 3. Translated by Neville Plaice, Stephen Plaice, and Paul Knight. Cambridge, MA: MIT Press.
Boyer, Dominic. 2019. *Energopolitics: Wind and Power in the Anthropocene*. Durham, NC: Duke University Press.
Bryant, Rebecca, and Daniel M. Knight. 2019. *The Anthropology of the Future*. Cambridge, UK: Cambridge University Press.
Choi, Vivian. 2015. "Anticipatory States: Tsunami, War, and Insecurity in Sri Lanka." *Cultural Anthropology* 30 (2): 286–309.
Choy, Timothy, and Jerry Zee. 2015. "Condition—Suspension." *Cultural Anthropology* 30 (2): 210–223.
Clancey, Gregory. 2006. *Earthquake Nation: The Cultural Politics of Japanese Seismicity, 1868–1930*. Berkeley: University of California Press.
Donaldson, Lindsay. 2020. "Covid-19, (In)visible Mothers, and the State." Covid-19,

Fieldsights, May 11. https://culanth.org/fieldsights/covid-19-invisible-mothers-and-the-state.

Escobar, Arturo. 1995. *Encountering Development: The Making and Unmaking of the Third World.* Princeton, NJ: Princeton University Press.

Feeny, David, Fikret Berkes, Bonnie J. McCay, and James M. Acheson. 1990. "The Tragedy of the Commons: Twenty-Two Years Later." *Journal of Human Ecology* 18: 1–19.

Ferguson, James. 1999. *Expectation of Modernity: Myths and Meanings of Urban Life on the Zambian Copperbelt.* Berkeley: University of California Press.

Fisch, Michael. n.d. "Mediations on the 'Unimaginable' (Soteigai)." In *The Space of Disaster*, edited by Erez Golani Solomon. Tel Aviv: Resling.

Fischer, Michael. 2009. *Anthropological Futures.* Durham, NC: Duke University Press.

Fisheries Agency. n.d. "Suisan butsu no houshaseibushitsu chosa no kekka ni tsuite" (About the results of the radioactive material survey of marine products). http://www.jfa.maff.go.jp/j/housyanou/kekka.html.

———. 2009. "Heisei 20 nendo suisan hakusho" (Fisheries white paper of 2008). http://www.jfa.maff.go.jp/j/kikaku/wpaper/h20/index.html.

Fortun, Kim. 2001. *Advocacy after Bhopal: Environmentalism, Disaster, New Global Orders.* Chicago: University of Chicago Press.

———. 2015. "Ethnography in Late Industrialism." In *Writing Culture and the Life of Anthropology*, edited by Orin Starn, 119–136. Durham, NC: Duke University Press.

Freeman, Carla. 2014. *Entrepreneurial Selves: Neoliberal Respectability and the Making of a Caribbean Middle Class.* Durham, NC: Duke University Press.

Fujitani, Takashi. 1998. *Splendid Monarchy: Power and Pageantry in Modern Japan.* Berkeley: University of California Press.

Fukunaga, Mayumi. 2019. *Sake o tsukuru hitobito: Suisan zoshoku to shigen saisei/ Futuring Salmon: Dreams of Marine Ranching in Ruins.* Tokyo: University of Tokyo Press.

Fukushima Study. 2016. "Tokyo Denryoku Honten no kishakaiken tekisuto: 2011 nen 3 gatsu 13 nichi 19 ji 53 fun kara 180 funkan" (Transcript of the press conference at the main office of Tokyo Electric Power Company [TEPCO], the 180 minutes from 19:53 on March 13, 2011). http://fukushimastudy.org/t0313_1953.

Gamburd, Michele Ruth. 2013. *The Golden Wave: Culture and Politics after Sri Lanka's Tsunami Disaster.* Bloomington: Indiana University Press.

Ghosh, Amitav. 2016. *The Great Derangement: Climate Change and the Unthinkable.* Chicago: University of Chicago Press.

Gill, Tom. 2013. "This Spoiled Soil: Place, People and Community in an Irradiated Village in Fukushima Prefecture." In *Japan Copes with Calamity*, edited by Tom Gill, Brigitte Steger, and David H. Slater, 201–233. Oxford, UK: Peter Lang.

Gluck, Carol. 1985. *Japan's Modern Myths: Ideology in the Late Meiji Period*. Princeton, NJ: Princeton University Press.

Güney-Frahm, Irem. 2020. "Neoliberal Motherhood during the Pandemic: Some Reflections." *Gender, Work, and Organization* 27 (5): 847–856.

Gupta, Akhil. 2015. "Suspension." Theorizing the Contemporary, Fieldsights, September 24. https://culanth.org/fieldsights/722-suspension.

———. 2018. "The Future in Ruins: Thoughts on the Temporality of Infrastructure." In *The Promise of Infrastructure*, edited by Nikhal Anand, Akhil Gupta, and Hannah Appel, 62–79. Durham, NC: Duke University Press.

Haraway, Donna J. 2008. *When Species Meet*. Minneapolis: University of Minnesota Press.

———. 2016. *Staying with the Trouble: Making Kin in the Chthulucene*. Durham, NC: Duke University Press.

Hardin, Garrett. 1968. "The Tragedy of the Commons." *Science* 162: 1243–1248.

Harding, Susan, and Daniel Rosenberg, eds. 2005. *Histories of the Future*. Durham, NC: Duke University Press.

Hecht, Gabrielle. 1998. *The Radiance of France: Nuclear Power and National Identity after World War II*. Cambridge, MA: MIT Press.

Helmreich, Stefan. 2009. *Alien Ocean: Anthropological Voyages in Microbial Seas*. Berkeley: University of California Press.

Hjort, Johan. 1914. "Fluctuations in the Great Fisheries of Northern Europe: Viewed in the Light of Biological Research." *Rapports et Procès-Verbaux des Réunions du Conseil Permanent International Pour L'Exploration de la Mer* 20: 1–228.

Honda, Teruyuki. 2001. "Kaiyo seibutsu chu no houshasei kakushu/Radionuclides in Marine Organisms." *Bulletin of the Society of Sea Water Science Japan* 55 (1): 11–20.

Howe, Cymene. 2019. *Ecologics: Wind and Power in the Anthropocene*. Durham, NC: Duke University Press.

Hughes, David M. 2014. "Energy." In *To See Once More the Stars: Living in Post-Fukushima World*, edited by Daisuke Naito, Ryan Sayre, Heather Swanson, and Satsuki Takahashi, 185–187. Santa Cruz, CA: New Pacific.

Ibaraki Prefecture. n.d. "Honken suisanbutsu ni kakawaru houshano kankei jouhou" (The Fukushima Daiichi Nuclear Power Plant accident's effects on this prefecture's fisheries products). http://www.pref.ibaraki.jp/nourin/gyosei/shinsaieikyou.html.

Ivy, Marilyn. 1995. *Discourses of the Vanishing: Modernity, Phantasm, Japan*. Chicago: University of Chicago Press.

Johnson, Chalmers. 1994. *Japan: Who Governs? The Rise of the Developmental State*. New York: Norton.

Karatani, Kojin. 2011a. "Rebekka Sorunitto 'Saigai yutopia,' Shohyo, Sogofujo no shutsugen, muhojotai de naku" (A book review of Rebecca Solnit's 'A Paradise Built in Hell': Mutual aid emerged, not anarchy). *Asahi Shimbun*, Feburary, 6, 2011.

———. 2011b. "Jishin to Nihon" (Earthquake and Japan). *Gendai Shiso* 39 (7): 22–25.

Kawashima, Shuichi. 2003. *Gyorou denshou* (The tradition of fishing). Tokyo: Hosei University Press.

Kelly, William W. 1990. "Japanese No-Noh: The Crosstalk of Public Culture in a Rural Festivity." *Public Culture* 2 (2): 65–81.

———. 1994. "Tractors, Television, and Telephones: Reach out and Touch Someone in Rural Japan." In *Re-Made in Japan: Everyday Life and Consumer Taste in a Changing Society*, edited by Joseph Jay Tobin, 77–88. New Haven, CT: Yale University Press.

Kimura, Aya. 2016. *Radiation Brain Moms and Citizen Scientists: The Gender Politics of Food Contamination after Fukushima*. Durham, NC: Duke University Press.

Kirby, Peter. 2011. *Troubled Natures: Waste, Environment, Japan*. Honolulu: University of Hawai'i Press.

Kirksey, Eben. 2015. *Emergent Ecologies*. Durham, NC: Duke University Press.

Kirksey, Eben, Nicholas Shapiro, and Maria Brodine. 2014. "Hope in Blasted Landscapes." In *The Multispecies Salon*, edited by Eben Kirksey, 29–63. Durham, NC: Duke University Press.

Klein, Naomi. 2007. *The Shock Doctrine: The Rise of Disaster Capitalism*. Toronto: Knopf Canada.

Komatsu, Masayuki. 2016. *Sekai to Nihon no gyogyoukanri* (Fisheries management of the world and Japan). Tokyo: Seizandoshoten.

Koselleck, Reinhart. 2004. *Futures Past: On the Semantics of Historical Time*. New York: Columbia University Press.

Latour, Bruno. 1996. *Aramis, or the Love of Technology*. Cambridge, MA: Harvard University Press.

———. 1999. *Pandora's Hope: Essays on the Reality of Science Studies*. Cambridge, MA: Harvard University Press.

Li, Tania Murray. 2007. *The Will to Improve: Governmentality, Development, and the Practice of Politics*. Durham, NC: Duke University Press.

Lien, Marianne Elisabeth. 2015. *Becoming Salmon: Aquaculture and the Domestication of a Fish*. Berkeley: University of California Press.

Martinez, D. P. 2004. *Identity and Ritual in a Japanese Diving Village: The Making and Becoming of Person and Place*. Honolulu: University of Hawai'i Press.

Marubeni. n.d. "Purojekuto sutori: PROJECT 07 Fukushima fukkou futaishiki youjou windo famu jissho jikken jigyou" (Project story: PROJECT 07 Fukushima reconstruction, the floating offshore wind farm demonstration research project). http://www.marubeni.co.jp/business/project_story/wind/index.html.

Matthews, Andrew. 2020. "Anthropology and the Anthropocene: Criticisms,

Experiments, and Collaborations." *Annual Review of Anthropology* 49: 67–82.
Mikuriya, Takahashi. 2011. "'Sengo' ga owari 'saigo' ga hajimaru" ("Postwar" ends, "postdisaster" begins). *Chūō Kōron* (May): 24–31.
Ministry of Economy, Trade, and Industry. 2020. "ALPS shorisui nitsuite" (About ALPS treated water). http://www.meti.go.jp/earthquake/nuclear/osensuitaisaku/pdf/2020/20200701a1.pdf.
Ministry of Health, Labor, and Welfare. 2011. "Shokuhin anzen no kinkyu torimatome o uketa shokuhinchu no houshasei bushitsu ni kansuru zantei kiseichi no toriatsukai nitsuite" (Food Safety Committee's emergency decisions on the tentative food safety standard with radioactive substances in food items). http://www.mhlw.go.jp/stf/houdou/2r98520000017tmu-att/2r98520000017trg.pdf.
Miura, Makoto. 2011. "Tokusan hirame chigyo houryu o dannen: Genpatsu onhaisui de shiiku" (Stocking of juvenile flounders, a local specialty, abandoned: Raising with nuclear power plant thermal discharge). *Yomiuri Shimbun*, May 5, 2011.
Miyazaki, Hirokazu. 2004. *The Method of Hope: Anthropology, Philosophy, and Fijian Knowledge*. Stanford, CA: Stanford University Press.
———. 2015. "Comments on Peter Pels's article, 'Modern Times.'" *Current Anthropology* 56 (6): 790–791.
Mori, Satoshi, and Masamichi Kagaya. 2015. *Houshasenzou: Houshanou o kashika suru* (Autoradiography: Visualizing radiation). Tokyo: Kouseisha.
Morimoto, Ryo. 2022. "A Wild Boar Chase: Ecology of Harm and Half-Life Politics in Coastal Fukushima." *Cultural Anthropology* 37 (1): 69–98.
Morris-Suzuki, Tessa. 2017. "Disaster and Utopia: Looking Back at 3/11." *Japanese Studies* 37 (2): 171–190.
Morton, Timothy. 2013. *Hyperobjects: Philosophy and Ecology after the End of the World*. Minneapolis: University of Minnesota Press.
Munn, Nancy D. 1992. "The Cultural Anthropology of Time: A Critical Essay." *Annual Review of Anthropology* 21: 93–123.
Murphy, Michelle. 2006. *Sick Building Syndrome and the Problem of Uncertainty: Environmental Politics, Technoscience, and Women Workers*. Durham, NC: Duke University Press.
Nading, Alex. 2020. "Living in a Toxic World." *Annual Review of Anthropology* 49: 209–224.
Nancy, Jean-Luc. 2012. *Fukushima no atode: Hakyoku, gijutsu, minshushugi* (After Fukushima: Catastrophe, technology, and democracy). Translated by Yotetsu Tonaki. Tokyo: Ibunsha.
———. 2014. *After Fukushima: The Equivalence of Catastrophes*. Translated by Charlotte Mandell. New York: Fordham University Press.
Ohno, Hirohito. 2011. "INTERVIEW Ulrich Beck: System of Organized

Irresponsibility behind the Fukushima Crisis." *Asahi Shinbun, Asia and Japan*, July 6, 2011. http://ajw.asahi.com/article/0311disaster/opinion/AJ201107063167.

Oliver-Smith, Anthony. 1999. "'What Is a Disaster?' Anthropological Perspectives on a Persistent Question." In *The Angry Earth: Disaster in Anthropological Perspective*, edited by Anthony Oliver-Smith and Susannah M. Hoffman, 18–34. New York: Routledge.

Oliver-Smith, Anthony, and Susannah M. Hoffman. 2002. "Introduction: Why Anthropologists Should Study Disasters." In *Catastrophe and Culture*, edited by Anthony Oliver-Smith and Susannah M. Hoffman, 3–22. Santa Fe, NM: School of American Research Press.

Omori, Taryo, ed. 1987. *Kaijin no dentō* (Traditions of marine people). Tokyo: Chuokoronsha.

Ostrom, Elinor. 1990. *Governing the Commons: The Evolution of Institutions for Collective Action*. Cambridge, UK: Cambridge University Press.

Ostrom, Elinor, Thomas Dietz, Nives Dolsak, Paul C. Stern, Susan Stonich, and Elke U. Weber, eds. 2002. *The Drama of the Commons*. Washington, DC: National Research Council.

Pacchioli, David. 2013. "Radioisotopes in the Ocean: What's There? How Much? How Long?" http://www.whoi.edu/oceanus/feature/radioisotopes-in-the-ocean.

Paredes, Alyssa. 2021. "Weedy Activism: Women, Plants, and the Genetic Pollution of Urban Japan." *Journal of Political Ecology* 28 (1): 70–90.

Pels, Peter. 2015. "Modern Times: Seven Steps toward an Anthropology of the Future." *Current Anthropology* 56 (6): 779–796.

Perrow, Charles. 1984. *Normal Accidents: Living with High-Risk Technologies*. Princeton, NJ: Princeton University Press.

———. 2011. "Fukushima, Risk, and Probability: Expect the Unexpected." *Bulletin of the Atomic Sciences*. https://thebulletin.org/2011/04/fukushima-risk-and-probability-expect-the-unexpected.

Petryna, Adriana. 2002. *Life Exposed: Biological Citizens after Chernobyl*. Princeton, NJ: Princeton University Press.

———. 2014. "Chernobyl." In *To See Once More the Stars: Living in a Post-Fukushima World*, edited by Daisuke Naito, Ryan Sayre, Heather Swanson, and Satsuki Takahashi, 68–73. Santa Cruz, CA: New Pacific.

Phillips, Sarah D. 2002. "Half-Lives and Healthy Bodies: Discourses on "Contaminated" Foods and Healing in Post-Chernobyl Ukraine." *Food and Foodways* 10 (1–2): 27–53.

———. 2004. "Chernobyl's Sixth Sense: The Symbolism of an Ever-Present Awareness." *Anthropology and Humanism* 29 (2): 159–185.

———. 2011. "Chernobyl Forever." *Somatosphere*. April 25. http://somatosphere.net/2011/chernobyl-forever.html.

Pigg, Stacy Leigh. 1992. "Inventing Social Categories through Place: Social Representations and Development in Nepal." *Comparative Studies in Society and History* 34 (3): 491–513.

Pálsson, Gísli. 1991. *Coastal Economies, Cultural Accounts: Human Ecology and Icelandic Discourse.* Manchester, UK: Manchester University Press.

Rikimaru, Sachiko. 2021. "'Akarui mirai no enerugi' kanban, tenji hajimaru: Fu no isan" (The heritage of loss in the "Energy of a Bright Future" billboard exhibit). *Asahi Shinbun*, March 25, 2021.

Rose, Deborah Bird. 2011. *Wild Dog Dreaming: Love and Extinction.* Charlottesville: University of Virginia Press.

Royce, William F. 1972. *Introduction to the Fishery Sciences.* New York: Academic Press.

Satsuka, Shiho. 2015. *Nature in Translation: Japanese Tourism Encounters the Canadian Rockies.* Durham, NC: Duke University Press.

Schnell, Scott. 1999. *Rousing Drum: Ritual Practice in a Japanese Community.* Honolulu: University of Hawai'i Press.

Scranton, Roy. 2015. *Learning to Die in the Anthropocene.* San Francisco, CA: City Lights.

Sekiya, Naoya. 2011. *Fūhyōhigai: Sono mechanizumu o kangaeru* (Reputational damage: Thoughts on the mechanism). Tokyo: Kobunsha.

Solnit, Rebecca. 2010. *A Paradise Built in Hell: The Extraordinary Communities That Arise in Disaster.* New York: Penguin.

Star, Susan Leigh, and Karen Ruhleder. 1996. "Steps toward an Ecology of Infrastructure: Design and Access for Large Information Spaces." *Information Systems Research* (7): 111–134.

Sternsdorff-Cisterna, Nicolas. 2019. *Food Safety after Fukushima: Scientific Citizenship and the Politics of Risk.* Honolulu: University of Hawai'i Press.

Strathern, Marilyn. 1991. *Partial Connections.* Lanham, MD: Rowman and Littlefield.

Swanson, Heather Anne. 2017. "The Banality of the Anthropocene." Member Voices, Fieldsights, February 22. https://culanth.org/fieldsights/the-banality-of-the-anthropocene.

———. 2022. *Spawning Modern Fish: Transnational Comparison in the Making of Japanese Salmon.* Seattle: University of Washington Press.

Takahashi, Satsuki. 2014a. "Hatchery Flounder Going Wild: Authenticity, Aesthetics, and Fetishism of Fish in Japan." *Food and Foodways* 22: 5–23.

———. 2014b. "Hero." In *To See Once More the Stars: Living in a Post-Fukushima World*, edited by Daisuke Naito, Ryan Sayre, Heather Swanson, and Satsuki Takahashi, 118–119. Santa Cruz, CA: New Pacific.

———. 2018. "Fukushima oki ni ukabu 'mirai' to sono mirai / The Future of 'Fukushima Future.'" *Bunka jinrui gaku* 83(3): 441–458.

Thomas, Julia Adeney, Mark Williams, and Jan Zalasiewicz, eds. 2020. *The Anthropocene: A Multidisciplinary Approach.* Cambridge, UK: Polity.

Thompson, Peter, and Slavoj Žižek, eds. 2013. *The Privatization of Hope*. Durham, NC: Duke University Press.

Tilt, Bryan. 2014. *Dams and Development in China: The Moral Economy of Water and Power*. New York: Columbia University Press.

Tsing, Anna Lowenhaupt. 2000. "The Global Situation." *Cultural Anthropology* 15 (3): 327–360.

———. 2014. "Blasted Landscapes (and the Gentle Arts of Mushroom Picking)." In *The Multispecies Salon*, edited by Eben Kirksey, 87–110. Durham, NC: Duke University Press.

———. 2015. *The Mushroom at the End of the World: On the Possibility of Life in Capitalist Ruins*. Princeton, NJ: Princeton University Press.

Tsing, Anna Lowenhaupt, Heather Anne Swanson, Elaine Gan, and Nils Bubandt, eds. 2017. *Arts of Living on a Damaged Planet: Ghosts and Monsters of the Anthropocene*. Minneapolis: University of Minnesota Press.

University of Tokyo. 2012. "Ashita no kaze ga umi ni fuku: Fukushima oki de hajimaru futaishiki youjou fuuryoku hatsuden no jissho kenkyu/Harvesting the Winds of Fukushima: Japan to Build World's First Floating Wind Farm." http://www.u-tokyo.ac.jp/focus/ja/features/f_00027.html.

Wada, Toshihiro. 2021. "Radiocesium Contamination of Marine and Freshwater Fish after the Fukushima Dai-ichi Nuclear Power Plant Accident." *Chikyukagaku (Geochemistry)* 55: 159–175.

Walker, Brett. 2008. *The Lost Wolves of Japan*. Seattle: University of Washington Press.

———. 2011. *Toxic Archipelago: A History of Industrial Disease in Japan*. Seattle: University of Washington Press.

Walley, Christine J. 2004. *Rough Waters: Nature and Development in an East African Marine Park*. Princeton, NJ: Princeton University Press.

West, Paige. 2006. *Conservation Is Our Government Now: The Politics of Ecology in Papua New Guinea*. Durham, NC: Duke University Press.

Weston, Kath. 2014. "Detectable." In *To See Once More the Stars: Living in a Post-Fukushima World*, edited by Daisuke Naito, Ryan Sayre, Heather Swanson, and Satsuki Takahashi, 8–11. Santa Cruz, CA: New Pacific.

———. 2017. *Animate Planet: Making Visceral Sense of Living in a High-Tech Ecologically Damaged World*. Durham, NC: Duke University Press.

White, Richard. 1995. *The Organic Machine: The Remaking of the Columbia River*. New York: Hill and Wang.

Williams, Raymond. 1973. *The Country and the City*. Oxford, UK: Oxford University Press.

Yoshikawa, Takashi, Nobuyuki Yagi, and Hisashi Kurokura. 2014. "The State of

Concentration of Radioactive Cesium in Marine Organisms collected from the Fukushima Coastal Area: A Species by Species Evaluation." *Nihon Suisan Gakkaishi* 80 (1): 27–33.

Zhang, Amy. 2020. "Circularity and Enclosures: Metabolizing Waste with the Black Soldier Fly." *Cultural Anthropology* 35 (1): 74–103.

INDEX

Page numbers in *italics* refer to illustrations.

abalones, 9–10, 117, 124–126
Abe, Shinzo, 126
Abélès, Marc, 108–109
"After Fukushima" (Nancy), 136
agents, fisheries. *See* fisheries agents
Akasaka, Norio, 149n4
Amba-sama (sea goddess), 43–47, 146n3
anchovies, young: declining catch sizes, 17–18, 32–33, 50, 62, 64; finding hope in, 137; at Fishermen's Mamas' Shop, 55, 69; fishing methods, 30–31; limits on fishing and, 49–50; pilot fishing program, 125; radiation testing, 102; reopening approval by METI, 95–96; on research fishing trip, 133–134; season for, 51, 52; at Tsukiji Fish Market event, 96, 96–100
Anthropocene, 13–14, 138–139, 151n2
anthropological shock, 90–91
Assembly to Talk about the Future of Ibaraki, 87–89, 103–104

backwardness: Amba-sama (sea goddess) and, 43–44, 46; fisheries agents on, 26; gender roles and, 56, 60–62; "hunter-gatherers," 110; interpretations of, 41; keeping ahead of, 42–43; octopus-potting rule and, 47, 49; urgency and, 63; yellow-light rule and, 49–50; young fishers and, 22–23, 26. *See also* modernization

beach erosion, 31–32
Beck, Ulrich, 90–91, 104
Benjamin, Walter, 149n6
Bloch, Ernst, 107, 117
bonitos, 132
bottom-trawling. *See* trawling
breams, 30
breeding programs, 27
brothels, 65
"Buy, Eat, and Support in Tsukiji!" disaster reconstruction event, 95–100, *96*

Chernobyl, 91, 92, 148n7, 149n5
Choi, Vivian, 148n1
Choy, Timothy, 137
Chthulucene, 151n2
citizen scientists, 93
citizenship, 99, 100, 148n7
clams, hard: as "bank of the sea," 29; beach erosion and, 31–32; collaborative survival and, 22–23; co-op project to save baby, 18–19, *38*, *39*; cut feet problem, 26–27; declining catch sizes, 17–18, 31, 62; dominant year class, 18, 82; gendered land tasks and, 61; income-pooling system, 27–29; as octopus prey, 35; population recovery, 141; radioactive accumulation in, 145; stocking, 29
clams, surf, 51–53

Coastal Fisheries Promotion Act, 25–26
collaboration, 13–14, 22–24
commons, tragedy of the, 30–31
community-based resource management (CBRM), 25
company jobs, 33–34
compensation: for damage by rumor, 89, 92; for depressed prices, 92; end of, 89, 133; history of, 8–9; as insufficient, 132; lawsuit over, 3, 84; moratorium extension and, 85; in natural vs. manmade disasters, 84; records required for, 84–85; wholesalers and, 125
competition and cooperation, 46–47
conch, 31
conservation, marine, 25–29
consumer fears of radiation in fish, 3–4, 88–89, 96, 140
consumption of fish, declining, 58
cooperation and competition, 46–47
co-ops: baby hard clams project, 18–19, 38, 39; "backward" rules, views on, 62, 63; conservation and, 25; Fishermen's Mamas' Shop and, 55, 68–69; gendered land-task rules, 59–62, 67; income-pooling system, 27–29; in northern Fukushima, 115–116; octopus fishing veto, 47–49; restaurant and, 71; temporary headquarters in Fukushima, 80; tsunami and, 76–77, 80; yellow-light rule, 49–50; YFAs and, 23
countryside mama (*kāchan*), 57
crabs, 30

damage by rumor (*fūhyō higai*): anthropological shock and, 90–91; "Buy, Eat, and Support in Tsukiji!" reconstruction event and, 95–100; defined, 89–90; Japanese history of, 91–92; "risk society" and, 93; uncertainty, risk, and, 92–94
debt, 63
Democratic Party of Japan (LDP), 126
dentōteki ("traditional fishing village"), 43–44, 64–65, 146n3
development, 21–22, 41
disaster capitalism, 112, 148n1
disaster futurism, 108–112, 123, 124
disaster nationalism, 112, 148n1
disasters: Anthropocene and, 138–139; industrial accidents as "normal," 144n4; legal procedures, familiarity with, 84; as processual, 2–3; sense of belonging and disaster citizenship, 148n7; visibility and, 139; vulnerabilities and, 144n3
disaster utopianism, 123
dolphinfish, 132–133
dominant year class: clams, 18, 82; defined, 34–35, 144n7; octopuses, 34–37, 36, 141
dredging, 26–28, 30, 61, 64

earthquake (2011), 77; aftershocks, xvii, 79; location of, 147n2 (chap. 4); narratives of, xvii–xviii, 75–77, 80–81
eco-futurism, 11–12, 111–112, 135
eels, 30
entrepreneurialism, 39–43, 56–57, 63, 147n1 (chap. 3). *See also* Fishermen's Mamas' Shop
environmental subjects, 25
Escobar, Arturo, 23
expectation(s) and the unexpected: anticipation vs., 73; deaths and revising, 79–82; following, during Fukushima tsunami, 75–79; historical, 74–75;

radiation contamination and, 82–86; TEPCO and, 73–74
extension agents. See fisheries agents

farmerization (*nōkō-ka*), 110. See also Fukushima offshore floating wind farm: farmerization and artificial reefs
Fischer, Michael, 20
fish: consumers fears of radiation in, 3–4, 88–89, 96, 140; consumption of, declining, 58. See also prices for fish; specific types of fish
Fisheries Agency: Assembly to Talk about the Future of Ibaraki, 87–89, 103–104; conservation and, 25–26; Fisheries Restoration Master Plan, 104; loans, low-interest, 88–89; self-responsibility rhetoric, 42–43; white papers, 25–26, 58; YFAs and, 24
fisheries agents: conservation and, 29, 31; Fishermen's Mamas' Shop and, 56–57; modernization and, 7, 26–27, 40–42, 56; restaurant and, 69–71; surf clams discussion, 51–53; as translators, 24; YFAs and, 23–24, 29
Fisheries Forum FY2006, 54–56
Fisheries Restoration Master Plan, 104
Fishermen's Mamas' Shop, 54–59, 62–64, 67–70, *70*
fish hatcheries: clam-stocking from, 29; Fukushima Fish Nursery Laboratory, 9–11, 111, 114, 131; modernization and, 111
fishing methods: about, 30–31; dredging, 26–28, 30, 61, 64; gill-netting, 31, 113, 116; longlining, 31, 47–48, *131*; modern, 22; multiple, 30–31; ocean farm idea and, 126; pot fishing, 47–48. See also purse-seining; rules; trawling

fishing moratoriums: end of, 14, 32, 95–96; extension of, 85; IAEA, 3; impacts of, 3; oil spills and, 17–18, 47, 51; practice of, 92; prolonged, after Fukushima nuclear crisis, xv–xvi, 19, 78, 82, 140; Tokaimura nuclear accident and, 3
fish markets, new vs. traditional, 123–125. See also Fishermen's Mamas' Shop; Tsukiji Fish Market, Tokyo
fish-stocking programs, 27, 114
flatheads, 31
flounder, 10–11, 31, 82, 100, 114, 116, 125
Freeman, Carla, 146n1 (chap. 3)
fūhyō higai. See damage by rumor
Fukushima Daiichi Nuclear Power Plant, 2, 9, 115–116, 132, 139
Fukushima Fish Nursery Laboratory, 9–11, 111, 114, 131
Fukushima FORWARD. See under Fukushima offshore floating wind farm
Fukushima nuclear crisis (3/11). See damage by rumor; earthquake; expectation(s) and the unexpected; fishing moratoriums; precarious seascape; radiation contamination; Tokyo Electric Power Company; tsunami
Fukushima offshore floating wind farm: budget, 106, 126, 129; farmerization and artificial reefs, 110–111, 130–134; fishers' views of, 112–119, 126–127; Fukushima FORWARD pilot project, 106–112, 122, 129–132, 140; futurism and, 11–12; map, 2; national project and local employment, 109–110; research fishing trip for data collection, 128–134, *131*; revised plans, 123, 126–127; special exhibition in tourist center, 121–122; symbiosis with fisheries, planned, 110–111, 126–127

Index 165

—turbines: Fukushima Future (Fukushima Mirai), *12*, 14, 15, 106, 109, 116–117, 119, 131–132, 140; Fukushima New-Wind (Fukushima Shinpu), 129, 130, 140; Fukushima Shore-Wind (Fukushima Hamakaze), 129, 140; removal of, 140, 151n4
Fukushima Offshore Wind Power Consortium, 106, 121, 126–127
Fukushima Prefecture projects, 106–107, *107*, 149n3
"Future from Fukushima"/"Let's Start from Fukushima" slogan, 106–107, *107*
futurism: Chernobyl and, 149n5; defined, 7; disaster, 108–112, 123, 124; Fukushima slogan and, 106–107; industrial and fisheries, 8–9; modernization and, 7–13; power of, 119–120; temporality of suspension and, 137; utopian, 107–109, 123. *See also* ecofuturism; modernization

gender politics, 56–62. *See also* mamas, coastal
gill-netting, 31, 113, 116
Gupta, Akhil, 123

halfbeaks, 30
Haraway, Donna, 137, 151n2
hatcheries. *See* fish hatcheries
Hoffman, Susanna, 2
hope: accumulated risks and possibilities and, 20–21; ambiguous views of, 112–117; anxiety, certainty, and uncertainty coexisting with, 134–135; Blochean, 107; dominant year classes and, 34–36; Fukushima Future futurism and, 107–108; Nancy's "After Fukushima" and, 136; offshore wind farm and, 123; placed in women and young people, 38; possibilities of survival, 141–142; in the precarious sea, 5, 13–16; in suspension of Fukushima FUTURE, 137
housing camp, temporary, 112–113
human-nonhuman relationship: Anthropocene and, 138; changed by disaster, 135, 144n3; collaborative, 13–14, 22–23; conservation and, 29; Fukushima disaster as chance for ocean to recuperate, 82, 125; Haraway on Chthulucene and, 151n2; modernization and, 6, 137; ocean farms and, 111; reconfiguration of, 141–142; temporality of suspension and, 123; Weston on intimacies of, 144n6. *See also* Joban Sea; precarious seascape
"hunter-gatherers," 110
husband-wife boats (*meoto bune*), 60, 64

Ibaraki, Assembly to Talk about the Future of, 87–89, 103–104
Ibaraki Prefecture website, 99, 102–103
income-pooling system, 27–29
International Nuclear Event Scale (INES), 3
Ishihara, Takeshi, 110–111, 126

Japan Aerospace Exploration Agency (JAXA), 147n3 (chap. 5)
jikosekinin (self-responsibility), 42–43, 57
Joban Sea (Jōban Oki): about, 1–2; disasters and resilience along, 4–5; map, 2; possibilities of survival, 141–142; seascape as increasingly ordinary, 138–139. *See also* precarious seascape
Johnson, Chalmers, 145n11

kāchan (countryside mama), 57
Kaku, Michio, 101
Karatani, Kojin, 150n1 (ep.)
Klein, Naomi, 6, 148n1
Koizumi, Junichiro, 41–42
Koselleck, Reinhart, 7

land tasks (*okamawari*), 59–62
laws and legal procedures: in case of disaster, 84; Coastal Fisheries Promotion Act, 25–26. *See also* damage by rumor lawsuits. *See* compensation
loans, low-interest, 88–89
longlining, 31, 47–48, *131*
Lucky Dragon incident, 91

mamas, coastal: at Fisheries Forum FY2006, 54–56; Fishermen's Mamas' Shop, 54–59, 62–64, 67–70, *70*; hard work, undervalued, 58; husband-wife boats, 60, 64; land tasks, gendered rules, and, 59–62; Mamas' Restaurant, 71–72; motherhood, rhetoric and role of, 54, 56–57, 72; newcomers, "originals," and history of Hama, 64–67
markets, fish, new vs. traditional, 123–125. *See also* Fishermen's Mamas' Shop; Tsukiji Fish Market, Tokyo
Marubeni Corporation, 109, 150n7
"Matasaburo of the Wind" (Kaze no Matasaburō, short story), 37
meoto bune (husband-wife boats), 60, 64
Mikuriya, Takashi, 136
Ministry of Economy, Trade, and Industry (METI), 15, 106, 129, 140, 151n4
Ministry of Health, Labor, and Welfare, 85, 95, 148n6

Miyazaki, Hirokazu, 145n12
modernization: accumulated risks and possibilities and, 20–21; Anthropocene and, 138–139; collaboration in, 22–24; conservation and, 25–29; decline in landings, ironic, 29–32; development history narratives, 21–22; expensive boats and, 74–75; Fisheries Forum FY2006 and, 54; Fisheries Restoration Master Plan and, 104; futurism and, 7–13; gender norms and, 57; Japan's history of, 145n11; justifications of, 6, 8; Minato vs. Hama and, 39–40, 43–44; neoliberal policies, 39–41, 56, 57, 72; new fish market and, 124; power infrastructure and, 8; self-responsibility rhetoric, 41–43, 57; surviving, 6–7, 15–16, 56, 120, 138–139, 144n9; symbiotic relationship with precarious seascape, 6–7; temporality of suspension and, 137; uncertain risks, addiction, and, 104; women and, 56; as work of translation, 40–41. *See also* futurism
monitoring, of radiation. *See* radiation contamination
moratoriums. *See* fishing moratoriums
motherhood, rhetoric and role of, 54, 56–57, 72. *See also* mamas, coastal
Munn, Nancy, 149n6

Nancy, Jean-Luc, 136
National Convention on Nurturing the Abundant Ocean, 10
neoliberalism, 39–43, 54, 56–57, 72
nōkō-ka ("farmerization"), 110
nonhuman species. *See* human-nonhuman relationship

normality: end of moratorium and, 14; future-oriented, 105; gestures of, 80; industrial accidents as "normal," 144n4; Joban seascape as increasingly ordinary, 138–139; Tokaimura accident and return of, 3–4; tsunami narrated as "normal," 81
nuclear fish hatcheries, 111

ocean farms, 111–112, 118
octopus: clams as prey of, 35; co-op veto on fishing, 47–49; dominant year class, 34–37, 36, 141; large catch, 20; potting vs. longlining, 47–48; radioactive accumulation in, 145
oil spills, 4, 17–20, 47, 51, 92
okamawari (land tasks), 59–62
okidashi ("to push offshore"), 74–82
Oliver-Smith, Anthony, 2

Pels, Peter, 145n12
Perrow, Charles, 144n4
Petryna, Adriana, 148n7, 149n5
Phillips, Sarah, 149n5
pilot fishing program, 125, 140
power infrastructure and modernization, 8
precarious seascape: changing circumstances and, 6; disasters, resilience, and hope, 4–5; hope and anxiety in, 13–16, 134–135; risks and possibilities, accumulated, 20–21; symbiotic relationship with modernization, 6–7. *See also* survival; uncertainty
precarity, defined, 16; disasters and, 3
prices for fish: damage by rumor and, 92; fishing strategies based on, 31; freshness and, 60; historical struggles, 27–28, 30; low, stagnant, or declining,

3, 58, 64, 89, 96, 105, 125; neoliberal logic on, 42–43; precarious sea and, 5; records on, 84; recovery, uncertain, 92, 133
purse-seining: landing declines, impact of, 59, 64, 67; land tasks for, 61; as method, 30; season of, 51; weather and, 49; wind farm and, 113; women and, 67

radiation contamination: "Buy, Eat, and Support in Tsukiji!" reconstruction event, 95–100, 96; coastal currents and, xvi; consumers' fear of, 3–4, 88–89, 96, 140; expectation and, 82–86; government estimations of dilution, 83; Ibaraki Prefecture website FAQ, 102–103; interpretation of data by consumers, 103; low-level, politics of, 90; *Lucky Dragon* incident, 91–92; possibilities of survival, 141–142; reductions and reopening of fishing, 14–15; rules for approval of reopening, 148n6; safety standards, 85–86, 92; seminar on promoting businesses with local fish, 100–101; testing and monitoring, 83–85, 92–93; test results, posting or announcement of, 99, 101–102; uncertainty and, 93–94, 115–116; visibility of, 93–94. *See also* damage by rumor; wastewater
radioactive metabolism of marine organisms, 142
recession, 29–30
reefs, artificial, 110, 130–134
restaurants, 70–72
risk: accumulated, 20–21; anthropological shock and, 90–91; damage by rumor

and, 91; modernization and, 104; "risk society," 90, 93, 104; uncertainty and, 93–94, 104. *See also* radiation contamination: consumers' fear of
ritual and religion, 44–45, 146n3
rules: conservation and, 31; gendered, 59–62, 63; octopus-potting and, 47–49; for radiation and reopening, 148n6; sea goddess Amba-sama and, 43–47; yellow-light, 49–50

sand lances, Japanese, xv, 85, 102
sardines, 69, 102
Satsuka, Shiho, 146n1 (chap. 2)
sea bass, 30
sea robin, 31
sea urchin, 10, 117, 125
Sekiya, Naoya, 91
self-responsibility (*jikosekinin*), 42–43, 57
sex industry, 65
Shimizu, Masataka, 73
shock doctrine, 6
Solnit, Rebecca, 150n1 (ep.)
squid, 55, 69, 95
Sternsdorff-Cisterna, Nicolas, 148n7
Suga, Yoshihide, 15
Sunday activities, 38, 69–70
survival: Abélès on politics of, 108–109; anthropological shock and, 90; collaborative, 13–14, 22–23, 137; experience-based knowledge of, 86; neoliberal politics of, 39–43, 54, 56, 72, 147n1 (chap. 3); possibilities of, 20–21, 141–142; precarity and, 5–6; revised expectations and, 79; and "survival subjects," 29; utopian futurism and, 123. *See also* modernization: surviving

suspension, temporality of, 123, 127, 137
Swanson, Heather, 138

tanker accidents (2006), 4, 17–20, 47, 51, 92
temporality of suspension, 123, 127, 137
testing, for radiation. *See* radiation contamination
thermal discharge, 10, 111, 131, 145n14
Three Mile Island, 3
Tokaimura nuclear accident (1999), 3–4, 5, 86, 92
Tokyo Electric Power Company (TEPCO): "beyond expectations" statement, 73–74; damage by rumor and, 89; lawsuit and compensation demand options against, 84–85; underwater leakage and dumping, 15, 105, 115–116, 135, 140. *See also* compensation
"traditional fishing village" (*dentōteki*), 43–44, 64–65, 146n3
tragedy of the commons, 30–31
translation, 24, 40–41
trawling (bottom-trawling): cut feet problem with clams, 26–27; ocean conditions for success of, 133; octopus-potting vs., 36; octopus fishing veto and, 48–49; wind farm and, 113–114, 130, 132–133
Tsing, Anna, 6, 145n10
Tsukiji Fish Market, Tokyo, 83, 95–100, 96, 144n2
tsunami (2011): fisher deaths in Fukushima Prefecture, 79–82; fish hatchery and, 11; harbor scene (Minato) day after, 76, 77; Mamas' Restaurant and, 71; *okidashi* ("to push offshore") and, 74–82; size of, 76; speed of, 75, 147n2 (chap. 4)

Index 169

turbines. *See* Fukushima offshore floating wind farm—turbines

uncertainty, 93–94, 104, 115–116
US Nuclear Regulatory Commission (NRC), 144n5
utopian futurism, 107–109, 123

wastewater: industrial, history of, 21–22; underwater leakage and dumping, 15, 105, 115–116, 135, 140. *See also* radiation contamination
weather, 49–50, 65, 128
Weston, Kath, 144n6

wholesalers, 124–126
wind farm, offshore. *See* Fukushima offshore floating wind farm
Women's Associations (WAs), 38, 55, 58–59, 68–69, 147n2 (chap. 3). *See also* mamas, coastal

yellow-light rule, 49–50
Young Fishermen's Associations (YFAs), 23–29, 38, 51–53

Zee, Jerry, 137
Zhang, Amy, 145n9

CULTURE, PLACE, AND NATURE
Studies in Anthropology and Environment

Fukushima Futures: Survival Stories in a Repeatedly Ruined Seascape,
 by Satsuki Takahashi
The Camphor Tree and the Elephant: Religion and Ecological Change in Maritime Southeast Asia, by Faizah Zakaria
Turning Land into Capital: Development and Dispossession in the Mekong Region, edited by Philip Hirsch, Kevin Woods, Natalia Scurrah, and Michael B. Dwyer
Spawning Modern Fish: Transnational Comparison in the Making of Japanese Salmon, by Heather Anne Swanson
Upland Geopolitics: Postwar Laos and the Global Land Rush, by Michael B. Dwyer
Misreading the Bengal Delta: Climate Change, Development, and Livelihoods in Coastal Bangladesh, by Camelia Dewan
Ordering the Myriad Things: From Traditional Knowledge to Scientific Botany in China, by Nicholas K. Menzies
Timber and Forestry in Qing China: Sustaining the Market, by Meng Zhang
Consuming Ivory: Mercantile Legacies of East Africa and New England, by Alexandra C. Kelly
Mapping Water in Dominica: Enslavement and Environment under Colonialism, by Mark W. Hauser
Mountains of Blame: Climate and Culpability in the Philippine Uplands, by Will Smith
Sacred Cows and Chicken Manchurian: The Everyday Politics of Eating Meat in India, by James Staples
Gardens of Gold: Place-Making in Papua New Guinea, by Jamon Alex Halvaksz
Shifting Livelihoods: Gold Mining and Subsistence in the Chocó, Colombia, by Daniel Tubb
Disturbed Forests, Fragmented Memories: Jarai and Other Lives in the Cambodian Highlands, by Jonathan Padwe
The Snow Leopard and the Goat: Politics of Conservation in the Western Himalayas, by Shafqat Hussain
Roses from Kenya: Labor, Environment, and the Global Trade in Cut Flowers, by Megan A. Styles

Working with the Ancestors: Mana and Place in the Marquesas Islands,
by Emily C. Donaldson
Living with Oil and Coal: Resource Politics and Militarization in Northeast India,
by Dolly Kikon
Caring for Glaciers: Land, Animals, and Humanity in the Himalayas, by Karine Gagné
Organic Sovereignties: Struggles over Farming in an Age of Free Trade,
by Guntra A. Aistara
The Nature of Whiteness: Race, Animals, and Nation in Zimbabwe, by Yuka Suzuki
Forests Are Gold: Trees, People, and Environmental Rule in Vietnam,
by Pamela D. McElwee
Conjuring Property: Speculation and Environmental Futures in the Brazilian Amazon,
by Jeremy M. Campbell
Andean Waterways: Resource Politics in Highland Peru, by Mattias Borg Rasmussen
Puer Tea: Ancient Caravans and Urban Chic, by Jinghong Zhang
Enclosed: Conservation, Cattle, and Commerce among the Q'eqchi' Maya Lowlanders,
by Liza Grandia
Forests of Identity: Society, Ethnicity, and Stereotypes in the Congo River Basin,
by Stephanie Rupp
Tahiti Beyond the Postcard: Power, Place, and Everyday Life, by Miriam Kahn
Wild Sardinia: Indigeneity and the Global Dreamtimes of Environmentalism,
by Tracey Heatherington
Nature Protests: The End of Ecology in Slovakia, by Edward Snajdr
*Forest Guardians, Forest Destroyers: The Politics of Environmental Knowledge
in Northern Thailand*, by Tim Forsyth and Andrew Walker
Being and Place among the Tlingit, by Thomas F. Thornton
Tropics and the Traveling Gaze: India, Landscape, and Science, 1800-1856,
by David Arnold
Ecological Nationalisms: Nature, Livelihood, and Identities in South Asia,
edited by Gunnel Cederlöf and K. Sivaramakrishnan
From Enslavement to Environmentalism: Politics on a Southern African Frontier,
by David McDermott Hughes
Border Landscapes: The Politics of Akha Land Use in China and Thailand, by Janet C. Sturgeon
Property and Politics in Sabah, Malaysia: Native Struggles over Land Rights,
by Amity A. Doolittle
The Earth's Blanket: Traditional Teachings for Sustainable Living, by Nancy Turner
The Kuhls of Kangra: Community-Managed Irrigation in the Western Himalaya,
by Mark Baker

CPSIA information can be obtained
at www.ICGtesting.com
Printed in the USA
BVHW040551120723
667077BV00006B/20